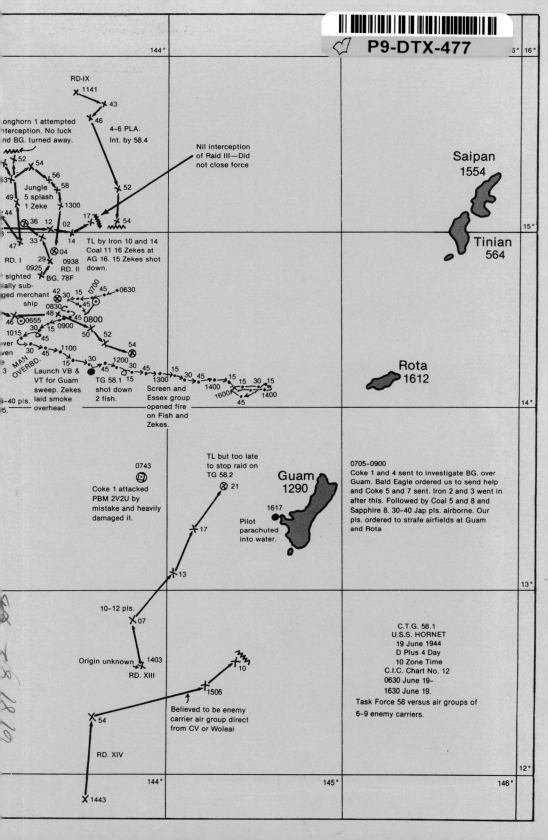

144°

P9-DTX-477

16°

RD-IX
✕ 1141

✕ 43

✕ 46

4–6 PLA.
Int. by 58.4

onghorn 1 attempted
nterception. No luck
nd BG. turned away.

Nil interception
of Raid III—Did
not close force

Saipan
1554

✕ 52
✕ 54

✕ 56
58

Jungle
5 splash
1 Zeke

✕ 52

✕ 1300

49
44

⊗ 36 12 02

14

✕ 54

17

Tinian
564

15°

47 33

⊗ 04

TL by Iron 10 and 14
Coal 11 16 Zekes at
AG 16. 15 Zekes shot
down.

RD. I

29 0938
0925 RD. II
BG. 78F

sighted
ally sub-
ged merchant
ship

42 30 15 45 ⊙ 0630
⊗ 30 45
0830 45
48 45
46 ⊙ 0655 0800
30 15 0900
1015 50 52
30 45
over 30 45 1100
3 MAN 15 30 1200
OVERBD. 15 30

0700

54

Launch VB &
VT for Guam
sweep. Zekes
laid smoke
overhead

TG 58.1 15
shot down
2 fish.

45 1300
30 45
1400
1600

15 30 15
45 1400

Screen and
Essex group
opened fire
on Fish and
Zekes.

Rota
1612

14°

–40 pls.

0743
⊞

Coke 1 attacked
PBM 2V2U by
mistake and heavily
damaged it.

TL but too late
to stop raid on
TG 58.2

⊗ 21

Guam
1290

1617

Pilot
parachuted
into water.

✕ 17

✕ 13

0705–0900
Coke 1 and 4 sent to investigate BG. over
Guam. Bald Eagle ordered us to send help
and Coke 5 and 7 sent. Iron 2 and 3 went in
after this. Followed by Coal 5 and 8 and
Sapphire 8. 30–40 Jap pls. airborne. Our
pls. ordered to strafe airfields at Guam
and Rota

13°

10–12 pls.
✕ 07

Origin unknown 1403
RD. XIII

✕ 10

✕ 1506

Believed to be enemy
carrier air group direct
from CV or Woleai

✕ 54

C.T.G. 58.1
U.S.S. HORNET
19 June 1944
D Plus 4 Day
10 Zone Time
C.I.C. Chart No. 12
0630 June 19–
1630 June 19.
Task Force 58 versus air groups of
6–9 enemy carriers.

RD. XIV

✕ 1443

144°

145°

146°

12°

DATE DUE

JAN 2 2 2004			

Red Sun Setting

Red Sun Setting

THE BATTLE OF THE PHILIPPINE SEA

By William T. Y'Blood

NAVAL INSTITUTE PRESS
Annapolis, Maryland

Copyright © 1981
by the United States Naval Institute
Annapolis, Maryland

Printed in the United States of America.

Library of Congress Cataloging in Publication Data

Y'Blood, William T. 1937–
  Red sun setting.

  Bibliograpy: p.
  Includes index.
    1. Philippine Sea, Battles of the, 1941. I. Title.
D774.P5Y34   940.54'26   80-84062
ISBN 0-87021-532-9

Contents

Preface

SURPRISINGLY, the Battle of the Philippine Sea has been somewhat neglected in the annals of history. Certainly, it is mentioned in books on World War II, but there is no truly comprehensive account of this action—the greatest carrier duel of the war. It is hoped this book will begin to rectify this omission.

This is not a study of the battle from the lofty perch of the strategic planners. Rather, this is the story of the battle from the viewpoint of the admirals, sailors, fliers, and ship's officers who were on the firing line, with a glance at the strategy and planning that led to this huge confrontation. It is also the story of the controversy that erupted after the battle, a controversy that still simmers today.

A work of this type is never the work of just one person; it is based on the experiences of hundreds or thousands of individuals. A look at the bibliography will show just how indebted I am to these individuals, especially to the largely unknown authors of the Action Reports and War Diaries.

In particular, however, I am indebted to the following: Dr. Dean C. Allard and his assistants, primarily Mrs. Gerri Judkins, at the Operational Archives Branch of the Naval Historical Center in Washington, for their patience and expertise in guiding me through the maze of records there; Mr. John W. Taylor at the Modern Military Records section of the National Archives; the staffs of the photographic libraries of the National Archives and the United States Naval Institute for their help in finding the photographs to go into this book; Dr. Paul S. Dull for his valuable comments on the manuscript; the Air Micronesia pilots who took the time during my visit to those islands to acquaint me with that special experience that is Micronesia; finally, but certainly not last, I would like to thank three very important people in my life—my wife, Carolyn, and my son and daughter, Kent and Laura. All three provided help, encouragement, and inspiration when I needed it.

NOTE: In this book the Japanese names are rendered in English order.

Glossary

AA	Antiaircraft fire
AP	Armor-piercing shell or bomb
ASP	Antisubmarine patrol
BatDiv	Battleship Division
BB	Battleship
Bogey(s)	Unidentified aircraft
CA	Heavy cruiser
CAP	Combat air patrol
CarDiv	Carrier Division
CCS	Combined Chiefs of Staff
CinCPac	Commander in Chief Pacific Fleet
CL	Light cruiser
CL(AA)	Antiaircraft light cruiser
C.O.	Commanding Officer
CruDiv	Cruiser Division
CV	Aircraft carrier
CVE	Escort carrier
CVL	Light carrier
DD	Destroyer
DE	Destroyer escort
DesDiv	Destroyer Division
DesRon	Destroyer Squadron

FDO	Fighter director officer
Flak	Antiaircraft fire
GP	General-purpose bomb
Hedgehog	Type of throw-ahead missile launcher
HF/DF	High frequency direction finding
IFF	Identification, friend or foe
JCS	Joint Chiefs of Staff
Jink(ing)	To take evasive action in an aircraft
LCI(G)	Landing craft, infantry (gunboat)
LSO	Landing signal officer
LST	Landing ship, tank
Magic	Code name of project to decipher Japanese codes
OTC	Officer in tactical command
SAP	Semi-armor-piercing shell or bomb
TF	Task Force
TG	Task Group
TU	Task Unit
USA	United States Army
USMC	United States Marine Corps
USN	United States Navy
USS	United States Ship
VB	Navy bomber squadron or single plane
VF	Navy fighter squadron or single plane
VSB	Navy scout-bomber squadron or single plane
VSO	Navy scout-observation squadron or single plane
VT	Navy torpedo-bomber squadron or single plane
XCV	Japanese hybrid battleship/carrier; i.e. the *Ise* and the *Hyuga*

Aircraft Types

United States

Avenger	Grumman/General Motors TBF/TBM torpedo plane
Corsair	Vought F4U fighter
Dauntless	Douglas SBD dive bomber
Hellcat	Grumman F6F fighter
Helldiver	Curtiss SB2C dive bomber
Kingfisher	Vought OS2U float scout plane
Liberator	Consolidated B-24/PB4Y heavy bomber or patrol plane
Mariner	Martin PBM flying-boat
Seagull	Curtiss SOC float scout plane
Wildcat	Grumman/General Motors F4F/FM fighter

Japanese

Betty	Mitsubishi G4M attack bomber
Emily	Kawanishi H8K flying-boat
Frances	Yokosuka P1Y night fighter
Hamp	Mitsubishi A6M3 fighter; later called Zeke 32
Helen	Nakajima Ki-49 heavy bomber
Irving	Nakajima J1N1 reconnaissance plane or night fighter
Jack	Mitsubishi J2M fighter
Jake	Aichi E13A reconnaisance floatplane
Jill	Nakajima B6N torpedo bomber
Judy	Yokosuka D4Y dive bomber
Kate	Nakajima B5N torpedo bomber
Nick	Kawasaki Ki-45 fighter
Oscar	Nakajima Ki-43 fighter
Tojo	Nakajima Ki-44 fighter
Tony	Kawasaki Ki-61 fighter
Topsy	Mitsubishi L4M/Ki-57 transport
Val	Aichi D3A dive bomber
Zeke	Mitsubishi A6M fighter

Red Sun Setting

Introduction

By June of 1944 the tide that had swept the Japanese forces across the Pacific to Wake, Guadalcanal, and New Guinea had begun to ebb rapidly. The Pacific War had begun impressively enough for the Japanese with a series of stunning victories at Pearl Harbor, Hong Kong, Singapore, in the Java Sea and the Indian Ocean, and in the Philippines. By these victories the Japanese had forced the U.S. Navy to rethink its strategic and tactical options. The battleship, beloved vessel of the "Big Gun" admirals, was pushed to one side and the aircraft carrier became the new capital ship. Unfortunately, United States carrier tactics were still very much in the formative stage. In a battleship-oriented navy, the tactics, administration, and other policies that make a carrier unit run efficiently were still being formulated when 7 December 1941 came. Then there was no time to go over procedures systematically; the carriers were sent out to fight. But by June 1944 the concepts, procedures, and policies had all fallen into place. Of this the Japanese Navy was only too aware.

The awesome victories for the Japanese continued for some months, but then came Coral Sea, Midway, and the furious series of actions on and around Guadalcanal. Besides the precious carriers that were lost in some of these battles, the Japanese had lost irreplaceable flight crews. Their airmen had been the best trained in the Pacific during the early days of the war, but they had been small in numbers. The Japanese had planned on quick conquests, using a small elite group of fliers. They had not planned to augment this group with additional trained airmen at a later time. As a result, few qualified fliers were available to take up the slack caused by the losses in these crucial battles, and it would be some time before a training program would become effective. The need for experienced airmen would become all too apparent to the Japanese military leaders in the months ahead. Indeed, lower-ranking Japanese would not be the only ones to fall in combat. On 18 April 1943 Admiral Isoroku Yamamoto's plane was ambushed by United States Army Air Force planes and the admiral was killed. As with Midway, this victory could be credited to the marvelous work of the American cryptanalysts.

By the end of 1943 the Solomons campaign was almost over and strategic interest now switched to the Central Pacific. In November 1943 the Gilberts were taken by the Americans. Heavy losses were sustained by the Marines at Tarawa, but by this point in the war the Americans were beginning to digest the lessons they had been force-fed by the Japanese. On 6 January 1944 the Fast Carrier Task Force (initially built around a core of six fleet and five light carriers but constantly increasing in size) became Task Force 58 under the command of Rear Admiral Marc A. Mitscher.

Task Force 58 began a series of attacks—the Marshalls, Truk, the Marianas, Palau, Hollandia—that kept the Japanese guessing and subtracted more aircraft and fliers from their order of battle. In May TF 58 was anchored at Majuro, in the Marshalls, for a well-earned rest. A big operation was just around the corner—Forager, the invasion of the Marianas. Not since the big fleet actions around Guadalcanal in 1942 had the Japanese sought a large-scale battle. Some Americans thought they never would. Others thought that with the right provocation the Japanese Navy would come out spoiling for a fight. It was hoped that Forager be the right provocation.

chapter 1

A Long Winding Road

UNITED STATES STRATEGIC PLANNING for Pacific operations during
World War II can be likened to a tortuous back road in the mountains.
Along the winding road on the way to Tokyo were a number of stops
and an occasional side road. One of these stops, in the Marianas, did
supply the provocation for the Japanese Fleet to seek a naval action
with the United States Fifth Fleet. However, the road to the Marianas
engagement was not a smooth one, and for some time thought was
given to taking a side road and bypassing these islands entirely.

Even before the war, the Marianas had figured importantly in U.S.
naval plans for the Pacific. In the event of a war with Japan the
pre-World War II Orange and Rainbow plans called for U.S. forces to
move across the Pacific via the Marshalls and the Marianas to the
Philippines.[1] It was assumed the latter islands would be under heavy
attack or even lost. American forces would move through the Central
Pacific to drive off the Japanese and relieve the Philippines.

The Pearl Harbor attack and the stunning early victories of the
Japanese in the Pacific threw out of balance these pre-war plans. The
direction of the Japanese attacks also tended to color U.S. strategic
planning in the first years of the war. With Japanese and United States
forces fighting in the South and Southwest Pacific during this time, the
attention of the U.S. strategists was drawn in that direction.[2] Operations in the Central Pacific were limited to weak raids on widely scat-

tered targets. Still, the "traditional Navy view of war against Japan in any case was that the major offensive would be across the Central Pacific rather than through the East Indies."[3]

Fortunately, the war plans issued were not cast in concrete. Circumstances changed and so plans changed. The operations against the Marianas showed just how flexible these plans could be.

At the time of the Casablanca Conference in January 1943 "there was no final, approved plan in existence for the defeat of Japan."[4] In August of the previous year the Joint United States Strategic Committee had begun work on a strategic plan for the defeat of Japan, but this plan was far from finished when the American and British leaders met at Casablanca. Although nothing was yet in solid form, Admiral Ernest J. King, Commander in Chief, U.S. Fleet and Chief of Naval Operations, undertook to present his views on the Pacific situation.

King's "ideas at this stage of the war closely followed the concept developed in the preceding years of war games at Newport and of successive plans named Orange."[5] An American advance, according to King, should be toward the Philippines—but by way of the Marshalls, Truk, and the Marianas, not via New Guinea and the Netherlands East Indies. These latter areas were not, in King's view, the proper places for the use of American naval forces. King stressed the Marianas as "the key of the situation because of their location on the Japanese line of communications."[6]

So it was here at Casablanca that King described to the Combined Chiefs of Staff (CCS) "the line of advance through the Central Pacific to the Philippines that was in fact to be the primary strategic pattern for the war against Japan."[7] King was sure that America's growing naval strength (which would see in 1943 a massive increase with the addition of the new *Essex*-class carriers and *Iowa*-class battleships) would eventually force the Japanese into submission without the terrible losses which would be incurred in an invasion of Japan.[8] It took many months of high-level wrangling before a Central Pacific route was approved, but King's confidence in his naval forces was well founded. When the fast carriers showed they could operate without land-based air cover, deep in enemy territory, the Central Pacific drive moved more rapidly and deeply into the Japanese defenses.[9]

It would take some time for King's ideas to be digested by the Combined Chiefs. In the meantime, General Douglas MacArthur, Commander in Chief Southwest Pacific, found King's plans thoroughly indigestible and wasted no time in criticizing it. In his campaign plan for the Southwest Pacific, Reno I issued in February 1943, he claimed that the route King favored would be "time consuming and expensive in . . . naval power and shipping."[10] A drive up the back of New Guinea and into the Philippines (under his command, of course) would be more successful.

MacArthur's protests had little effect. In March 1943, representatives of the three major areas (South, Southwest, and Central) met in Washington for a Pacific Military Conference. Most of the agenda was taken up with operations in the South and Southwest Pacific and the endless debate over the division of resources between Europe and the Pacific. However, King and Admiral Chester W. Nimitz's representative, Vice Admiral Raymond A. Spruance, were able to put in a few words for a Central Pacific offensive. King pointed out indirectly that major Navy units could be more valuable in the Central Pacific than in the Solomons–New Guinea area. Spruance then pointed out that with Japanese naval forces still afloat, Pearl Harbor remained a tempting target. Ships from the South Pacific, along with the new vessels just becoming available, could launch an assault on the Gilberts and Marshalls, and remove the threat of an attack on Hawaii.[11] (Left unsaid but very likely considered by King was the thought that a Gilberts or Marshalls operation would provide the opening for the Navy to push through to the Joint Chiefs of Staff (JCS) more reasons for a Central Pacific offensive.)

At the Trident Conference held in Washington in May 1943, a Central Pacific route was tentatively approved by the CCS. In the "Strategic Plan for the Defeat of Japan" presented to and approved by the Combined Chiefs, however, it appeared that the planners were leaning toward MacArthur's views. In this plan Nimitz's forces were given a secondary role of capturing the Gilberts, Marshalls, and Truk, while protecting MacArthur's right flank. MacArthur, in turn, would be rolling up New Guinea into the Celebes and Sulu Sea areas.[12] But MacArthur was still upset that *any* planning would be considered for a Central Pacific drive. Nevertheless, he did not argue too strongly against the invasions of the Gilberts and the Marshalls since they would remove a threat to his flank. Any further moves through the Central Pacific would be another matter, however.[13]

In the meantime King was still fighting to get the Marianas targeted by the CCS. At the Trident Conference King tried once again. His intense interest in the Marianas "stemmed from a realization on his part that the true importance of this target was not unanimously felt. Significant in this connection is the fact that the Marianas had not been prescribed as a specific objective even at this time."[14]

For the Navy to undertake an offensive in the Central Pacific, major naval units would have to be transferred from the South Pacific to join with the new construction just appearing. MacArthur and Vice Admiral William F. Halsey, Commander in Chief South Pacific, definitely opposed this idea as did one of Nimitz's deputies, Vice Admiral John H. Towers. As Commander Air Force Pacific Fleet, Towers believed that Rabaul (still in the plans to be assaulted) was the best Japanese base for American use in operations against enemy bases in the Carolines and sea routes between Japan and Malaysia.[15] Nevertheless, Admiral King was for the redeployment of certain naval units, and this movement did take place.

Following the Trident meetings King reviewed the plans that had been proposed and urged that a timetable be set up for Central Pacific operations. Shortly the Joint Staff Planners agreed to prepare an outline plan for the capture of the Marshalls in November of 1943. Nimitz was directed by the JCS to submit an operational plan and target date for the Marshalls. A tentative plan was received in July. [16]

The Joint Strategic Survey Committee presented to the JCS in late June a memorandum covering Pacific operations to that time and making several recommendations for the future conduct of the war. In the Committee's view the war against Japan had fallen into a strategy of attack from the South and Southwest Pacific because the defense of Australia had required so much of the available resources. This, coupled with "certain psychological and political considerations"[17] and a lack of U.S. naval forces, had tended to spotlight an offensive strategy from Australia. It had originally seemed that an offensive in the Bismarcks–Solomons–New Guinea area would be fairly successful. This turned out not to be the case, however. Strong Japanese bases in the area had made the offensive slow and relatively costly. But now it appeared that, with U.S. naval strength growing, a drive through the Central Pacific, supported by these naval forces, would be more successful and offer greater strategic advantages.[18]

By this time in the war, after the losses in the Solomons and the Aleutians, the Japanese began to worry that they were overextended. And there was a gnawing fear of an American offensive in the Central Pacific. Thus the Japanese withdrew their main defensive line into a perimeter extending from western New Guinea through the Carolines to the vital Marianas. This line was to be held at all costs.[19]

Though the Marianas were very important to the Japanese, and Admiral King also considered them so, many planners in the Army and Navy had not been convinced that the Marianas needed to be taken. This was obvious in Quebec at the Quadrant Conference in August 1943 where the islands were not "mentioned in the written plans" of the Joint Chiefs.[20] This state of affairs would change as some major strategic alterations were brought about by the talks.

At Quebec the Combined Chiefs suggested timing the defeat of Japan within a twelve-month period after the fall of Germany. This concept would mean accelerating operations in the Pacific, and perhaps extending their reach.[21] In line with this reasoning, the decision was made to bypass Rabaul. Also, with King again vocal on the subject, the Marianas were approved, somewhat halfheartedly, as a target. The Marianas were conspicuously absent from a proposed timetable for operations. King, however, was able to offer a modification of the timing of operations by inserting into "Specific Operations in Pacific and Far East" this statement: "It may be found desirable or necessary to seize Guam and the Japanese Marianas, possibly the Bonins, in conjunction with the seizure of the western Carolines, and in particular with the attack on the Palaus. The Mariana–Bonin attack would have profound effects on the Japanese because of its serious threat to the homeland."[22] (It should be noted here that though the Combined Chiefs considered Pacific operations, strategic control of this theater had in fact been turned over to the American Joint Chiefs.)[23]

King gained an important ally at Quebec: General Henry H. Arnold, commander of the Army Air Forces. Arnold's new weapon, the B-29, had been mentioned at Quebec, but its importance was not yet understood. This would shortly change. The Quebec decisions and the apparent alliance between King and Arnold indicated to MacArthur that he and the Southwest Pacific might soon be playing second fiddle to Admiral Nimitz in the Central Pacific. MacArthur intensified his opposition to the Central Pacific route.

On 4 October 1943 Brigadier General Laurence S. Kuter USA, of the Joint Staff Planners, wrote a memorandum concerning the B-29, pressing for the capture of the Marianas. In it he stated, "Current Planning in the Pacific treats the seizure of the Marianas as a subordinate operation. . . ."[24] He continued that if this was the case, the planners ought to forget about the Marianas, for the operation would serve no purpose. But the new B-29s had the capability of reaching and bombing Japan—from the Marianas.

Another paper, originated by the Joint War Plans Committee and titled "Outline Plan For The Seizure of The Marianas, Including Guam," was also circulating in JCS upper echelons about this time. The paper predicted, as had Admiral King earlier (and both correctly), that the Japanese Navy would probably come out and fight in defense of the islands.[25]

The next meeting of the Combined Chiefs (Sextant) was held in Cairo in late November–early December 1943. General MacArthur sent his chief of staff, Major General Richard K. Sutherland USA, to oppose any more Central Pacific operations. MacArthur, through Sutherland, argued that amphibious operations in that area would take too long to mount; land-based air support would be unavailable because of the distances involved; and carrier-based air would not be strong enough to maintain pressure on the enemy. Therefore, Nimitz's forces should be used to support MacArthur.[26]

On the other hand, proponents of an offensive through the Central Pacific argued that such a route would require fewer and longer moves; could bypass enemy strongholds far easier than an army tethered to the range of land-based fighters; would be more direct; would cut Japanese sea communications more effectively; would provide a base (the Marianas) for the B-29s; and would probably draw the Japanese Navy out for a decisive naval engagement.[27]

Along with King, General Arnold brought his influence to bear on the Combined Chiefs on the matter of the Marianas. Basing the B-29s in China, as was then planned, promised to be a headache, and Arnold had little confidence in the Chinese's ability to defend the airfields. The Marianas would be easier to defend and supply. And he assured the CCS that the B-29s could bomb Japan from Guam, Tinian, or Saipan.[28]

The Sextant Conference brought about some far-reaching agreements pertaining to operations in the Pacific. Two documents were particularly important in this regard: "Specific Operations for the Defeat of Japan" and "Over-all Plan for the Defeat of Japan." "Specific Operations" set up a timetable for execution. It was strictly for planning purposes and took into account the fact that circumstances might change drastically. It called for the invasion of the Marianas on 1 October 1944, with the start of B-29 attacks from there in December.[29] The "Over-all Plan," which was approved in principle at Cairo, was used as a jumping-off place for later studies. This plan "established the strategic concept within the Pacific."[30]

The revised Combined Chiefs plan was sent to Nimitz and MacArthur on 23 December 1943. In it a two-pronged plan was formulated. Each prong would be mutually supporting, and each would be executed in conjunction with the other. One prong would be led by MacArthur up the back of New Guinea, through the Netherlands East Indies, and into the Philippines. Meanwhile, Nimitz would lead the Central Pacific prong, which would stab through the Japanese Mandated Islands. Both routes would converge on the Luzon–Formosa–China area in the spring of 1945. The Central Pacific route would be favored if there was any conflict in the operations.

The planners believed that the Central Pacific route offered the advantages of a "more rapid advance toward Japan and her vital lines of communications," with the "earlier acquisition of strategic air bases (i.e., the Marianas) closer to the Japanese homeland." Finally, the planners repeated the point that an advance in this area would be "more likely to precipitate a decisive engagement with the Japanese Fleet."[31]

Based on the directive of 23 December 1943 Admiral Nimitz issued his tentative campaign plan, code-named Granite, four days later.[32] This was quickly followed by another Granite plan on 13 January 1944. There were a few differences in the two plans. The sequence of operations was to be as follows:

Operation	Tentative Target Date
Kwajalein	31 January 1944
Air attack on Truk and capture of Kavieng	20 March 1944 (changed to 24 March)
Manus	20 April 1944 (changed to 24 March)
Eniwetok	1 May 1944
Mortlock (160 miles southeast of Truk)	1 July 1944 (changed to 1 August)
Truk	15 August 1944 (changed to 1 August)
Palaus	(not mentioned in first plan; added for 1 August)
Saipan, Tinian, and Guam	15 November 1944 (changed to 1 November)[33]

In this formulation, an invasion of the Marianas would take place rather late in the year, and the U.S. forces would have to backtrack from the Palaus to attack the Marianas. This sequence was soon dropped, however. Nimitz also pointed out in Granite that a major fleet action, even if it delayed an operation for a time, would be very likely to speed up those that followed.[34]

On 27 and 28 January 1944 senior officers of the South, Southwest, and Central Pacific commands met at Pearl Harbor to discuss and plan forthcoming operations. Before the meeting Admiral Towers had sent Admiral Nimitz a memorandum endorsed by Rear Admirals Charles H. McMorris and Forrest P. Sherman (Nimitz's chief of staff and planning officer), opposing the Marianas operations. Towers pointed out that the Japanese could easily send bombers escorted by fighters through Iwo Jima and Chichi Jima to attack the southern Marianas, whereas American efforts towards Japan would have to be without fighter escort. The lack of harbors in the Marianas would be a point against these targets also. Towers recommended that the Pacific Fleet go by way of the Admiralties and the Palaus, bypassing Truk and the Marianas, and striking for the Philippines.[35] "Thus, he agreed precisely with what MacArthur had been recommending."[36] Nimitz concurred with the recommendation and sent it on to King. There it would get a chilly reception.

During the meetings on the 27th and 28th Admiral Nimitz proposed two alternative timetables for future operations. These were:

(A) Truk, 15 June; Marianas, 1 September; Palaus, 15 November.

(B) Truk, bypass; Marianas, 15 June; Palaus, 10 October.[37]

Most of the officers present were not enthusiastic about a Central Pacific offensive, and opposition to the capture of the Marianas was almost unanimous.[38]

Towers presented his views again, and Sherman continued complaining about the poor harbors and the cost in lives of such an operation. Major General George C. Kenney, USA, who hoped to get B-29s under his control in the Southwest Pacific, thought that operating the big planes out of the Marianas was "just a stunt."[39] With everyone present against a Marianas attack, Nimitz said he would recommend to Washington a single prong attack, using the New Guinea–Mindanao approach as the line of advance.[40]

When he heard the results of the conference, MacArthur was elated, believing he had finally won the ballgame. But there was one heavy hitter yet to come to bat—Admiral King. MacArthur went about making his plans, including an obvious one to make himself the supreme commander of all forces in the Pacific. But with King yet to bat, MacArthur's plans were presumptuous and his hopes were soon dashed.[41]

King meanwhile had written a blistering letter to Nimitz, saying in part:

> Apparently, neither those who advocated the concentration of effort in the Southwest Pacific, nor those who admitted the possibility of such a procedure, gave thought nor undertook to state when and if the Japanese occupation and use of the Marianas and Carolines was to be terminated. I assume that even the Southwest Pacific advocates will admit that sometime or other this thorn in the side of our communications to the western Pacific must be removed. In other words, at some time or other we must take out time and forces to carry out this job. . . .
>
> The idea of rolling up the Japanese along the New Guinea coast, throughout Halmahera and Mindanao, and up through the Philippines to Luzon, as our major strategic concept, to the exclusion of clearing our

Central Pacific line of communications to the Philippines, is to me absurd. *Further, it is not in accordance with the decisions of the Joint Chiefs of Staff. . . .*[42] (Italics added.)

King's last sentence is crucial. No matter how much the commanders in the Pacific talked, without solid evidence against a Marianas invasion, the views of the JCS—particularly King and Arnold—would prevail.

Nimitz was already having second thoughts about a drive across the Central Pacific, having been buoyed by the successful Marshalls landings. Still, he was concentrating on Truk, not the Marianas. King was again not pleased, having himself eliminated Truk as a target some time before. He again prodded Nimitz toward a Marianas decision, saying, "We should not do so [mount a Truk invasion] unless and until all other measures have been fully examined."[43]

General MacArthur had kept up his fight against the Central Pacific route, dispatching General Sutherland to Washington in early February, in a last-ditch effort to change the Joint Chiefs' minds. It was a futile effort, however, and MacArthur had to accept the inevitable. To the end, however, he believed that the Central Pacific route was the wrong way to defeat Japan.

Another visitor to Washington in March was Admiral Nimitz, also there to present his views and plans on upcoming operations to the JCS. The Marianas were discussed in detail, particularly regarding their lack of harbors. Eniwetok would be too small for full development and would be too far east for operations west of the Marianas. Nimitz mentioned Ulithi, about four hundred miles southwest of the Marianas, as a possible fleet base. (Ulithi was finally taken in September during the Palaus invasion and proved to be an excellent anchorage for the Pacific Fleet in its later operations.)[44]

A speedup of operations was considered by the JCS, but Truk at first remained a stumbling block. Nimitz felt that "an assault on Truk should be avoided if possible,"[45] but this was a measure not to be taken lightly. Until the carrier strikes on Truk in February showed what to expect there, the original timetable had to be followed. When the TF 58 raids on 17 and 18 February showed that Truk was not the bastion it was thought to be, it was obvious that Pacific operations could be expedited.

Besides the Truk strikes, a number of factors entered into the Joint Chiefs' decision to accelerate the offensive. The Marshalls operation had taken less time and had been less difficult than anticipated. MacArthur, perhaps hoping to get the jump on Nimitz and also show the JCS an attack in his area would be cheaper and faster, advanced the date of his invasion of the Admiralties from 1 April to 29 February and proposed bypassing Wewak and Hansa Bay to strike directly at Hollandia. With Truk obviously weak, Nimitz was now recommending an attack on the Marianas in mid-June, to be followed by an assault on the Palaus around 1 October. Finally, General Arnold was still pushing for the early capture of the Marianas to deploy the B-29s there sooner. [46]

Taking into account these new factors, the Joint Chiefs issued a directive on 12 March 1944. In it MacArthur was ordered to cancel the Kavieng landings and instead isolate that island and Rabaul. Hollandia was to be targeted for 15 April 1944. All Pacific Fleet combat and service vessels, which had been allocated for the Kavieng–Hansa Bay–Manus attacks, were to be returned to Nimitz by 5 May. Following Hollandia MacArthur was to undertake further operations up the New Guinea coast and to prepare to assault Mindanao and support the Central Pacific attack on the Palaus.

In the same directive Admiral Nimitz was ordered to "institute and intensify to greatest practicable degree" bombings of the Carolines and to make carrier attacks on the "Marianas, Palaus, Carolines, and other profitable targets."[47] The southern Marianas were to be seized, with a target date of 15 June 1944, and B-29 bases and secondary naval bases established. Nimitz was also ordered to cover MacArthur's Hollandia attack and other operations in that area. Both commanders were ordered to "prepare plans for the coordinated and mutual support" of these operations.[48]

The day after receiving the JCS directive Admiral Nimitz sent a secret dispatch to his major subordinates. In it he ordered that planning for the Truk assault be halted and all effort be given to preparing for the Marianas. A week later a CinCPOA Forager Joint Staff Study was issued. In it was outlined the purpose of the operation. Specifically, it was to "establish bases from which to attack the enemy's sea-air communications, support operations for the neutralization of by-passed Truk, initiate B-29 bombing of the Japanese home islands, and support further offensives against the Palaus, Philippines, Formosa and China." Generally, it was to "maintain unremitting military pressure against Japan" and to "extend our control over the Western Pacific."[49]

A new campaign plan, Granite II, was issued on 3 June. There was a marked difference between this and the original Granite plan, particularly in the timing of operations. The tentative schedule was now:

Operation	Tentative Target Date
Capture of Saipan, Guam, and Tinian	15 June 1944
Capture of Palau	8 September 1944
Occupation of Mindanao	15 November 1944
Capture of Southern Formosa and Amoy	
or	
Capture of Luzon	15 February 1945[50]

When this plan was issued the invasion of the Marianas was less than two weeks away. The forces on the long winding road to Tokyo were approaching their next stop—the Marianas. Despite the roadblocks, despite the side roads and detours, the Marianas had become vital (inevitably so, given King's insistence) to the conduct of the war in the Pacific.

chapter 2

Operation A-GO

WITH ADMIRAL ISOROKU YAMAMOTO'S DEATH in April 1943 a successor to the command of Combined Fleet had to be chosen, and the man picked was Admiral Mineichi Koga. While not of the same caliber as Yamamoto, Koga was highly qualified. Though his policies varied little from his predecessor, he was thought to be more conservative, with a cooler temperament.

One of the first operational plans Koga became concerned with was the Z plan. This was prepared in May 1943 and envisioned the use of the Japanese Navy to counter U.S. naval forces threatening the Japanese outer defense perimeter. (This line extended from the Aleutians down through Wake, the Marshall and Gilbert Islands, Nauru, Ocean, the Bismarck Archipelago, New Guinea, then westward past Java and Sumatra to Burma.)[1] When their position in the Solomons disintegrated, the Japanese modified the Z Plan by eliminating the Gilberts–Marshalls and the Bismarcks as vital areas to be defended by the Navy. They then based their possible actions on the defense of an inner perimeter (including the Marianas, Palau, western New Guinea, and the Dutch Indies).[2]

Koga survived Yamamoto slightly less than a year. While retreating from Palau just before TF 58 attacked that anchorage at the end of March 1944, his plane disappeared en route to the Philippines. As great as Koga's loss was, it was compounded by the loss and subsequent capture of a top secret Z Plan copy and its coding system. Koga's chief of staff, Admiral Shigeru Fukudome, left Palau separately from Koga on 30 March. In his possession was the Z Plan copy. The two planes ran into a storm (which probably killed Koga) and Fukudome's crashed just off Cebu. Fukudome was captured by Filipino guerrillas and his precious documents seized. Although the guerrillas soon were forced to give up their prisoner, the documents found their way to U.S. forces via submarine. They were a priceless find. After recovering Fukudome, the Japanese realized that their operations plan was compromised and a new one needed.

Admiral Shigetaro Shimada, Chief of the Naval Staff in Tokyo, immediately began preparing a new plan. Based on a preliminary draft by Admiral Koga, the plan was known as Operation A-GO, and it was under this directive that the Japanese fought the Battle of the Philippine Sea. (Literally, A-GO means the "A" Operation, but for this book a redundant form, Operation A-GO, will sometimes be used.)

Before A-GO went into effect, however, another important change took place in the Japanese Navy. Though the Navy had been a world leader in carrier development, many of its top commanders were battleship or "Big Gun" adherents. However, by early 1944 these commanders had finally accepted the fact that the carrier was the new capital ship. With this realization came a change in fleet organization.[3]

On 1 March 1944 the First Mobile Fleet (or as more commonly known, the Mobile Fleet) was organized under the command of Vice Admiral Jisaburo Ozawa. Joining the carriers in the Mobile Fleet instead of remaining in separate fleets were most of the first-string battleships, cruisers, and destroyers in the Navy. The Japanese had finally accepted the concept (adopted by the U.S. Navy almost two years earlier) of entrusting a task force including battleships and cruisers to the tactical command of a carrier admiral.

A month passed after Koga's death before a new commander of Combined Fleet was named. He was Admiral Soemu Toyoda, a sarcastic, but brilliant and aggressive officer. He raised his flag on the light cruiser *Oyodo*, anchored in Tokyo Bay, on 3 May. Toyodo received the A-GO plan from Shimada the same day and immediately issued the general order for Operation A-GO.

As with so many of the previous plans, A-GO envisioned a "decisive" fleet action. This time the "decisive battle areas" were deemed to be the Palaus and the Western Carolines. It was in these areas that the Mobile Fleet, along with heavy land-based air, would be concentrated. If by chance the U.S. fleet attacked the Marianas, its ships would be pounced upon by land-based planes in that area. Then the enemy would be

Vice Admiral Jisaburo Ozawa, the redoubtable commander of the Mobile Fleet during the Battle of the Philippine Sea. (U.S. Navy)

lured into the areas where the Mobile Fleet could defeat him. There "a decisive battle with full strength (would) be opened at a favorable opportunity. The enemy task force (would) be attacked and destroyed for the most part in a day assault."[4]

The framers of the A-GO plan were nothing if not optimistic: "As soon as the enemy is damaged, he will be pursued. The strongest air force that can be used will be immediately deployed at land bases and ceaseless air attacks will be waged day and night. . . . Complete success is anticipated."[5]

In conjunction with Operation A-GO, Admiral Shimada came up with a plan to use planes from the home islands. This plan was known as TO-GO. The land-based naval planes of First Air Fleet or Base Air Force were to have an important role in this plan. Prior to the "decisive" battle these planes were to destroy at least one-third of the enemy carriers. Deployment of these planes started 23 May and was completed by early June. However, because of the proposed battle area, the majority of the aircraft were stationed in the Carolines–Philippines area. Only 172 aircraft were based at the point of attack, the Marianas.[6] However, a number of planes from the Hachiman Air Unit in Japan could be sent into the Bonins (including Iwo Jima) and thence south to the Marianas if danger developed there. Clearly, the Japanese placed a great deal of faith in their land-based planes for the coming action. However, though TO-GO was good theory, it failed miserably in practice.

The Japanese had every reason to hope, even to pray, that the "decisive" battle would be fought in the Palaus–Western Carolines area. They were running out of fuel for the Navy! Even though an enemy attack on the Marianas was not out of the question, there was not enough fuel for the Mobile Fleet to steam there and fight a battle. American submarines had recently been making Japanese tankers special targets and they had been doing very well at it. In the first five months of 1944 the U.S. subs had sent twenty-one tankers to the bottom. The oil Japan and her Navy so desperately needed was not reaching the Home Islands.

Oil was available to the Navy from the Borneo oilfields of Tarakan and Balikpapan—oil pure enough to be delivered unprocessed directly into the ships' fuel bunkers. But this unprocessed oil was also highly volatile and therefore dangerous to use. Also, it contained some impurities that tended to foul boilers. For these reasons it was ordered that this oil be processed by refineries in Sumatra and Borneo before being issued to the Mobile Fleet.

Following the distribution of the A-GO plan, senior staff officers from all the concerned commands met on Saipan between 8 and 11 May. During discussions of the plan the disturbing question of a possible American attack on the Marianas came up. At first the high command ruled out the possible sortie of the Mobile Fleet to the Marianas because of the fuel situation. The nagging problem remained, however. Toyoda, therefore, decided to take the admittedly daring step of authorizing the use of unprocessed Borneo oil for the Mobile Fleet units. With this fuel the Fleet would now be able to give battle off the Marianas. But the use of this volatile fuel would have a serious effect on the Mobile Fleet during the Battle of the Philippine Sea. To be nearer the supply of oil the Mobile Fleet began congregating at Tawi Tawi in mid-May. This fine anchorage is on the westernmost island of the Sulu Archipelago, only 180 miles from Tarakan.

Ozawa's own Carrier Division (CarDiv) 1, consisting of the fine new 29,300-ton armored-deck carrier *Taiho*, plus the veteran heavy carriers *Shokaku* and *Zuikaku*, sailed from Lingga Roads south of Singapore, where it had been training for over two months, on 11 and 12 May.

(For the coming battle Ozawa would wear two hats: one as commander of the Mobile Fleet; the other as CarDiv 1 commander.) On the 11th CarDiv 2, comprising the 24,140-ton sister ships *Junyo* and *Hiyo* and the converted 13,360-ton *Ryuho*, and CarDiv 3, with the 11,262-ton *Zuiho* and the 11,190-ton former seaplane tenders *Chitose* and *Chiyoda*, left the Inland Sea. After fueling their destroyers at Okinawa, these two divisions proceeded to Tawi Tawi, arriving on the 16th.

The air units assigned to each carrier division were the 601st, 652nd, and 653rd Naval Air Groups. These were largely green organizations. The 601st had been shattered at Rabaul in November 1943 and, newly reformed, did not join CarDiv 1 until February 1944. The 652nd had also been smashed at Rabaul in January and was not reformed until March. Carrier Division 3's 653rd Naval Air Group was an entirely new outfit, having been formed about the first of February.

These air groups were sorely lacking in training time, ranging between only two to six months. Training at Tawi Tawi for these inexperienced groups was hampered considerably by the lack of a suitable airfield there. Flight training had to be cancelled in May, and the air groups would consequently not be ready for the impending battle. An important factor in these units' training was that most of the crews, would be flying newer and "hotter" aircraft—D4Y Judy dive bombers, B6N Jill torpedo planes, and the improved Zeke 52 fighters. So, with its pilots lacking time in their new aircraft, combat experience, night qualifications, and coordination between (and within) their groups, the outlook for the air arm of the Mobile Fleet was not a happy one. And besides the lack of an airfield, there was another big disadvantage to Tawi Tawi—one the Japanese were to learn the hard way. It was easily accessible to submarines.

The movement of the Mobile Fleet to Tawi Tawi did not go unnoticed by the Americans. The capture of the Z Plan had already given intelligence officers of Vice Admiral Thomas C. Kinkaid's Seventh Fleet an inkling of coming events. On 11 May they commented, "A powerful striking force is believed to be gathering in the northern Celebes Sea, using anchorages in the vicinity of Tawi Tawi. It is believed that the assembly of this force will be completed by 15 May."[7]

Although close to the facts, this was still just speculation on the Americans' part. More hard evidence was needed. This evidence was beginning to trickle in, however. The submarine *Lapon*, patrolling off the west coast of Borneo, spotted at least three carriers, five cruisers, and a number of destroyers steaming by about six miles away on the morning of 13 May. The sub couldn't get into an attack position but was able to send a contact report that evening.

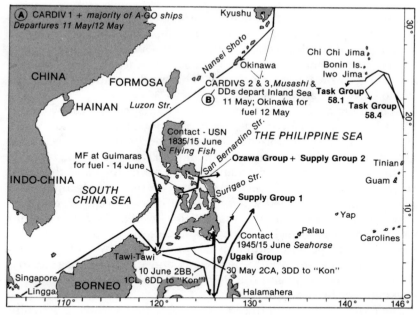

Movements of the Mobile Fleet, May to 16 June 1944.

Following the *Lapon* report, Commander Submarines Southwest Pacific (or in Navy lingo, ComSubSoWesPac) ordered the *Bonefish*, skippered by Commander Thomas W. Hogan, to take a look at Tawi Tawi. Hogan brought his sub south from the Sulu Sea, where he had been patrolling, at full speed. Early on the morning of the 14th Hogan spotted a convoy of three tankers and three destroyers. It appeared they were heading for Tawi Tawi. Creeping up on the convoy, Hogan fired five torpedoes from 1,300 yards. Two of them hit—one in a tanker and one in the 2,090-ton destroyer *Inazuma*, which went down. The remaining destroyers pounded the *Bonefish* for a time, but the sub was able to slip away.

A little before noon the next day, while the *Bonefish* was lying submerged some forty miles northwest of Tawi Tawi, a large group of ships passed by, headed for the anchorage. Possibly the force that the *Lapon* had seen, it contained one large carrier, two battleships, many cruisers, and about ten destroyers. Hogan got off a contact report that night.

Hogan was not finished looking over Tawi Tawi. The next day he moved in closer, raised his periscope, and saw a sight mouthwatering for a submariner: "Six carriers, four or five battleships, eight heavy cruisers, light cruisers, and many destroyers."⁸ But the *Bonefish* had only one torpedo left, so this would remain but a tantalizing target. Hogan moved south during the night and sent out another report. Two enemy "tin cans" must have been listening, for they immediately came out after the *Bonefish*. Hogan took his sub deep, however, and was able to evade his attackers.

To help the *Bonefish* keep Tawi Tawi under surveillance, two more subs (the *Puffer* and *Bluefish*) were ordered into the area. While approaching Tawi Tawi on the morning of the 22nd, the *Puffer*, under the command of Lieutenant Commander Frank G. Selby, found a group of vessels on training maneuvers. Two flattops and three destroyers could be seen as Selby crept in. Carefully setting up on one carrier, Selby was startled when the other carrier swept by, only 500 yards astern. Breaking off the attack, Selby brought the *Puffer* around for another approach. Finally, at a range of 1,400 yards he fired a spread of six torpedoes. Although one, and possibly two, torpedoes hit the *Chitose*, they apparently were duds and did no damage to the carrier. All that Selby and the *Puffer* got for their effort was a good working-over by the escorts.

The *Puffer* made up for the attack on the *Chitose* by sinking two ships on 5 June. The 4,465-ton *Takasaki* and 7,951-ton *Ashizuri* were valuable ships designed to operate with the carrier forces, furnishing the flattops with supplies while at sea. They even provided aircrew quarters and aircraft repair facilities.

Another submarine, the *Cabrilla*, visited the Tawi Tawi area a few days after the *Puffer*'s action with the *Chitose*. During an attack on a group of three carriers and three battleships maneuvering outside the anchorage, the sub's skipper apparently took too long a look at his targets. The sub was suddenly depth-charged by a plane, and was violently shaken up. The enemy vessels were able to retire safely to Tawi Tawi.

U.S. submarine operations in this area had been reasonably successful so far and were far from being finished. One important result of the subs' attentions was that the Mobile Fleet's maneuvers were curtailed considerably in the month before it sailed for battle. On the other hand, Japanese submarine operations during A-GO can hardly be considered successful. At least twenty-five enemy subs were used for scouting and supply purposes in the operation; seventeen were sunk. No useful information was obtained and not one American ship was even damaged.

The Japanese began their submarine operations on 14 May, the day the *Bonefish* moved into the Tawi Tawi area. Still convinced that an

American attack would be aimed at the Palaus, the Japanese set up a scouting line (the NA line) of seven submarines starting at a point about 120 miles northeast of the Admiralties. Other subs were stationed in the Marshalls and Marianas area. The NA-line submarines were decimated by U.S. hunter-killer groups (particularly that of the *England*). Other Japanese submarines suffered equally poor results.

The *I-176* was on a supply mission to Bougainville when it was pounced on by the destroyers *Haggard, Franks, Hailey,* and *Johnston.* After holding the sub down for about twenty hours, the destroyers began taking turns on attack runs. Following five separate attacks, the *Franks* began another run shortly after midnight on 17 May. A full depth-charge pattern was sown, and the unfortunate sub was blown up and sunk northeast of Green Island. One sub down. The *RO-42,* patrolling off Eniwetok, survived three salvos of hedgehogs (a type of throw-ahead projectile more accurate than the conventional roll-over-the-side depth charge) from the destroyer escort *Bangust* on 10 June, but could not survive a fourth. Two down. While steaming on the surface north of the Admiralties on 11 June, the *RO-111* was surprised by the destroyer *Taylor.* After taking numerous 5-inch and 40-mm hits, the Japanese boat crash-dived and was put under permanently by the "tin can's" depth charges. Three down. On 16 June the destroyer escort *Burden R. Hastings* made contact with a surfaced submarine about 120 miles east of Eniwetok. The sub suddenly submerged, and the destroyer escort fired two hedgehog salvos followed by four depth charges. A violent explosion accompanied the second salvo, and the depth charges finished the job of breaking up the enemy vessel. At daylight an aluminum nameplate with *RO-44* written on it was found. Four down.

In the Marianas the Japanese were no luckier. A picket line manned by the *I-10, I-185,* and *I-5* was set up east of Saipan, but it did not last long. The *I-5* simply disappeared, the *I-185* was sunk by the destroyers *Chandler* and *Newcomb* on 22 June, and the *I-10* came out on the short end of a battle with the destroyer *David W. Taylor* and destroyer escort *Riddle* on 4 July. Three more vessels had been crossed off the list of operational Japanese submarines.

On 13 June the destroyer *Melvin* met the *RO-36* near Saipan and pelted the sub with 5-inch fire and depth charges. The destroyer *Wadleigh,* with help from the *Melvin,* sent the *RO-114* down on the 16th. The next day a Liberator of VB-109, flying out of Eniwetok, bombed and sank the *RO-117* cruising on the surface. Another surfaced submarine, the *I-184,* ran afoul of an Avenger from the escort carrier *Suwannee* on 19 June and never returned to Japan to report the attack. A total of eleven Japanese submarines had been lost so far. Six more were to be sunk during this period, and all six belonged to the destroyer escort *England*.

The *England*, commanded by Lieutenant Commander Walton B. Pendleton, was a brand-new ship with only about ten weeks sea experience. At Purvis Bay (on Florida Island across Ironbottom Sound from Guadalcanal) she was assigned to Escort Division 39 along with the destroyer escorts *Raby* and *George*. The officer in tactical command (OTC) was Commander Hamilton Hains, riding in the *George*. Armed with excellent information on the NA line provided by American codebreakers, the three ships left Purvis Bay on 18 May and headed north to attack the line. However, the first unfortunate to test the *England*'s inexperienced crew was not a member of the NA line, but a submarine on a supply mission to Bougainville. At 1335 on the 19th, the *England* picked up the sub (the *I-16*) on her sonar. Five hedgehog attacks were made with hits being made on the second and fifth runs. Following the last attack, a violent explosion threw men to the deck and lifted the *England*'s fantail out of the water. At first the *England*'s crew thought they had been torpedoed; then they realized the *I-16* had blown up.

Early on the morning of the 22nd the three destroyer escorts ran across the *RO-106* cruising on the surface. The Japanese submarine dove, but it could not escape. When the *George*'s first attack was unsuccessful, the *England* took over and sent the enemy submarine to the bottom with two hedgehog salvos. Twenty-four hours later the *RO-104* became the quarry. Detected on the surface, she plunged and then played cat and mouse with the *Raby* and *George*. As the hunters closed the wily submarine skipper "pinged" back at his "pinging" attackers, hoping to foul up their runs. He also maneuvered his vessel skillfully. The *Raby* spent over half an hour in fruitless attacks, and the *George* made five runs without hitting anything. Finally tiring of the game, the OTC ordered the *England* in. Her first pass was unsuccessful but on the second her hedgehogs tore the *RO-104* apart. Shortly after this action another enemy submarine was detected, but this one was lucky; it escaped.

By this time Commander Charles A. Thorwall, commanding Escort Division 40 and riding in the *England*, was ready to change the *England*'s call sign from "Bonnie" to "Killer-Diller."[9]

Moving south toward Manus, the three little ships had still more excitement ahead for them. A little after midnight on the 24th the *George*'s radar locked onto a surface target, range 14,000 yards. The target submerged, but at 0150 sonar contact was made. The captain of this sub was good, too—but not quite good enough. The *England* was forced to make two dry runs because of shrewd evasive tactics by the enemy skipper, but the third pass scored. At least three hedgehogs hit and only bits and pieces of the *RO-116* surfaced again.

On 25 May this crack hunter-killer group received orders to proceed to Seeadler Harbor in the Admiralties, to refuel and load more hedgehogs. At 2303 the *Raby*'s radar picked up another sub 14,000 yards away. Within minutes the other two ships also had the target. When the range closed to 4,000 yards the sub dove. Sonar contact was quickly made, and the *Raby* was given first chance this time, but she muffed it. The *England* didn't. Her first salvo snuffed out the *RO-108*'s life some 250 feet below the surface. At daybreak oil and debris were discovered gushing to the surface.

Arriving at Seeadler Harbor on the afternoon of the 27th, the three ships loaded more hedgehogs from their sister destroyer escort, the *Spangler*, which now joined them. After fueling, the four ships sortied the next afternoon to join a hunter-killer group built around the escort carrier *Hoggatt Bay*. Escorting the carrier were the destroyers *Hazelwood* and *McCord*.

Early on the morning of the 30th, as the task group was steaming north, the *Hazelwood* made radar contact with the *RO-105*. The destroyer forced the sub to dive, but a depth-charge attack gave no conclusive results. The *Hazelwood* maintained contact until 0435 when the *Raby* and the *George* arrived to assist. The two destroyer escorts were asked to make attacks while the *McCord* acted as contact keeper. (These two destroyer escorts were still part of Escort Division 39, while the *England* and the *Spangler* were now Escort Division 40 under the command of Commander Thorwall.) By now the other destroyer escorts were getting an inferiority complex, so Commander Hains was trying to give them a chance at a kill. The *Raby* and *George* each made a number of passes over the unlucky *RO-105* and several explosions indicated the sub was hit. But it was apparently only wounded. The two ships spent the rest of the day holding the *RO-105* down.

Shortly after the sun dipped below the horizon, the Americans heard three heavy underwater explosions. No debris or oil floated to the surface, so it was thought the Japanese skipper had become cagy and had fired torpedoes to throw his pursuers off the track. The ruse did not work, for contact was soon regained and maintained the rest of the night. By now the task group really wanted this submarine, but it was decided to wait until daylight to make any more attacks.

When dawn broke the *George*, followed by the *Raby* and *Spangler*, attacked. They all missed. Time was growing short, for the ships had received word to clear the area, as they might get jumped by enemy planes. Finally, the OTC called in the *England*. This young "old pro" did not miss. At 0729 on the 31st her sonar operator reported contact with the sub. Six minutes later a full salvo of hedgehogs connected with the enemy vessel. A huge explosion followed and the *RO-105* went down for the last time. Only an oil slick and a few pieces of debris marked her passing.

Six Japanese submarines had been sunk by the *England* in thirteen days. It was a masterful performance which earned the ship a Presidential Unit Citation. Commander Thorwall congratulated the *England* and her crew with the comment, "As a result of your efforts Nip recording angel working overtime checking in Nip submariners in joining Honorable Ancestors."[10]

The submarine phase of Operation A-GO had completely miscarried. Not only were seventeen submarines lost, but no submarines would now be available for quick action against the U.S. fleet off the Marianas. The destruction of the NA line and other losses in the area also tended to lead Japanese officers back to their preconceived opinion that any American attack would be launched at the Palaus.

The Japanese were now rapidly becoming aware that a major American offensive was at hand. But where? Even with the submarine losses south of Truk indicating a drive west from there, more substantial evidence was needed. Task Group 58.6, consisting of the carriers *Essex, Wasp, San Jacinto*, five cruisers, and twelve destroyers, struck Marcus on 19 and 20 May. Results were not overwhelming, but the attack prompted Admiral Toyoda to place TO-GO in motion. However, when TG 58.6 raided Wake on the 23rd it was obvious that these two forays were not full-scale attacks and Toyoda cancelled TO-GO.[11]

Toyoda issued his preparation order for A-GO on 20 May. The Mobile Fleet was placed on a six-hour alert. Falling back on one of their favorite tactics, the "bait" force, the Japanese commanders ordered the battleship *Fuso*, cruisers *Myoko* and *Haguro*, and a pair of destroyers to be ready to sortie as a decoy force. They were to lure the Americans into the Palau–Ulithi area where they could then be destroyed by naval and air forces concentrated there. Finally, Base Air Force was ordered to intensify its reconnaissance efforts.

Base Air Force conducted several reconnaissance flights over American bases. On 27 May one plane flew from Truk via Buin (thought by the Americans to be knocked out) to Tulagi, where Rear Admiral Richard L. Conolly's Southern Attack Force was staging for the Guam landing phase of the Marianas invasion. Two other Truk-based planes staged through Nauru to take a look at Majuro and Kwajalein, where most of the invasion forces were gathering. The day before TF 58 sortied from Majuro another intrepid pilot took a peek at the lagoon and reported an impressive array of warships there. The Japanese now had the Americans located, but they were not quite sure of what to do next.

Following the receipt of "Start A-GO," which actually meant "Begin preparations," Admiral Ozawa held a meeting on his flagship *Taiho* for all his commanders. He reminded them that the coming action was to be decisive, and that they were to press on despite any damage suffered. Regarding the latter point, Ozawa declared that for A-GO to succeed, individual units had to be considered expendable. The officers present also discussed proposed tactics for the battle. A massed grouping of carriers much like the disposition used by the Americans was considered, or an "encirclement" using an inverted-V arrangement of three groups. But the final disposition chosen for the Mobile Fleet involved dividing the force into a Main Body and a heavily armed Vanguard.[12]

The Japanese now watched and waited. Then came the invasion of Biak on 27 May. The Japanese high command felt that this move should not go unchallenged. In the first place, the loss of the three airfields on this island off the coast of New Guinea would be a serious blow to the air units of A-GO. The Japanese also reasoned that an attempt by them to recapture Biak would lure the U.S. fleet into "The Decisive Battle near Palau." But the Combined Fleet intelligence officer, Commander Chikataka Nakajima, was not convinced Biak was the major offensive. He thought the landings were just a subsidiary operation and the main American effort would be aimed at the Marianas. His superiors did not agree with him, though, and the Japanese prepared a relief operation for Biak designated Operation KON. The KON plan called for warships to transport about 2,500 troops to Biak from Mindanao. The battleship *Fuso*, the heavy cruisers *Myoko* and *Haguro*, and five destroyers were to act as the screen for a transport section of one heavy and one light cruiser, and three destroyers.

The movement of the enemy ships, coming mainly out of Tawi Tawi, did not escape notice. Allied intelligence officers, using "Magic" intercepts, already knew that a landing attempt would be made on Biak around the fourth or fifth of June and that the *Fuso, Myoko,* and *Haguro* would be in the force. The reports by the submarines *Cabrilla* and *Bluefish* of enemy vessels leaving Tawi Tawi merely confirmed the "Magic" reports.[13]

The transport section, now augmented by two minelayers and a small transport, picked up its troops at Zamboanga on 31 May and proceeded to Davao, where it rendezvoused with the heavy cruisers and three destroyers. The units then headed for Biak, the *Fuso* and two destroyers taking a more northerly course. On the morning of 3 June the submarine *Rasher* spotted part of the force and sent off a contact report. The message was intercepted by the Japanese, who were disturbed at being discovered so far from their target. When a Wakde-based PB4Y began shadowing them, the Japanese decided to call off the attempt.

But this abortive effort would not end happily for the Japanese. While the transport section proceeded to Sorong, on New Guinea's western tip, to disembark troops, the *Fuso, Myoko, Haguro,* and two destroyers retired to Davao. As this force approached Davao on the night of 8 June, they ran into the path of the submarine *Hake.* Commander John C. Broach waited until a destroyer crossed his sights, then fired a spread of torpedoes that ripped open the 2,077-ton *Kazagumo* and sank her.

While the first attempt to reinforce Biak by sea had stalled, action in the air over the island had heated up considerably. Since the Japanese had been anticipating that the next major U.S. offensive would be in the Carolines–Palaus sector, much of their air strength was situated in or near this region. When the Biak landings "confirmed" their suspicions, they began rushing planes in to reinforce their 23rd Air Flotilla. A number of these planes came from the Marianas—reducing the air strength there at a time when they would most be needed.

This one fact illustrates the effectiveness of the Joint Chiefs' concept of a dual thrust across the Pacific. No longer could the Japanese mass their forces in a particular area against an enemy thrust, for now they could be outflanked by another enemy movement.

A number of air strikes were flown against U.S. positions on Biak and Wakde; one attack in particular, on 5 June at Wakde, was very successful. But the Japanese could not keep up the intensity of their attacks and in the process lost planes that could have been used more profitably elsewhere. Also, quite a few pilots came down with malaria at this time, greatly limiting their usefulness.

The Japanese were not about to give up on Biak, though, and a second attempt to reinforce it was quickly mounted. On 7 June Rear Admiral Naomasa Sakonju led a force of six destroyers, distantly screened by two cruisers, on the reinforcement mission. Three destroyers carried six hundred troops, while the remaining destroyers provided an escort and also towed a landing barge each.

Sakonju's second effort (he had led the first attempt) was to be even less successful. On the 8th ten B-25s from Hollandia, escorted by P-38s, spotted Sakonju's ships sliding in toward Biak. In a low-level bombing and strafing attack, the B-25s sent the 1,580-ton *Harusame* to the bottom and damaged the *Shiratsuyu, Shikinami,* and *Samidare.* Sakonju pressed on, but not for long. At 2340 a lookout on one of Sakonju's ships picked up an Allied cruiser and destroyer force, led by Rear Admiral Victor A. C. Crutchley, RN, which was out looking for just these ships.

Sakonju decided that discretion was the better part of valor. After casting off the barges, his force fired a volley of torpedoes at the Allied ships and then high-tailed it to the northwest. Involved in a stern chase and having to dodge torpedoes occasionally, the Allied destroyers were unable to close the distance enough to be effective. The *Shigure* was hit five times by 5-inch fire and the *Shikinami* also had some casualties, but that was the extent of damage to both sides. Most of the troops—who must not have been very happy about what was taking place around them—were taken back to Sorong. The second attempt to reinforce Biak had been turned back.[14]

While the Japanese were vainly trying to reach Biak, a lone U.S. submarine was making her presence felt near Tawi Tawi. Commander Samuel D. Dealey was on his fifth patrol in the *Harder.* This patrol he had been assigned a dual mission: scout Tawi Tawi and pick up a group of guerrillas on northeast Borneo.

As the *Harder* was transiting Sibutu Passage (just south of Tawi Tawi) on the night of 6 June, a convoy of three tankers and two destroyers was picked up. Closing the convoy on the surface, the sub was suddenly spotlighted for the nearest destroyer, when the moon broke through the clouds. The Japanese destroyer charged in for an "easy" kill. Dealey waited until the enemy ship was only 8,500 yards away before submerging. When the ship got within 1,100 yards, Dealey let her have three "fish" from the stern tubes. The *Minazuki,* a 1,590-ton vessel, was stopped cold by two torpedoes, blew up, and went down fast. A second try at the convoy by the *Harder* was frustrated by the other destroyer, and Dealey turned back toward Sibutu Passage.

Shortly before noon the next day, Dealey saw another destroyer in the Passage. And the destroyer saw the *Harder!* This time Dealey let the 2,077-ton *Hayanami* come in close to point-blank range—650 yards— before firing three torpedoes "down the throat." Two of them disembowled the *Hayanami,* and nine minutes after the first sighting she sank, stern first. But Dealey and the *Harder* were not home free. A second destroyer came boiling over to the spot and spent the next two hours rolling depth charges around the sub. None hit, but when six more Japanese destroyers showed up, Dealey decided it was time to leave. He cleared the area and on the night of 8 June picked up his group of guerrillas. He then returned through Sibutu Passage and took up station off Tawi Tawi.

Two more Japanese destroyers showed up in the *Harder's* periscope the following night. Dealey made a submerged approach on the ships and when the targets overlapped, he fired four torpedoes. Two hit the 2,033-ton *Tanikaze*, which literally fell apart. The other two "fish" were thought to have hit the second destroyer, but there is no record of this ship being lost or even damaged.

Dealey and the *Harder* had made a big dent in Ozawa's destroyer forces. Three destroyers had been sent to the bottom in four days by "The Destroyer Killer" (as Dealey was later nicknamed). The U.S. submarines congregated around Tawi Tawi had hurt Ozawa and, thus, Operation A-GO. Along with the destroyers Dealey had sunk, several others had been lost or would soon be. Destruction of these destroyers would mean that the Mobile Fleet would be inadequately screened by these critically important, versatile ships during the coming battle. It was a situation other American submarines would take advantage of in the Philippine Sea.

In the meantime, following the second failure to reinforce Biak, Ozawa was more determined than ever to force his way to the island and land troops that would push the invaders back into the sea. To this end he assembled a new force to carry out Operation KON. It was not a puny force. Included in it were the superbattleships *Yamato* and *Musashi*, three heavy and two light cruisers, seven destroyers, two minelayers, and a number of support and transport vessels.

Under the command of Vice Admiral Matome Ugaki, this force sortied from Tawi Tawi on the afternoon of 10 June. Their departure was noted by Sam Dealey. As the *Harder* closed in for an attack, the sub's periscope was seen and a destroyer charged in. Dealey was not impressed and waited for the enemy ship to close the range. At 1,500 yards three torpedoes were fired "down the throat."

As the *Harder* went deep, a series of explosions were heard. Dealey thought he had gotten another destroyer, but Japanese records do not confirm this. If not sunk, this unidentified destroyer must have been badly damaged. The other escorts and covering aircraft were not about to let the *Harder* off the hook, but she did escape after undergoing a succession of furious counterattacks. After dark, Dealey was able to surface and send a contact report about the enemy's departure from Tawi Tawi.

The Japanese ships continued on to Batjan, just south of the island of Halmahera, where they arrived on the 11th. The run to Biak was scheduled to be made on the 15th. This time the troops were to be landed at all costs, and the big guns of the heavy ships were to be used in a smashing bombardment of U.S. positions on the island.

But fate, and the U.S. Fifth Fleet, were again to stall the reinforcements for Biak. On the 11th and 12th TF 58 planes pounded Saipan and Guam. The Japanese now realized they had been outfoxed; the Americans were aiming for the Marianas, not the Palaus. At 1830 on 12 June Admiral Toyoda ordered the start of A-GO. Operation KON, although only "temporarily" called off, was never resumed.[15]

Admiral Ozawa's Mobile Fleet began moving out for the fateful meeting in the Philippine Sea.

chapter 3

Operation Forager

AT MAJURO, where the waters of the lagoon shimmer from the darkest cobalt to the brightest emerald, TF 58 awaited the moment to sortie for the invasion of the Marianas. The months of wrangling about which course of action to follow were over, and the day for the assault was drawing near.

The invasion of the Marianas, with the first target to be Saipan, was set for 15 June. The landings on Guam and Tinian would follow as the situation dictated. Forager would be one of the largest operations of its type mounted in World War II. Over 127,500 troops (built around four and one-half reinforced divisions) would be carried by 535 combat vessels and auxiliaries. The logistics alone were awesome. All the men and material had to be shipped from Guadalcanal, Eniwetok, or Pearl Harbor—the latter being about 3,500 miles from Saipan.

One of the striking features about Forager was its timing. In just a little under a two-week period, three major attacks were launched at opposite ends of the earth. On 4 June Rome was entered by elements of the United States Fifth Army. On the 6th came the mightiest assault of them all—the Normandy landings. Finally came the landings on Saipan on 15 June. In this short space of time, hundreds of thousands of American soldiers, sailors, and airmen opened the drives that eventually led to the destruction of the Axis powers. These three massive operations, coming so close together, were an amazing demonstration of American strength, particularly in logistics. It was a demonstration of power, strategic and tactical, that may never be seen again.

Commanding Forager was Admiral Raymond A. Spruance, Commander Fifth Fleet. In intellectual ability Spruance was "unsurpassed among the flag officers of the United States Navy."[1] There were two attack forces under Spruance's command, designated for the assaults on Saipan/Tinian and Guam. The Southern Attack Force (TF 53), under the command of Rear Admiral Conolly, staged out of the Guadalcanal area. When the Japanese Navy came out to fight, the Guam landings were postponed; TF 53 took little part in the Battle of the Philippine Sea.

Vice Admiral Richmond K. Turner commanded the Northern Attack Force (TF 52), as well as TF 51, the Joint Expeditionary Force. Task Force 52 staged out of the Hawaiian Islands. The makeup of the two Attack Forces was one of the reasons why TF 58 was involved in the Marianas assault. Although TF 58's main job was to attack and destroy enemy ships, planes, and troops, it also had the responsibility of protecting the invasion groups from attack. The Northern and Southern Attack Forces were covered by a group of old battleships (primarily used for shore bombardment) and a number of escort carriers; it was thought these might not be sufficient to handle a full-scale naval action.

The time had finally come for TF 58 to depart Majuro and set course for the Marianas. Japanese reconnaissance planes missed the sortie by one day, being over Majuro at midday on the 5th. On 6 June the ships

Admirals Raymond A. Spruance and Chester W. Nimitz.

weighed anchor and slowly steamed out the lagoon entrance. It was a magnificent sight. Task Force 58 was such a huge force—seven fleet and eight light carriers, seven fast battleships, three heavy and seven light cruisers, and sixty destroyers—that it took almost five hours for this aggregation to clear the lagoon.

Commanding TF 58 was Vice Admiral Marc A. Mitscher. The task force was divided into four task groups. Task Group 58.1 was commanded by Rear Admiral J. J. "Jocko" Clark, and had the carriers *Hornet, Yorktown, Belleau Wood,* and *Bataan.* The four carrier air groups—2, 1, 24, and 50, respectively—had 267 planes spread among them.

Rear Admiral Alfred E. "Monty" Montgomery commanded TG 58.2. His task group had the carrier *Bunker Hill* with the ninety-three planes of Air Group 8, the *Wasp* with Air Group 14's eighty-nine planes, the *Monterey* with twenty-nine Air Group 28 planes aboard, and the *Cabot* with Air Group 31's thirty-three aircraft.

Rear Admiral John W. "Black Jack" Reeves, Jr., led TG 58.3. His force had the veteran carrier *Enterprise* plus the *Lexington, San Jacinto,* and *Princeton.* Air Group 10 on the "Big E" had sixty-nine planes. Air Group 16 on the "Blue Ghost" had ninety-four planes. The two light carrier air groups, 51 and 27, had thirty-two and thirty-three aircraft

Vice Admiral Marc A. Mitscher and his chief of staff, Captain Arleigh A. Burke.

VF(N)-101 Corsair night fighters are among the aircraft clustered on the Enterprise's *deck during the Forager operation.*

on board, respectively. (The *Princeton* VF-27 planes were unique in having "sharks' mouths" painted on the cowls of the Hellcats. VF-27 was probably the only Navy squadron during the war to carry such colorful and exotic designs on its planes.)

The last task group, TG 58.4, was the smallest in TF 58. Rear Admiral William K. "Keen" Harrill had only three carriers under his command. The *Essex* had Air Group 15 aboard with its ninety-nine planes. On the *Langley* was Air Group 32 with thirty-two aircraft. The *Cowpens* had the thirty-two planes of Air Group 25.

The 902 planes carried on the flattops of TF 58 made that force a formidable one indeed. Most of the fighters were the superb F6F-3 Hellcats. Three radar-equipped F4U-2 Corsairs were on the *Enterprise* for night operations. The majority of the dive bombers were the new SB2C-1C Helldivers (known as "2Cs" or "Beasts" to their pilots). The venerable SBD-5 Dauntlesses would be making their final appearance with the fast carriers during this operation. Both the *Enterprise* and *Lexington* would have Dauntlesses as their dive bombers, and the *Yorktown*, surprisingly, would have four SBDs listed among her complement of forty-four dive bombers. The torpedo planes would be the efficient TBF/TBM Avengers.

Besides the striking power of its aircraft, TF 58 fairly bristled with 5-inch/38-caliber, 40-mm, and 20-mm guns. An *Essex*-class carrier held over eighty of these weapons. The other vessels also carried a vast number of these guns. An enemy plane attempting to attack TF 58 would have to brave an awesome display of firepower.

One vital weapon that TF 58 and the entire U.S. Navy used effectively during the war was radar. During the coming action ship-borne radar (coupled with some excellent direction by the TF 58 fighter director officer and the task group FDOs) provided valuable information that was used to help decimate the attacking Japanese formations.

After TF 58 cleared Majuro, some planes that had been sent ashore for training or to provide extra Combat Air Patrol (CAP) returned to their carriers. At 1630 the task groups rendezvoused near Lat. 7°22'N, Long. 170°57'E and congealed into TF 58. Initially a course of 225 degrees was taken up, heading indirectly for Point Roger where the task force was to fuel from the oilers of Service Squadron 10. Point Roger, an arbitrary fix, had been picked to be the fueling rendezvous because it was considered to be outside the range of enemy search planes from Truk and Marcus.

On the 7th and 8th all the air groups flew training missions, and the ships held gunnery drills. For the *Yorktown*'s Air Group 1 these missions were very useful, for Forager would be its first operation. Carrier operations are always hazardous, even during training, and operational losses are not rare. The task force suffered a pair of such losses on the 8th, when the *Bunker Hill* lost an SB2C-1C and the *Cabot* an Avenger.

On 8 June TG 58.7 (the battle line), which had been operating separately, was disbanded and the big-gun ships and their escorting vessels distributed throughout the other task groups. At 1400 course was changed to 330 degrees. Later that afternoon the oilers of TG 50.17 joined, and the next day TF 58 fueled. The oilers were divided between the task groups, with the *Sabine* fueling the ships of TG 58.1, the *Platte* and the *Guadalupe* with TG 58.2, the *Caliente* with TG 58.3, and the *Cimarron* and *Kaskaskia* with TG 58.4. The fueling took about ten hours as the ships headed east.

Vice Admiral Mitscher, sitting facing aft on the *Lexington*'s flag bridge as was his custom (it was said he didn't like the wind in his face) ended the fueling about 1530 and turned his force toward the Marianas. The *Indianapolis*, carrying Admiral Spruance who had been visiting facilities on Roi and Eniwetok, joined TG 58.3's screen about 1400.

Mitscher fully expected to be picked up by snoopers from Saipan or Guam on either the 11th or 12th, and that TF 58 would have to fight its way in. Mitscher's chief of staff, Captain Arleigh "31-Knot" Burke, and assistant chief of staff, Captain Truman Hedding, were not too keen about being discovered. Normal American carrier tactics had pre-scribed a dawn fighter sweep of enemy airfields. Following this plan, the attack would be made on the morning of the 12th. If the task force was discovered a day or two before this (and it was), the Japanese would obviously be waiting for just an attack and would try to throw a punch of their own before the Americans could send in planes.

Weather forecasts, however, had indicated that it would be possible to top off the task force's destroyers while headed west on 11 June. If this forecast held up, it meant that TF 58 would be within fighter range of the Marianas on the 11th, and the Americans might still get the jump on the enemy.

Task Force 58's air operations officer, Commander Gus Widhelm, and his assistant, Lieutenant Commander John Myers, came up with a trio of plans to help achieve surprise. In Plan Gus, several destroyers were to be detached from the force and sent twenty miles ahead of the leading task groups to provide radar surveillance, fighter direction, and rescue chores. Plan Johnny called for a maximum-range fighter sweep of the four important islands on the afternoon of the 11th, rather than the planned sweep on the morning of 12 June. The third plan, Jeepers, was named after an oft-used expression of gunnery officer Lieutenant Commander Burris D. Wood. It would bring the regular morning bombing strikes back into operation for 12 June.

Spruance provisionally accepted the three plans, provided TF 58 was not spotted on 10 June. Mitscher was not about to be put off, saying, "Recommend Plan Johnny to be carried out regardless contact. Enemy has assembled considerable number dive bombers and fighters on fields. Plan is to try to prevent coordinated attack on our carriers while planes are on deck fueled and armed. Believe unscheduled operation will be most disturbing. We have left over 200 fighters to protect fleet while Plan Johnny effective. Believe expenditure fuel is warranted. Hope Plan Jeepers will take care of any planes that may be flown in during night."[2] Spruance concurred and the plans went into effect.

Aboard the fifteen carriers of TF 58 the pace quickened as crews scrambled to get the planes ready for the strikes. Each flight deck was a kaleidoscope of color that formed, broke apart and reformed again as the red, yellow, blue, and green-shirted deck crews went about their jobs. Occasionally the whine of an elevator would stand out from the general monotone of noise, as it brought up another plane from the hangar deck, where it had been checked and readied for battle. The deck crews or a small tractor would then pull and push the plane into position on deck.

On the edge of the flight deck or in strategic locations on the carrier's islands, the lookouts and gun crews took little notice of the commotion going on around them. Their attention was focused outward, away from the ship, for they were in enemy waters and a Japanese plane could suddenly appear out of that cloud over there or out of the sun shining directly overhead.

Bogeys began popping up with increasing frequency on the 10th. Several encounters with enemy planes occurred during the day primarily by land-based long-range search planes. VB-108 and VB-109 PB4Ys shot down three enemy planes, including two Bettys, only 50 to 65 miles west of the task force. A *Princeton* fighter got into the act late in the afternoon by dropping another Betty, also 50 miles west. The day was not without loss to the Americans. In the morning an *Essex* night fighter crashed near the task group, and the pilot was not recovered.

11 June came up a beautiful day. Unfortunately, it was also the kind of day a group of ships the size of TF 58 could be seen by snoopers miles away. And TF 58 was seen.

Lieutenant (jg) Charles A. Sims, a Japanese language expert on the *Lexington*, monitored transmissions from an enemy plane about midmorning that made it quite plain that TF 58 had been sighted. More evidence of the presence of snoopers was provided by the smoke trails of the enemy aircraft as they were shot down by CAP Hellcats. Several Emilys, Bettys, and Helens, plus a sprinkling of other planes went down around TF 58. One of the Emilys destroyed by *Yorktown* fighters near a pair of picket destroyers provided some information. The destroyer *Burns* picked up two survivors, charts, and mail from the debris of the crashed plane. The unlucky flying-boat had been evacuating personnel from Buin to Saipan, via Truk, when it stumbled into TF 58's path.

The 8 June forecast held up and the destroyers were able to be topped off while TF 58 headed west. The fueling was completed by 0900, three hours earlier than had been figured. The task force was able to draw almost fifty miles closer to the target than had been expected. Under Plan Gus the destroyers moved out to take their positions in a picket line. At 0937 Mitscher ordered Plan Johnny into operation, advancing the launch time one hour.

The sweep was set to go at 1300. Clark's TG 58.1 would hit the Guam and Rota airfields, while the other task groups would take on Saipan and Tinian. On the carriers the planes were already spotted for takeoff. The Hellcats would go in alone, escorted only by a few SB2Cs or TBFs for rescue work. In the cockpits the pilots sat ready for the

command to start engines. Although everyone appeared to be out-
wardly calm, an atmosphere of tension permeated the ships.

At 1300 TF 58 was in the vicinity of 13°45'N, 148°50'E and about
192 miles from Guam and 225 miles from Saipan. Over the loudspeakers came the command, "Start engines!" Tentatively at first, one
engine began to turn over, then settled into a throaty roar. It was
quickly followed by the sound of other engines running up. Soon the
flight decks were throbbing with the deep bellow of the Hellcats'
engines.

The deck signalmen now took over, signalling each plane into
takeoff position. On some carriers the Hellcats would be launched by
catapult; on others the fighters would roll down the deck. Under the
wings of each plane was a plane handler ready to pull the chocks from
in front of the wheels when the plane was guided forward. When the
chocks were pulled the handler crouched, rolled or crawled away from
his plane. To stand up could mean quick death to an unwary sailor.

As each Hellcat moved into takeoff position, the head signalman
started whirling his hand over his head in a tight circle. The pilot ran
up his engine and went through his final check. When everything was
okay, the pilot nodded to the signalman. Still twirling his hand over his
head but in a larger circle, the signalman finally snapped his arm down
and pointed forward. With brakes released, the fighter started to roll
forward slowly, gradually picking up speed. After takeoff the pilot
began a slight turn to starboard and began climbing toward the rendezvous.

The fifteen carriers launched a deckload strike of 213 Hellcats
(many carrying bombs), with ten Helldivers and Avengers joining in.
Three planes had to return with mechanical problems. Following the
launch, TG 58.1 broke off to proceed independently to Point Attic, its
launch position for the next day's strikes.

A little over an hour after launch the fighters were in sight of their
targets. Scattered low clouds dotted the area, but visibility was good.
The *Bataan*, hampered throughout the operation by a balky forward
elevator that could only be used in an emergency—and then only at
slow speed—sent twelve VF-50 Hellcats against Rota. Little activity was
noted on the island, but the 3,262-ton *Kinposan Maru*, a trawler, and a
number of trucks on the airfield were strafed.

Sixteen *Hornet* and eight *Belleau Wood* fighters, with two SB2Cs
supplying rescue support, attacked Agana field on Guam. No enemy
planes were seen airborne when the attackers arrived but the flak was
relatively heavy. The enemy fighters did show up, but "as usual, no

difficulty was encountered in destroying the enemy once he was found."³ VF-2 from the *Hornet* tangled with over twenty-five Japanese planes which tried popping out of clouds against the Hellcats strafing the field. The tactic didn't work and the "Rippers" wound up claiming twenty-three planes destroyed, including three Zekes and a Jack shot down by the squadron commander, William A. "Bill" Dean. Dean reported that the Jack, a new arrival from Japan, burned as easily as a Zeke. Fighting 2 did lose Lieutenant (jg) Howard B. Duff, Jr., when he was shot down by flak and had to ditch off Port Apra. Although he was seen to get out of his plane and swim away, he was not recovered.

Over Orote field the fifteen depth-charge or fragmentation-cluster-carrying Hellcats of VF-1 and four VF-24 fighters were met with intense antiaircraft fire. The flak didn't stop the attackers, however, and the *Yorktown* planes claimed three enemy planes shot down and four damaged on the ground. All four of the *Belleau Wood* pilots scored, getting two Zekes and two "Tojos."

The heaviest fighting of the day took place over Saipan and Tinian, where the other three task groups had sent their planes. Task Group 58.2 was assigned the airfields on Tinian and sent fifty-five fighters and two Helldivers against the targets. The *Bunker Hill* sent sixteen, and the *Monterey* twelve Hellcats against Gurguan field. They met no air opposition and only one antiaircraft gun was firing. A division of VF-8 fighters also attacked the field after runs on the Ushi Point airfield.

Monterey Avengers are guided into position for launch against targets on Tinian, *11 June 1944.*

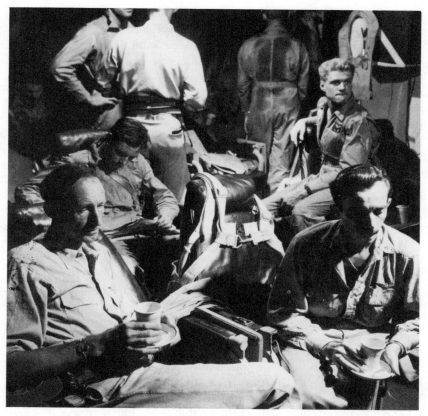

Captain Stuart H. Ingersoll (left), skipper of the light carrier Monterey, *and Lieutenant Commander Roger W. Mehle, Air Group 28's commander, anxiously await word of VB-28's attack on Tinian, 11 June 1944. Other pilots also wait quietly for the first word. (National Archives)*

Following their passes on Gurguan, the pilots of Fighting 28 noticed several Bettys trying to land on the field. The pilots patiently waited until all the Bettys were in the landing circle, then pounced on the enemy bombers. The *Monterey* pilots claimed three Zekes and nine Bettys destroyed and seven other planes as probables. The *Bunker Hill* fighters claimed four enemy planes in the air and thirteen on the ground.

Over the Ushi Point airfield were twenty-seven Hellcats (fifteen VF-8 and twelve VF-31) with two *Wasp* dive bombers for rescue work. When the bomb-carrying Hellcats from the *Cabot's* fighter squadron arrived over Tinian, the two divisions at 10,000 and 12,000 feet were jumped by twenty to thirty Zekes diving out of an overcast. An alert pilot saw the rapidly closing enemy fighters and called out the warning, "Skunks!" The VF-31 fliers quickly jettisoned their bombs and turned into the attack.

As the Zekes came screaming in, the Americans began the scissoring maneuver known as the Thach Weave. In this maneuver two pilots could cover each other's tail. When an enemy plane attacked, the two pilots would then turn toward each other and be in position to shoot the attacker down. About eight Zekes jumped Lieutenant Doug Mulcahy and his wingman, Lieutenant (jg) J.M. Bowie, but with no success. Mulcahy and Bowie immediately began scissoring and Bowie flamed one Zeke that was trying to escape Mulcahy's fire. The enemy pilots left, looking for easier game. Mulcahy and Bowie gave chase after another Zeke, with Mulcahy doing the honors this time from point-blank range.

When the *Cabot* fliers returned to their ship they claimed fourteen Zekes, with three more as probables and one damaged. One Hellcat was shot down by the Zekes but the pilot, Ensign Richard G. Whitworth, was able to bail out. He was finally rescued some eighty hours later by the destroyer *Caperton*.

The fifteen planes of VF-8 each carried 350-pound depth charges and used them to beat up the Ushi Point strip. A Japanese NCO was not impressed with their efforts, however, recording in his diary, "Air raid for an hour beginning at 1500. They took their time bombing and strafing places where there weren't any Japanese planes."[4]

Task Groups 58.3 and 58.4 worked over Saipan. The sixty fighters of TG 58.3 were sent primarily against Aslito field. The field was attacked about 1430 by Hellcats of VF-27, VF-10, VF-16, and VF-51, plus two VT-10 Avengers. The *Enterprise*'s fighters, "The Grim Reapers," tangled with a group of defenders and proceeded to knock down six Zekes, a Betty, and an Emily which had stumbled into the fray at the wrong time. Following the brush with the Zekes, the Fighting 10 pilots dropped down to the deck to strafe the airfields at Aslito, Marpi Point, and Charan Kanoa. After the first pass the Japanese lit smoke pots on the eastern shore, the smoke blowing west across the island and obscuring Tanapag. The two Avengers were able to get under the smoke at 500 feet and photographed considerable shipping clustered in Tanapag Harbor.

Though enemy air opposition melted away, flak was still very heavy and three planes were knocked out of the sky by it. The *Lexington*'s Lieutenant (jg) W.E. Burckholter was able to ditch, but when trying to get out of his sinking plane, he got snagged and was pulled down. The

Enterprise lost two fighters, but one pilot was rescued by a destroyer and the other was picked up by an *Indianapolis* SOC.

On the receiving end of the American attacks, a Japanese soldier wrote in his diary: "At a little after 1300, I was awakened by the air raid alarm and immediately led all men into the trench. Scores of enemy Grumman fighters began strafing and bombing Aslito airfield and Garapan. For about two hours, the enemy planes ran amuck and finally left leisurely amidst the unparalleledly inaccurate antiaircraft fire. All we could do was watch helplessly."[5]

Task Group 58.4 launched thirty-nine fighters and two dive bombers to work over the Tanapag Harbor–Marpi Point area. Seven of the fighters carried depth charges. Antiaircraft fire was intense and this group suffered the most combat losses of the day. Lieutenant (jg) L.T. Kenney, from the *Essex*, was hit during his initial dive and went straight in. The *Langley* lost two planes in the same run. Lieutenant (jg) Donald E. Reeves and Lieutenant M.M. Wickendoll were both hit by flak while making a second pass on the target. Wickendoll was lucky—he was able to ditch and was picked up by the destroyer *Thatcher*. Reeves was killed. Fighting 25's Ensign P.A. Parker did not return from a scrape with Zekes.

When Hellcats from other carriers arrived after the initial fighter pass, they found few targets airborne. Using their 500-pounders and

Bombed-out hangers and pieces of enemy flying boats litter the Tanapag seaplane base following the first strikes on Saipan.

.50-caliber machine guns, they bombed and strafed the airfields on Saipan and Tinian. Few planes could be seen on the ground, but fierce antiaircraft fire was received, especially at Aslito. One pilot who did hit a grounded plane was Lieutenant Bert Morris, better known to moviegoers as actor Wayne Morris. He set afire an Emily on the water. (Afterwards, with tongue in cheek, he argued that since the Emily had four engines, he should get credit for four kills.)

Not all the action was over the islands. Two *Bataan* pilots had an lively time while guarding a lifeguard submarine. Several Zekes took an inordinate interest in the sub, and the two fliers had to discourage them by shooting down three.

About 1630 the fighters began arriving over the task force. They were quickly brought aboard and as soon as the pilots reached their ready rooms the intelligence officers were tabulating the claims. When the totals were finally compiled, the fighter pilots had claimed eighty-six aircraft destroyed in the air, thirty-three more on the ground, with twenty-six probables and seventy damaged. This total included ten planes shot down by the combat air patrol. Eleven Hellcats and six pilots had been lost in combat. One *Lexington* Dauntless had taken the barrier on landing and had to be pushed overboard. Another twenty-two planes had been damaged by flak and fighters.

(It is interesting to note that a number of pilots claimed to see and shoot down Oscars, Tonys, and Tojos—Army fighters. Since no Army fighters were in the Marianas, it is evident they did not see what they thought they saw. Aircraft identification, in all theaters of war, was a problem that continued through the war.)

Although the Japanese reported the loss of only thirty-six planes and the shooting down of sixty-five U.S. planes, Vice Admiral Kakuji Kakuta's Base Air Force had been seriously hurt. Close to one-third of the total Japanese air strength had been put out of action on this day. Only with help from Japan and the Carolines would the enemy be capable of any effective action against TF 58. And yet, Kakuta was already telling Toyoda and Ozawa how well his forces had handled the Americans. His misplaced optimism (or, perhaps, face-saving) would play an important part in the battle.

Mitscher and his subordinates were very pleased with the day's results. Admiral Montgomery later wrote, "The afternoon VF sweep of D-4 Day is considered to have been tactically sound in all respects. . . . The fact that there was no air opposition for the next three days may be attributed to the success of the initial sweep."[6]

After the recovery of planes, TF 58 retired for the night, with TG 58.1 heading south and the other groups retiring to the northeast.

The Japanese tried hard to sink some U.S. vessels on the morning of the 12th but were unsuccessful. Ten Bettys from Truk started stalking the northern groups at 0315, but did not appear to want to mix it up. This "attack" was executed with the usual Japanese flair—lots of float lights and strings of flares—but with little else. At 0405 one Betty got a bit too close and was promptly downed by fire from the *New Jersey*. Fifteen minutes later TG 58.2's ships turned on their red truck lights and the *Wasp* and *Bunker Hill* began launching their first missions of the day. The sight of the lighted ships and the fighters taking off, running lights on also, must have frightened off the attackers for they quickly opened the distance and were soon off the radar screens.

For TF 58 the day's activities started early as the *Hornet* and *Yorktown* launched night fighters at 0230 to heckle Rota and Guam. The three northern task groups began launching planes shortly after 0400, while TG 58.1 (some seventy-three miles off Guam) began sending its planes off at 0525. While the *Bataan* furnished the CAP, antisubmarine patrol (ASP), and antisnooper patrol during the day, the other three carriers launched 464 planes on sweeps and strikes. *Bataan* pilots got two Judys within fifteen minutes of each other around 0600. The 0525 launch was a combined fighter sweep and strike, with the *Belleau Wood* planes working over Rota and the *Hornet/Yorktown* aircraft going against Guam targets. The sweep was productive, with the Hellcats claiming seven Zekes, two "Tojos," and an Irving.

Flak over Orote was extremely intense and accurate throughout the day. Fighting 24 pilots reported "the heaviest AA fire encountered by (the) squadron in nine months of combat experience." The batteries "were firing continuously up into the few holes in the clouds through which the attackers were coming."[7] VF-2 lost only one pilot when his fighter was hit by a large shell and exploded, but the *Yorktown* air group lost a number of planes during the day. Lieutenant (jg) Arthur M. Payton's Hellcat crashed into the water a few miles west of Orote Point and he was apparently trapped in his sinking plane. Lieutenant Norman N. Merrell's Avenger was last seen diving over the target with its engine blazing. Two Helldivers (but not their crews) were also lost. Before the day was over the intense flak claimed eleven American planes. Four others had been lost operationally. Twenty-three more planes had been damaged.

Many pilots in TF 58 were less than enchanted about attacking airfields, especially well-defended ones. One pilot stated, "Continued duels between aircraft and well-protected gun crews can have but one ending and that will be an unhappy one for the aircraft. . . . Bombing of runways and AA installations is considered futile." In the same vein another pilot said, ". . . It would be far cheaper to deny the airfields and airfield installations on Guam, Rota, Tinian and Pagan by surface-ship bombardment rather than by the relatively ineffective air bombing by carrier-borne planes."[8] Finally, a *Princeton* pilot commented, "The use of delayed action fuses on bombs dropped on the runways, and the maintenance of CAP over the fields at night to prevent reinforcements being flown in . . . would be more effective than constant cratering of runways, which requires great expenditures of bombs and permits the Japanese to display their ability to fill in holes."[9]

Besides attacking Guam and Rota, TG 58.1 sent morning and afternoon searches 325 miles to the west. Although these were generally unproductive, an enemy convoy was found 134 miles west of Guam in the afternoon and a strike was sent against it at 1500. The fifteen Hellcats, six "2Cs", and nine "Turkeys" (as the torpedo planes were known to their crews) were unable to find the convoy and dropped their bombs on Guam instead. The enemy vessels were not out of the woods yet, however.

The last strike of the day over Orote cost the *Belleau Wood* an F6F and pilot. Though he got out of his burning plane and his comrades circled over him in the water until dusk, he was not recovered. Air operations were generally completed by 1900. Six *Yorktown* Helldivers that were low on fuel settled on the *Hornet*, returning to their own ship the next day. There was a little excitement on the *Bataan* when she was landing her fighters. As the last plane touched down, an accidental burst of its .50-calibers was triggered. Crewmen hit the deck but five were a bit slow and received minor injuries. The ship's island structure above the bridge was riddled, and a radar antenna put out of commission.

Up north, TG 58.2 was working over Tinian while TGs 58.3 and 58.4 shared attacks on Saipan. Task Group 58.4 also sent strikes against Pagan. Task Group 58.2 sent 408 sorties over Tinian (only 65 miles away). The first sweep and strike was launched at 0418, even as the Truk-based Bettys were congregating around the task group. Seven strikes were flown by the task group's planes during the day with mixed results. Only three planes on the ground were claimed destroyed, with two others as probables and eight damaged. No enemy planes were seen in the air. Two *Bunker Hill* Avengers and their crews went down over Tinian, as did a *Wasp* Hellcat. Another fighter made it back to its carrier, but had been so badly damaged that it had to be jettisoned.

VB-14's skipper, Lieutenant Commander J.D. Blitch, was pleased with the work of his pilots, reporting: "After the second strike, AA fire fell off markedly in volume, which may be partly attributable to the effectiveness of VB attacks. . . . It is believed that pilots have overcome most of their earlier nervousness in attacking defended targets and are able to press their attacks with increased accuracy."[10]

With D-Day only three days away TGs 58.3 and 58.4 hit targets on Saipan heavily on the 12th. Even though 186 less sorties than planned were flown, TG 58.3 put 465 sorties over the Aslito and Charan Kanoa areas, while TG 58.4 contributed another seventy-two for the Marpi Point, Tanapag, and Charan Kanoa areas. Pickings were slim for the Americans as they roared in over Saipan on the fighter sweep. Only one Zeke was in the air and was quickly shot down. It was too dark to see any planes on the ground. *Princeton* planes, providing CAP and ASP for TG 58.3, bagged a Nick in the morning. For the entire day only four enemy planes were shot down and two more destroyed on the ground, against a loss of three planes in combat and three operationally. Four pilots and two crewmen were lost.

Against enemy shipping on the 12th the *Enterprise* pilots were unusually enterprising. Two pilots hit a medium-sized freighter in Tanapag Harbor with 1,000-pounders. A third pilot's SBD was hit by flak, though, in the attack and it went straight in. Lieutenant (jg) C.R. Largess was credited with sinking a large freighter with two 500-pounders, and Lieutenant (jg) C.B. Collins sent a medium freighter under with one 500-pound bomb. Fifteen miles northwest of Saipan, Lieutenant (jg) S.W. McCrary saw a small freighter heading for the island. Two 500-pound bombs took care of it and its load of fuel drums. Sixty-six survivors were later rescued.

Admiral Harrill's group was being kept busy with a variety of tasks. Although only seventy-two sorties were flown against Saipan targets, the TG 58.4 fliers found other things to keep them occupied. The *Essex* and the *Cowpens* launched fighter sweeps against Saipan shortly after 0400. These were shortly followed by another strike. The *Langley* spent the day providing CAP and ASP. One of the *Cowpens* Avengers had its elevators shot up over Saipan, and the pilot had to ditch near the flattop upon his return. Two of the crew were recovered by the destroyer *Wilson*.

The next strike was sent against targets on and around Pagan. This attack was expensive, costing the *Essex* an Avenger and the *Cowpens* two fighters but only one *Cowpens* pilot was lost. A large sampan flotilla northwest of the island was almost completely destroyed. But the biggest action of the day was against a convoy found shortly after 1000, northwest of the island.

This convoy (twelve Marus and ten escorts, joined at sea by sixteen fishing boats) had left Tanapag just before the Hellcats had swept over Saipan on the afternoon of the 11th. When spotted it was about 160 miles from Saipan and its sailors probably thought they were out of range of U.S. planes. They were wrong.

A strike originally intended for Saipan was instead diverted to hit the convoy as soon as possible. The *Essex* launched thirty-seven planes and the *Cowpens* sent along twelve fighters and seven Avengers. One *Essex* Helldiver just made it off the carrier before it went into the water, soaking the crew. The remaining planes came in on the unfortunate convoy at low level, decimating it. A number of hits and near-misses staggered the frantically maneuvering vessels. In the afternoon a twenty-seven-plane strike inflicted more damage on the convoy. Other strikes the next day finished the job. After TG 58.4 was through, ten cargo ships, three small escorts, the 840-ton torpedo boat *Ootori*, and several fishing boats had been sunk.

The attack on the convoy had not been without loss. The Hellcat of Air Group 25's skipper, Lieutenant Commander Robert H. Price, was hit and he had to ditch near the convoy. When the afternoon strike went after the ships, twelve *Cowpens* fighters tagged along to look for Price. He was seen and a life raft dropped to him. Unfortunately, a search by a floatplane failed to turn him up and a search the next morning was also unsuccessful. Price was considered lost and his friends aboard the *Cowpens* began dividing his belongings.

Another "Mighty Moo" pilot was rescued on the 12th, but for a time it was nip-and-tuck. The flier was being picked up west of Pagan by a *Houston* OS2U when the plane suddenly capsized. Now there were three men in the water! A second OS2U took over but was unable to take off with the extra weight. The plane radioed for help. Shortly the destroyers *Charles Ausburne* and *Thatcher* appeared and took the three drenched fliers aboard. The two "tin cans" also took time out from the rescue to knock off a pair of sampans that got in the way.

The day of 12 June had been costly for the Americans. During the day 1,472 target sorties had been flown. Twenty-three planes had been lost in combat and eight in operational crashes. Seventy-six more had been damaged. Sixteen pilots and eight crewmen had been lost. Japanese losses were not great—only about thirty-five planes claimed destroyed, with eleven more as probables and thirty-six damaged. But it was apparent that the Japanese air units in the Marianas were now hurting. Heavy and very accurate antiaircraft fire was now the main threat to the attackers. Especially vulnerable to the flak were the Avengers, because of the tactics used in glide-bombing attacks and runs with the new 3.5-inch rockets.

The bombing and rocket attacks by the torpedo planes were found to be extremely dangerous and results were well below expectations. A number of pilots and even Captain E.W. Litch, skipper of the *Lexing-*

ton, vented their feelings after the battle. Litch said, "The use of TBFs for glide-bombing AA emplacements has proven a costly undertaking. This is considered a needless loss of aircraft and personnel in view of the unsatisfactory results obtained from such bombing. Rocket firing with TBFs has proven costly also. Because of the shallow dive necessary and resulting lack of speed, rocket-firing planes are very vulnerable to AA fire."[11]

Lieutenant N.A. Sterrie, who took command of Torpedo 16 after Commander Robert H. Isely was shot down in a rocket attack, continued: "Weighing damage done against damage received in rocket attacks, it is the considered opinion of this command that . . . the rocket is a weapon of dubious merits penalizing an airplane (TBF) already extremely vulnerable to the attacks demanded of it."[12] To compound the problem, some Avengers had to carry both bombs and rockets, and the pilots found they couldn't aim the rockets and drop the bombs at the same time. Consequently, the pilots "chose to aim the bombs and fire the rockets promiscuously in their dives and pullouts."[13]

That night, while TGs 58.1 and 58.4 remained to the east of the Marianas, the other two groups passed north of Saipan to be in position to launch missions against the islands from the west the next day. On 13 June, TF 58's planes and battlewagons were used to pound Saipan. Under the command of Vice Admiral Willis A. "Ching" Lee, the seven new battleships, several screening destroyers, and Admiral Spruance in the *Indianapolis* peeled away from TGs 58.2 and 58.3 shortly before 0700 and stood off Saipan for the first scheduled bombardment of the island. The old battleships, experts in fire support, were not due to arrive until the next day; thus the new battlewagons (under a CAP from the *Wasp* and *Bunker Hill*) were given the job of starting the bombardment.

It was a failure. The fast battleships just did not know how to conduct a shore bombardment. The pilots of their spotter planes had not been trained in picking out ground targets, and the dust and smoke thrown up by the gunfire added to their difficulties. Then, because the big ships were considered too valuable to risk close in, they had to fire at a range of between 10,000 and 16,000 yards. (The fire-support battleships closed to less than 8,000 yards, and in some instances even closer, when they took over the shelling the next day.) The 2,432 16-inch and 12,544 5-inch shells that the fast battleships threw at Saipan largely went astray, and little of military importance was destroyed. One sailor described the bombardment as "a Navy-sponsored farm project that simultaneously plows the fields, prunes the trees, harvests the crops, and adds iron to the soil."[14]

While the battleships were busy adding "iron to the soil" of Saipan,

TF 58 planes were congregating over the island making intensive prelanding strikes. Enemy air opposition had been beaten down and though some officers thought "the greatest danger to our planes . . . was the damage of collision with our own spotting planes over the island,"[15] the flak was still murderous.

The *Enterprise*'s first strike of the day was led by Commander William I. Martin, Torpedo 10's skipper. Just north of Marpi Point, Saipan's northernmost projection, Martin's planes rendezvoused with a strike group from the *Lexington* led by Commander Robert H. Isely. The two leaders planned a joint attack on the Aslito airfield–Charan Kanoa area so as to prevent the Japanese gunners from concentrating on either group. The VT-10 Avengers were armed with 500-pound bombs, while the VT-16 torpedo planes carried the infamous rockets. Martin's target was a flak battery at Charan Kanoa; Isely's was an installation on Aslito field.

The two men began their attacks from 12,000 feet and at about the same time. Martin took a steep dive and Isely came in the flat, slow rocket pass. Both Avengers were hit by flak at almost the same time. At 4,000 feet, Isely's plane burst into flames, then crashed and exploded on the south edge of the airfield. There were no survivors. (Aslito would later be named Isely Field.)

Martin had just released his bomb from 3,500 feet when a burst of flak caught his plane. There was a savage shudder and the Avenger began swapping ends. Martin was thrown violently around the cockpit, unable to reach the mike to tell his crew to get out. He could feel heat and knew the plane was on fire. Somehow he got out of the cockpit, pulled the ripcord of his chute, straightened his body, and pointed his toes. Just before he hit the water his chute popped open, slowing his fall slightly. He landed at an angle of about forty-five degrees in four feet of water, bounced off the bottom and immediately began to gather his chute.

A few yards away, close enough for him to feel the heat and choke on the smoke, was what remained of his Avenger. Pieces of the plane's tail section were still falling around him. Inside the wreckage were the bodies of the two crewmen who had flown with him since 1942, AR1C Jerry T. Williams and AO2C Wesley R. Hargrove. But Martin had only a moment to mourn their deaths. Just a little over two hundred yards from the beach, he suddenly became aware of splashes and buzzing around him. Turning to face the shore, he saw Japanese soldiers, some standing, some prone, firing at him. Several were cheering. Quickly he ducked under the water and finished collecting his parachute. Then he headed for the reef and open sea—a half mile away.

Although a strong swimmer, Martin was hampered by his Mae West and parachute harness, with the life-raft seat pack still attached, and he refused to let go of his water-soaked parachute. He swam underwater, coming up for air at intervals. His seat pack bobbled along behind him on the surface of the water.

About halfway to the reef the water became deeper but the Japanese riflemen still peppered the water around Martin with bullets. The seat pack was creating a target for them. He came up for a breath and saw two boats coming after him. His arms and legs ached and every breath was torturous, but he knew he must reach the reef. Inspired by the oncoming boats, he set out again.

Nearly exhausted and with 250 yards still to go to the reef, Martin surfaced and found the leading boat only 200 yards away. He dove again, fully expecting to be captured the next time he came up for air. But when he came up again he discovered the leading boat had turned back. A pair of Avengers were low overhead, apparently searching for him. The second boat was still some distance away. Flak bursts bloomed around the Avengers and shell fragments splattered into the water around Martin.

Martin finally reached the reef, physically exhausted but still mentally alert. A second strike of planes was going in and the second boat turned back. He wearily rested on a piece of coral with only his eyes and nose above the water. He knew he was off Beach Green One, where troops of the 2nd Marine Division would be landing in two days, so he used the opportunity to make some observations of the landing area.

Martin picked out four objects that could be located on target maps and mentally set up cross bearings for his position. Working quickly with only his brain as his writing tablet, he plotted the positions of several antiaircraft batteries that had not previously been noted by the pilots. He jotted down on his mental tablet the depth of the water, the texture and firmness of the bottom and its gradient from the beach, and the lack of a current inside the reef.

Suddenly Martin was straddled by two large shells and he decided it was time to get out of there. Even as he dashed across the reef, chute still under his arm, his mind counted nineteen steps across the reef, that it felt like hard rubber, and that there was a foot and a half of water covering it.

Diving into the surf, Martin felt for the first time reasonably safe. He inflated his Mae West and slowly swam seaward. Once out of range of small-arms fire, he inflated his raft and climbed aboard. Figuring that any search for him would be concentrated off Green Beach One, Martin rigged a sea anchor and then trailed his chute from the raft to kill any drift. Soon he was relaxing about a mile off the reef.

Just about the time he was getting settled into his raft, a Hellcat and

Avenger came in from the west. Martin poured some dye marker and flashed his signal mirror at them. They caught the flash and came in low toward him. The planes flew so low and slow that he could recognize each pilot as being from the *Enterprise*. As the two planes passed, two flak bursts snapped overhead and shrapnel peppered the sea around his raft. Martin dove overboard but quickly climbed back in.

The Avenger made one more pass and dropped an emergency kit which Martin recovered. Deciding that the flak would make any rescue dangerous for both him and his rescuers, Martin headed out for sea. Pulling in his sea anchor and his extraordinarily useful chute, he put the chute to use one more time by fashioning a small sail from two of its panels.

His raft bounced over the waves and out to sea. One of the pilots overhead reported that Martin was "making three knots on a course of 290 degrees, not zigzagging."[16] Around noon a pair of SOC Seagulls from the *Indianapolis*, covered by two Corsairs from the *Enterprise*, approached. One Seagull landed and taxied over to Martin. Martin clambered on and began to pull his raft, chute and other gear up. The Seagull pilot, not too keen on remaining in dangerous waters, did not want to take the time to gather in the gear. After a few seconds of heated discussion, Martin saw his raft and beloved parachute (both full of holes so they would sink and not mislead other rescuers) dip beneath the waves.

The floatplane had to take off east, into the wind and toward the island, and for a few uncomfortable minutes was within range of the antiaircraft batteries of the island. The gunners, however, were inaccurate and the puffs of flak were well ahead.

Soon Martin was aboard the *Indianapolis* in dry clothing and with a couple of shots of medicinal alcohol under his belt. Martin's observations so impressed Admiral Spruance that they were sent to all other units. In the afternoon Martin was transferred to the destroyer *MacDonough* for return to the *Enterprise*. But before he would step onto the deck of his carrier, Martin and the destroyer had a job to do. The *MacDonough* took up position off Green Beach One and, with Martin helping direct the fire, plastered the antiaircraft battery which had shot him down. The next morning Martin, along with a wounded survivor from one of the enemy ships that had been sunk in the last two days, was transferred to the "Big E." Martin was home again.[17]

American losses on the 13th had not been as bad as the day before, but they were bad enough. Besides Martin's and Isely's Avengers, eight more planes had been lost in combat with two other pilots and four more crewmen. Twenty-six planes had been damaged by the heavy

Commander William I. Martin, VT-10's leader, is returned to the Enterprise *by the* MacDonough *after being shot down off Saipan on 13 June 1944. (National Archives)*

antiaircraft fire. Only eleven enemy planes were destroyed on the ground. Three Emilys at the Flores Point seaplane base made up the major portion of the five probables also claimed.

With the landings on Saipan only two days away, the three northern groups spent much of the day hitting gun emplacements and defense installations on the west coast of the island. The few times Japanese guns fired on the minesweepers working close inshore, TF 58 planes were quickly on the spot to force the gunners to duck and hold their fire.

Launchings were again early, with sweeps being sent out before 0430. Attacks this early in the day brought only mixed results. Much of TF 58's effort was spent against the installations around Charan Kanoa and Garapan. In the afternoon the *Enterprise* sent five Avengers, followed later by six more torpedo planes and eight fighters, to set fire to Garapan, hoping to eliminate antiaircraft fire in that area and "forcing [the enemy] to fight fire all night," thereby exhausting him.[18]

Task Group 58.4 planes spent most of the day attacking any Japanese shipping that was sighted. They also continued a fruitless search for Lieutenant Commander Price. *San Jacinto* planes discovered six sixty-foot trawlers forty-five miles west of TG 58.3. Four torpedo planes and two fighters were sent to work them over. With four more Hellcats joining in the strafing attacks and the Avengers dropping depth charges, five of the trawlers were badly damaged and had to be abandoned.

Tinian was not left alone. Task Group 58.2 sent 126 sorties over the island during the day. Two Hellcats were lost to the flak, including the plane of Lieutenant Commander Roger W. Mehle, Air Group 28's skipper. Both pilots were recovered. Mehle's plane had been hit when he had pressed his attack against a troublesome four-gun battery at extremely low level. Though the gunners got his fighter, Mehle's pass was apparently very successful, for only one gun of the battery was firing three hours later. But there were other guns. Pilots reported moderate flak at Ushi Point and intense and accurate flak at Gurguan Point. It appeared that some of the antiaircraft fire came from "new locations indicating the possibility of mobile units having been moved in during the night."[19]

About noon TGs 58.2 and 58.3 passed through an area of wreckage from one of the convoys attacked the day before, and sixty-six survivors were plucked from the water. Toward dusk the two groups also passed several burning trawlers, victims of the *San Jacinto's* planes earlier in the day.

Off Guam, TG 58.1 had not been inactive on the 13th; in fact the task group flew the most target sorties of the day for TF 58—339. The day had begun early as Clark's carriers launched eight night fighters (two for night CAP, four as hecklers, and two to search for the convoy seen the previous day) at 0258. The enemy ships had obligingly remained near their position of the day before, and were seen at 0803 slowly heading south. A special convoy strike, partially diverted from another mission, was launched at 1110. The convoy was about 350 miles away.

Two night fighters of VF(N)-76 led the attack, with fourteen VF-1 and six VF-2 Hellcats making up the strike force. Two Beasts from VB-2 tagged along for rescue work. The night fighters found the ships at 1340, but the ensuing attack was hardly brilliant. The fighter pilots, rusty in the art of bombing ships, almost completely missed the moving vessels. Only one *Hornet* pilot was able to score and, although the convoy was heavily strafed, only minor damage was inflicted. The convoy continued to Guam where it landed reinforcements.

Attacks against Guam and Rota continued throughout the day, with TG 58.1 drawing closer to the islands with every strike. By 1455 Guam was only forty-three miles from the *Hornet*. But there were some U.S.

ships even closer. One of them, the submarine *Stingray*, took part in an amazing rescue just off Guam's Orote Point.

Ensign Donald C. "Red" Brandt, from Fighting 2, was attacking Agana field when his fighter was hit by flak and he had to bail out. He landed in the water about a mile offshore. A Helldiver pilot dropped him a raft, and Brandt scrambled into it. Japanese shore batteries then began using him for target practice.

The *Stingray*, acting as a lifeguard submarine, was ordered to attempt a pickup of Brandt. Lieutenant Commander Sam C. Loomis, Jr., brought his sub barreling in on the surface. When Loomis arrived off Orote Point, he could see that Brandt was in trouble from the guns. Then a shell exploded just 400 yards from the submarine. Loomis "pulled the plug" and went down fast.

At periscope depth Loomis began inching the *Stingray* toward the downed pilot. The plan was for Brandt to wrap the line of his raft around the sub's periscope and be towed to safety. This plan had been briefed to the pilots but no one had ever tried it. Loomis recorded the pickup this way:

> 1233: Sighted pilot dead ahead. Had to approach from lee or across wind. Velocity 10 to 12 knots.
>
> 1235: Two shell splashes ahead.
>
> 1238: Two more splashes and burst of AA fire near pilot. Can see him ducking in rubber boat.
>
> 1240: Pilot has sighted us and is waving. Holding up left hand which shows a deep cut across the palm.
>
> 1303: Approached with about ten feet of number one scope and about three feet of number two scope out of water. Pilot very close and no signs of line ready for scope. Pilot so close I have lost him in number one field. Headed directly for him. Missed.
>
> 1319: Three shell splashes on port quarter.
>
> 1347: Heard shell land close aboard.
>
> 1349: Heard another close one.
>
> 1352: Almost on top of pilot. Now, he's paddling *away* from periscope. Missed.
>
> 1418: Planes commenced bombing Agana field and shore batteries.
>
> 1424: Heard shell splash.
> Heard another close one.
> Heard another close shell.
> Heard two more.
> Heard one shell.
>
> 1440: Heard and saw two splashes close aboard.
>
> 1453: Pilot missed the boat again. On this try, he showed the first signs of attempting to reach the periscope. Maybe shell fire has made him

think that a ride on a periscope might be right after all. I am getting damned disgusted, plus a stiff neck and a blind eye.

1500: Heard another shell.

1516: Fourth try. Ran into pilot with periscope and he hung on! Towed him for one hour during which time he frantically signalled for us to let him up. His hand was cut badly and it must have been tough going hanging onto the bitter end of the line with one hand while bumping along in the whitecaps.

1611: Lowered towing scope, watching pilot's amazed expression with other periscope.

1613: Surfaced.

1618: Picked up Ensign Donald Carol Brandt, USNR, suffering from deep wound in left hand. Glad to finally get him aboard. He said that during first and third approaches he was afraid periscopes were going to hit him and he tried to get out of the way and come in astern of me. He had been briefed on a rescue like this, but guess the shock of getting hit at 14,000 feet and falling upside down in his parachute from 12,000 feet was too much. And then the shell-fire shouldn't have done him much good either. He's taken quite a running, and taken it well. We're on speaking terms now, but after the third approach, I was ready to make him captain of the head.[20]

During her stint as lifeguard submarine the *Stingray* rescued five fliers.

The 13th had brought news from the submarine *Redfin* of the movement of the Japanese Fleet from Tawi Tawi, and TF 58 searchers had been busy. Although the Japanese were well out of range of American planes at this time, there seems to have been no thought given by the Americans to extending their planes' search patterns out from the standard 300–325 mile range. An early-morning search mission by six *Hornet* "2C's" had ended disastrously for the dive bombers. Unable to reach their carrier because of low fuel, four of them landed on the *Bataan*. The last plane's landing was bad and the Helldiver bounced over the barrier, smashing into the other *Hornet* aircraft and a *Bataan* Avenger. The damage was so great that all four of the Helldivers had to be pushed over the side. Two *Bataan* F6Fs also made emergency landings on the *Hornet*, but they were so damaged that they too had to be jettisoned.

The Japanese were on the move, but where they were moving was still unknown. A number of people in TF 58 were sure the Japanese would not even be heading their way. "Prevailing opinion in the fleet was that the Japanese Navy would not come out to defend the Marianas."[21] In his Forager operations plan Admiral Turner had stated, "It is believed that these units of the Japanese Fleet will not interfere with our operations against (the Marianas) except for 'hit and run' raids on detached units of our forces, but will conserve their strength until a time when they can go into action in waters nearer their main bases."[22]

Nevertheless, it looked to Admirals Spruance and Mitscher that this time the Japanese meant business. But after plotting the probable course and speed of the enemy, the two admirals figured they had at least three, maybe four, days of complete freedom of action before a confrontation with the enemy.

Spruance knew from intelligence reports (he apparently had in his possession a copy of the Japanese Z Plan) and just plain common sense that the Japanese were intending to fly planes from Japan to the Marianas. The planes were to be refueled at Iwo Jima. From there they would fly to Saipan, attack the American carriers and continue to Palau and Truk. After refueling and rearming at their landing bases the planes would return to Saipan for attacks, finally landing on Guam. In conjunction with these attacks, smaller raids would be made from Yap and Truk. In theory this plan appeared to be quite sound to the Japanese and it was christened Operation TO-GO. In practice it turned out to be a miserable failure.[24]

Spruance directed Mitscher to send two of his task groups north to the Bonins to pull the teeth of any possible threat from there. Mitscher selected Clark's TG 58.1 (the *Hornet, Yorktown, Belleau Wood,* and *Bataan*) and Harrill's TG 58.4 (the *Essex, Langley,* and *Cowpens*).

Neither commander was very enthusiastic about going north. Clark, a fighter, thought he would miss the main action against the enemy fleet. Harrill complained that his group was low on fuel, though his staff disagreed. It is possible Harrill was more concerned with the task force staying together. Splitting TF 58 to attack widely separated targets did not follow the "by the book" approach of concentration of forces.

But was Spruance taking a chance by this move? Not really. Having spent some time at the Naval War College teaching tactics and being, as Clark Reynolds says, "battleship-trained in the formalist tradition," Spruance knew he still had several days before an engagement.[25] He could recall the two task groups before this time. When TF 58 rejoined he would again have a concentration of forces.

Mitscher and his staff resorted to different methods to induce the two task group commanders to take the job. With Clark they used a psychological ploy. Captain Burke told Clark that Mitscher's staff understood his reluctance to head north since it was going to be such a dangerous mission. This turned Clark into a convert; he vowed to destroy completely the enemy aircraft in the Bonins. With Harrill,

Mitscher kept it simple and to the point. He *ordered* him to go. Harrill's reluctance and apparent non-aggressiveness would eventually cost him command of his task group.

Mitscher set up a rather unusual command arrangement for the Bonins strike. Neither Clark nor Harrill, four years senior to Clark, were given tactical command of the operation, but were instructed to operate independently yet stay "tactically concentrated."[26]

Both groups began fueling on the morning of 14 June. Task Group 58.1 was fueled from the *Caliente, Guadalupe,* and *Platte*, while TG 58.4 took on fuel from the oilers *Cimarron, Sabine,* and *Kaskaskia*. Accompanying the oilers was the escort carrier *Copahee*. The carrier brought new planes and pilots for the fast carriers while taking on the worn-out or damaged planes. (This method of replacement was to prove an invaluable manner of supply the remainder of the war, enabling the combat units to remain in action much longer.) After fueling northeast of Pagan, the two task groups set course for the over six-hundred-mile run to the Bonins.

During the fueling Harrill had informed Clark that he was still reluctant to go north. A stunned Clark had immediately flown from his flagship, the *Hornet*, to Harrill's *Essex*. Upon confronting Harrill, Clark found him ready with many excuses—lack of fuel, the possibility of missing the main battle, the chance of bad weather in the target area, etc. For several hours Clark and Harrill's chief of staff tried to talk Harrill into following orders. Finally in disgust, Clark told Harrill, "If you do not join me in this job I will do it all myself."[27] Realizing his position, Harrill at last agreed to come along.

On the evening of the 14th Spruance informed the two commanders that the Japanese were definitely on the way and instead of strikes on the 16th and 17th, only one day of attacks (the 16th) could be allowed. The two groups were to rendezvous with the other TF 58 forces off the Marianas on the morning of the 18th.[28]

Clark rushed north, hopeful of getting in an extra strike on the 15th, while Harrill tagged along. The targets were to be the Iwo, Chichi, and Haha Jimas. The main target would be Iwo Jima for it had the best airfields and the most installations. Hitting the island would be a dangerous proposition. On its fields were about one hundred planes, mostly Zekes of the 752nd Air Group, with a scattering of medium bombers sent from Japan, all under the command of Captain Kanzo Miura.

The weather began to kick up as the Americans drew closer to Iwo Jima. On 16 June squalls passed over the ships intermittently, and the wind picked up to force 6 speed. The ocean was rough, with a fifteen-foot swell, and the carriers pitched and rolled. It would be difficult to launch planes.

A pair of unlucky Japanese vessels strayed across the Americans' path. First, a sampan was sunk by *Langley* planes at 1016; then about an hour later the 1,900-ton freighter *Tatsutagawa Maru* was sighted only thirty miles ahead of TG 58.1. Antisnoop and ASP teams from the *Bataan* pounced on her, strafing and dropping depth charges. A depth charge dropped by an Avenger blew the bow off the freighter but didn't sink her. Finally, the destroyers *Boyd* and *Charrette* were called in and finished the job with forty rounds of 5-inch fire. A surprising 112 survivors were pulled from the water.

About noon the weather began abating enough to try a launch. At 1330 Clark and Harrill started sending their planes off toward the targets. Task Group 58.4 sent a twenty-two-plane fighter sweep and a fifty-nine-plane strike against Iwo Jima, while TG 58.1 launched a sweep against Iwo Jima and two deckloads for targets on Chichi Jima and Haha Jima.

After rendezvousing, the forty-four F6Fs of the sweep set course for Iwo Jima, 135 miles away. The fighters carried 135-pound fragmentation clusters to sprinkle over the airfields. When they thundered in over the island the fighters found a welcoming committee—thirty-seven Zekes, warned either by the *Tatsutagawa Maru* or radar.

Commander Bernard M. "Smoke" Strean's Fighting 1 Hellcats were the first over Iwo Jima. The "Top Hatters" took on the defenders, and the battle quickly disintegrated into a wild scuffle. Lieutenant Paul M. Henderson and his wingmen, Lieutenant (jg) John Meharg and Ensign Alden P. Morner, were among the first to open fire on the Zekes. Henderson flamed a Zeke on his first pass and then bagged three more before he became separated from Meharg and Morner. The last anyone heard of Henderson was his comment on the radio, "I knocked down four and I've got thirty more cornered."[29]

Meharg and Morner had not been doing too badly themselves. In a fight in which he said he made all the mistakes, Meharg claimed four Zekes. One plane blew up in his face and he had to fly through the debris. His last kill was chased down to the water where he was able to dunk it with only one gun firing. During the entire combat Meharg had been carrying his fragmentation cluster. Finally he dropped it and scooted for home.

Although claiming two kills and a probable, Morner had a hard time. His fighter was pretty well riddled by enemy fire. One 20-mm shell exploded just in front of his instrument panel and peppered him with shrapnel. His engine began smoking and streaming oil. A Zeke came in close and its pilot eyed Morner. Either out of ammo or deciding the American would not make it back to his carrier, the Japanese flier executed a slow roll around the Hellcat and disappeared. Morner made it back to the *Yorktown*, however. With his hydraulics shot out and unable to lower his gear, Morner brough his F6F in for a safe belly landing on the pitching deck.

Following on the heels of the *Yorktown* fighters came the Hellcats from the *Hornet* and *Essex*. Though the Japanese planes were still madly cavorting about the sky, they were doing little damage to the Americans. One group of four Zekes trapped Lieutenant (jg) Earling W. Zaeske, but he was able to get away, picking off one of the enemy planes in the process. Top scorer of the day was Lieutenant Lloyd G. Barnes, from the *Hornet*, with five kills.

After knocking down twenty-eight of the thirty-seven Zekes in the air, the Hellcats went down on the deck to strafe the approximately eighty-six planes that could be seen on the ground. The antiaircraft fire was not too heavy but was focused on the leading attackers with great skill. Two Avengers, a Hellcat, and an SB2C were shot down by the flak.

While the attack on Iwo Jima was progressing, more planes from Clark's carriers were bombing Chichi Jima and Haha Jima. No air opposition was encountered, but the enemy flak took its toll. One *Hornet* Helldiver went straight in during its dive. The antiaircraft fire also got a *Yorktown* Avenger. The crew made it into their raft, but search planes could not find them later and they were not recovered. In the harbor at Chichi Jima three small freighters were sunk, twenty-one seaplanes were destroyed, and numerous shore installations were hit.

Around 1700 the planes began returning and recovery operations commenced. The weather and damaged planes combined to make the landings very hazardous. Aboard the *Langley* a Hellcat crashed into the barrier when its tail hook did not engage the arresting gear. Another fighter caught the deck during an upswing and slammed down, breaking its tail and right landing gear. The ship's Avengers were roughly handled by the flak, with two airmen dying of wounds. Two of the torpedo bombers, along with one of the damaged fighters, had to be jettisoned.

The *Yorktown* lost an SB2C during the landings when the plane crashed astern the ship, but the crewmen got out and were picked up by the destroyer *Izard*. The *Bataan* also had a TBM ditch after taking a waveoff from the *Langley*, but the crew was also picked up by one of the ever-present destroyers.

The *Belleau Wood* had more than her share of excitement. At 1712 one of the ship's fighters crashed into the port catwalk. Almost two hours of relative quiet prevailed before another fighter took the barrier. A third Hellcat sliced through the barrier at 1920 and smashed into the island, bursting into flames. The mobile crane was knocked overboard, the flag bag carried away and the signal flags destroyed, the number one and two TBSs and a radar antenna put out of commission. After some twenty-three minutes of fighting the fire on the wet and pitching deck, the crew snuffed it out.

After recovering planes, both forces retired to the east-southeast for the night. That evening Clark was told by Harrill that he was suspending operations and was going to rejoin TF 58. A surprised and angry Clark replied that he didn't care what Harrill did, but *he* would stay and finish the job. "A tense moment of silence followed on the *Essex* flag bridge, after which Harrill let out an agonized wail, clutching his hands to his temples and bemoaning Clark's severe indictment."[30] Harrill decided to stay with Clark.

During the recovery operations the sea had been fairly rough, but in the night it got even worse. A typhoon was churning up the waters of the Pacific, and it was too close for comfort. The flattops were pitching and rolling so much that the launch of just a few planes was an adventure. Even the topping off of the destroyers in the morning was difficult. At 0450 Clark cancelled the planned morning strike on Chichi Jima (there was little of value there, anyway); but he still hoped to get in an attack on Iwo Jima in the afternoon. His perseverance was rewarded, for about noon the wind fell to force 4 and the sea moderated somewhat. At 1258 the *Hornet*, *Yorktown*, and *Bataan* began launching the fighter sweep, followed by two deckload strikes. The *Essex* and *Cowpens* sent a smaller sweep and strike at 1340.

The attackers came in over Iwo Jima unmolested, as the Japanese apparently expected no attack in such rotten weather. The enemy planes were lined up neatly on both sides of the runways when the U.S. planes roared over. With the fighters strafing and three waves of Avengers and Helldivers bombing, most of the grounded planes were destroyed or so badly damaged as to be useless for some time. Admiral Kakuta would miss these planes in the next few days. The bombing of the airfields was of little value though, as the craters were filled shortly. Damage to several gasoline tanks was more useful.

Once over their surprise, the Japanese put up a heavy curtain of flak. One pilot was lost when his fighter was hit by ground fire and spun into the sea. Ensign Hal Crabb brought "half" a Hellcat back to the *Yorktown*. With his hydraulics shot out, he could not get his gear down or his flaps to work. During the ensuing belly landing the tail hook of his fighter caught one of the arresting cables. The sudden shock over-stressed the Hellcat and it broke in half. The rear section stayed neatly in place restrained by the cable, while Crabb and the front section took a sleighride up the deck. The remains of the F6F were pushed over the side.

A Torpedo 1 Turkey took a large shell through one of its wings, leaving a ragged two-foot hole. All the way back to the ship the pilot was quite vocal in complaining that one of his wings was missing.

Ensign Tom Elliott almost got his Helldiver back to the carrier. Elliott's big Beast was hit by flak just as he pulled out of his dive. The Japanese gunners did a good job on his plane. The bomber's hydraulic lines were cut, causing the bomb bay doors to stay open and the dive flaps to remain half extended. The spinner and pitch adjustment mechanism of the propeller had been blown off, as was the tip of one of the prop blades.

The flight back to the *Yorktown* was not looking too good for Elliott. With the drag of the open doors and the flaps, and with only high pitch to control the prop, he could coax only 100 knots out of his plane. Since climbing was out of the question, he had to stay too low for comfort. After many minutes of sweating it out, Elliott finally sighted the *Yorktown*. Settling into the groove for landing, he lowered his landing gear. That was a mistake. The extended gear created too much additional drag. When Elliott found he was looking up, not down, at the Landing Signal Officer (LSO), he knew he would have to ditch. The SB2C splashed into the heaving sea. Elliott and his gunner scrambled out of their sinking plane and were quickly picked up.

Elliott was luckier than Lieutenant (jg) John R. Ivey. Ivey and his wingman were strafing when Ivey's Hellcat was hit by flak. He was able to pull out, but his flying quickly became erratic. His wingman and another pilot who had joined up could see Ivey had a large face wound. Both pilots shepherded Ivey back to the *Essex* but over the carrier they could neither get him to land nor bail out. They were finally ordered to land and Ivey flew off. A CAP fighter found only an oilslick and marker dye thirty-five miles from the *Essex*.

Anxious to return to TF 58, Harrill recovered his planes while steaming away from the Bonins. Clark, still hopeful of completing the destruction of Iwo Jima, stayed until a little after 1700. At that time, after topping off some of his destroyers, he turned and headed for Saipan. The excursion north had been fairly costly to the Americans. Twelve planes had been lost, but the destruction that had been caused more than balanced these losses. Almost one hundred Japanese aircraft had been destroyed or severely damaged in the two-day attack. Operation TO-GO had been effectively sidetracked for the time being. But Admiral Kakuta (down on Tinian) was sending Toyoda and Ozawa glowing reports on the number of aircraft he had available to attack the Americans. These reports, coupled with Kakuta's over-optimistic estimates of damage to the enemy, would certainly not help Ozawa in his plans for the coming battle.

As TGs 58.1 and 58.4 ran south, they received orders from Mitscher to head southwest and search for the Japanese Fleet. Clark had already sent some searches 200-250 miles to the west and north during the last two days, but on the morning of the 17th the two groups joined in search missions extending out to 350 miles. When the planes returned with negative results, it was planned that the two groups would turn southeast and rendezvous with the rest of TF 58. Admiral Clark, however, had a more daring plan in mind.

His plan called for TGs 58.1 and 58.4 to continue to the southwest, come in behind Ozawa's advancing force, and block its retreat. In this position the enemy would be caught between two large carrier forces and destroyed. The situation would be somewhat similar to that encountered by Vice Admiral David Beatty at the Battle of Jutland in 1916, where Beatty almost succeeded in cutting the German battle cruisers off from their homeports. Clark saw himself with a chance of cutting off the Japanese from their ports and, thus, becoming the Beatty of World War II.[31]

Clark was aware that there was no threat to his ships from an enemy fleet in the Philippines or Japan. But land-based air was another matter, and the two task groups were not well protected by escort vessels. There was also the possibility that the Japanese would turn on one or the other of the widely separated TF 58 units and defeat them in detail.

Clark was used to taking risks, but this plan truly needed permission from his higher commanders, and he could not get it because of the need to maintain radio silence. Although Clark and Rear Admiral Ralph Davison (on the *Yorktown* as an observer) saw eye-to-eye on the plan, Harrill wanted nothing to do with it. Harrill also said he was fed up with Clark's independent actions and was taking his ships with him to the rendezvous. Since this left Clark with only four carriers, including two of the light ones, he had no choice but to return also. Mitscher later thought Clark's plan had been a good one, but the two admirals agreed that Spruance would never have approved it for it would have gone against Spruance's strong belief in the principle of a concentration of forces in the face of an enemy.[32]

Harrill and Clark headed for the rendezvous, planned for the 18th. Prior to then TG 58.4 was to be fueled east of the Marianas. Enroute to the fueling, TG 58.4 launched a strike at Pagan. No enemy air activity was noted. Before TG 58.4 could be completely fueled, Harrill received an urgent order from Admiral Spruance calling off the fueling. Instead, the task group was to rendezvous as soon as possible with the rest of TF 58. Big events were about to break.

chapter 4

"The Rise and Fall of Imperial Japan Depends on This One Battle"

ON THE MORNING OF 11 JUNE Admiral Ozawa received the first reports of TF 58's strikes on the Marianas. At first he thought these raids were nothing more than diversionary attacks meant to take the heat off the Biak landings. The next day, however, brought more detailed reports about the American forces attacking the islands.

Japanese reconnaissance planes had snooped TF 58 and had estimated the composition and position of the attacking forces as: two carriers, one light carrier, and one battleship ninety miles east of Saipan; two more carriers ninety miles northeast of Saipan; a third group of two carriers, two light carriers, and three battleships ninety miles southeast of Saipan; and a final group of five carriers at an unreported position.[1]

These reports painted an accurate picture of the disposition of the American forces, and Ozawa now knew that TF 58 was out in force. However, until it could be clearly confirmed that the Marianas were actually the target of a full-scale invasion, Ozawa was limited in his actions. Biak was still a slim possibility for a fleet action, and Ozawa's big battleships, the *Yamato* and *Musashi*, were tied down at Batjan for the KON Operation.

On the 13th the situation became clearer to the Japanese. American battleships were reported shelling Saipan. It was now obvious the island was to be the target for an amphibious landing. At 0900 on the

13th the Mobile Fleet weighed anchor and began to sortie from Tawi Tawi, bound for Guimaras anchorage between Panay and Negros. Actually this sortie was not a reaction to the U.S. incursion into the Marianas, as it had already been planned. The increasing attention U.S. submarines had been paying to the area—and the paucity of destroyers to combat them—along with the lack of airfields for the training of the green flight crews had made Tawi Tawi a poor spot for massing the Mobile Fleet. Therefore, on 8 June Ozawa decided to move his fleet to Guimaras, or even Manila. That same day the 2nd Supply Force, which had been sent to a position east of the Philippines on the 3rd, was ordered to Guimaras.

As the Mobile Fleet steamed out of Tawi Tawi on the 13th, it was picked up by the submarine *Redfin*. Commander M.H. "Cy" Austin, the sub's skipper, attempted to close the advanced force—destroyers and a pair of heavy cruisers—but their maneuvers kept him out of range. Two hours after the first vessels left Tawi Tawi, the main body came steaming out. Again Austin was unable to get into an attack position, but he could observe the movements of the Japanese and was able to send a vital contact report at 2000 that night. Nimitz, Spruance, and Mitscher now knew that six carriers, four battleships, several cruisers, and a number of destroyers were on the move.[2]

Ozawa began consolidating his forces on the 13th. At 1727 the order "Prepare for A-GO Decisive Operation" was sent. Five minutes later the KON Operation was "temporarily" suspended and the *Yamato, Musashi, Myoko, Haguro, Noshiro,* and five destroyers were told to rendezvous with the rest of the Mobile Fleet in the Philippine Sea.[3] Both supply forces were put on a thirty-minute standby status, and the battleship *Fuso* began transferring most of her fuel to the oilers of the 1st Supply Force at Davao. This last step is an indication of how strapped the Japanese were for oil.

The sortie of the Mobile Fleet was cursed by misfortune from the start. Just after the fleet left Tawi Tawi an inexperienced pilot made a bad landing on the flagship *Taiho* and crashed into some parked aircraft. The ensuing fire destroyed two Zekes, two Judys, and two Jills. This accident was thought to be a bad omen; a bad beginning for this all-important battle.

A second mishap struck the Japanese one day later. The 1st Supply Force departed Davao late on the 13th bound for a refueling rendezvous in the Philippine Sea. Just after midnight on the 15th sailors on the destroyer *Shiratsuyu* thought they detected an enemy submarine and the destroyer began to maneuver radically. Unfortunately, one of her turns brought the *Shiratsuyu* close, too close, across the bow of the

Seiyo Maru. The oiler sliced the fantail off the destroyer and the *Shiratsuyu* quickly went down. There was no time to set depth charges on "safe" and these exploded as the ship sank, killing many in the water. Over one hundred of her crew were lost.

Ozawa's main force reached Guimaras at 1400 on the 14th and began fueling from the *Genyo Maru* and *Azusa Maru.* The fueling and resupply was quickly and efficiently done. Early the next morning Ozawa was ready to leave Guimaras.

Marines of the 2nd and 4th Divisions had waded ashore on Saipan at 0844 on the 15th against heavy opposition. At 0855 Admiral Toyoda sent Admiral Ozawa the following message: "On the morning of the 15th a strong enemy force began landing operations in the Saipan-Tinian area. The Combined Fleet will attack the enemy in the Marianas area and annihilate the invasion force. Activate A-GO Operation for decisive battle."[4]

Five minutes after this order Toyoda sent a further message; one that all Japanese knew by heart: "The rise and fall of Imperial Japan depends on this one battle. Every man shall do his utmost." Thirty-nine years earlier, Admiral Togo had uttered these same words just before his fleet crushed the Russian Baltic Fleet at Tsushima.[5]

With fueling completed, Ozawa led the Mobile Fleet from Guimaras at 0800 on the 15th. The force crossed the Visayan Sea and headed for San Bernardino Strait, between Samar and Luzon. Although neither man probably expected the Mobile Fleet to escape being spotted early on, Admirals Toyoda and Ozawa hoped that the sortie would be undetected until the Japanese were upon the Americans. Their hopes were not to be realized.

Filipino coastwatchers kept an eye on the Mobile Fleet as it moved into San Bernardino Strait. At 1100 one such watcher reported three carriers, two freighters, and sixteen other vessels. Seven and one-half hours later another coastwatcher reported three battleships, nine carriers, ten cruisers, eleven destroyers and two submarine chasers passing through the strait. (Unfortunately, it took two days for these reports to reach Spruance.) In the strait itself was a U.S. submarine, the *Flying Fish.* Lieutenant Commander Robert Risser had brought his submarine to the area for the very purpose of watching for the Mobile Fleet.

On the afternoon of the 15th the *Flying Fish* was submerged just inside the eastern entrance to the strait. At 1622 he saw the Japanese ships passing about eleven miles away. They were staying close to shore. Risser's mouth watered as he counted the juicy targets—three carriers, three battleships, and the usual cruisers and destroyers. But

his orders were to report first, attack later. Risser tried to stay with the
enemy as best he could, but the submarine's best submerged speed was
no match for Ozawa's ships. That evening Risser surfaced and sent his
important contact report. His message would be the first received by
Spruance showing that the Japanese were definitely approaching the
Philippine Sea.

As Risser took the *Flying Fish* back to Brisbane low on fuel, a second
U.S. submarine was watching another part of the Japanese forces.
Lieutenant Commander Slade D. Cutter was bringing the *Seahorse* up
from the Admiralties to cover Surigao Strait at the southern end of
Leyte. At 1845 Cutter saw smoke on the horizon. The *Seahorse* was
about two hundred miles east of Surigao Strait at the time.

Cutter immediately went to his best surface speed and started to
close with the target. As the *Seahorse* drew nearer, Cutter was able to
figure the course and speed of the enemy force. Then, when the
Seahorse was 19,000 yards away, one of her motors cut out, and the sub's
speed dropped off to 14½ knots. The Japanese ships pulled away into
the darkness.

Because of effective jamming by the Japanese, Cutter was unable to
get off a contact report until 0300 on 16 June: "At 1330 GCT task force
in position 10-11 North, 129-35 East. Base course 045, speed of advance 16.5. Sight contact at dusk disclosed plenty of battleships. *Seahorse* was astern and could not run around due speed restrictions
caused by main motor brushes. Radar indicates six ships ranges 28 to
39,000 yards. Carriers and destroyers probably could not be detected
at those ranges with our radar."[6]

Cutter had found the *Yamato* and *Musashi* racing north from Batjan.

Back off Saipan much had been happening the past few days. When
TGs 58.1 and 58.4 had steamed north to attack the Bonins, the other
two task groups had remained off Saipan to support the landings.
Although most of the close support work was now being done by the
"jeep" carriers of TG 52.14 (the *Fanshaw Bay, Midway, White Plains,
Kalinin Bay*) and TG 52.11 (the *Kitkun Bay, Gambier Bay, Nehenta Bay*),
the fast carriers were also kept busy.

Destroyers were fueled on the morning of the 14th while both
groups sent strikes against all four of the major islands. Over four
hundred sorties were launched during the day with few losses to the
attackers. The two groups then retired to the west of Rota for the night.

15 June 1944, D-Day (or Dog Day, as it was known for this operation), was a beautiful day, but it is doubtful if many of those present
were thinking how lovely it was. When the Marines stormed ashore in
the morning they found that many targets had not been touched by the

An Avenger takes off from the Monterey *to attack installations on Saipan on 14 June 1944.*

prelanding bombardment or the aerial strikes. Fighting was savage and losses heavy. By the 18th, though, the beachhead was secure and the Marines were there to stay.

Task Groups 58.2 and 58.3 were active on the 15th supporting the landings. Ninety-five sorties were sent over the beaches by TG 58.2 at H minus 90, followed by sixty-four *Lexington* and *Enterprise* planes at H-Hour. The two groups flew 579 target sorties. Only three planes and one pilot (all from TG 58.3) were lost during the day, but a number of others received varying degrees of damage from the still-heavy flak.

Around dusk Japanese planes began congregating near the American ships. The two U.S. groups were recovering planes about forty miles west of Saipan when the first group of enemy planes was detected. At 1800 a division of *San Jacinto* planes was vectored out to investigate a bogey at 20,500 feet. A "Nick" was found and quickly shot down. Ten minutes after the first vectors a second division was sent to investigate bogeys fifty-two miles away. At 1820 the *San Jacinto* planes contacted six "Tonys." (Again misidentifications. These planes were probably Zekes or Jills.) In the ensuing combat at 22,000 feet, five of the enemy planes were destroyed and the last one damaged. One of the Fighting 51 pilots had stayed high with a malfunctioning engine when the other pilots jumped the enemy planes. He was in a good position to see two more Japanese planes—Hamps—diving on his friends below. Pushing over, he got on the tail of one Hamp and splashed it. The other plane fled.

A big attack sent in from Yap came shortly after the sun went down. Task Group 58.2 beat off an attack by a few planes with accurate antiaircraft fire, but the main attack was against the carriers of TG 58.3. A pair of *Enterprise* F4U-2N Corsair night fighters had been launched at 1845 and at 1905 were vectored toward some bogeys. The target was only five miles away. Lieutenant Commander Richard E. Harmer and his wingman, Lieutenant (jg) R.F. Holden, soon picked it up—eight of the new Frances bombers with four or five fighters as escorts.

Harmer attacked the formation from the side but could not see the results of his attack in the darkness. Then Holden warned him of a fighter on his tail. Tracers streaking past Harmer's fighter confirmed this warning. As Harmer tried to evade the enemy fighter, 20-mm fire from one of the bombers hit his Corsair, shorting his formation lights "on." Holden finally knocked the enemy plane off Harmer's tail, the fighter corkscrewing down from 1,500 feet. Two more enemy planes attempted to get the Americans, but they were easily evaded. Harmer, unable to turn his lights off and feeling highly visible not only to the Japenese but to the gunners on the ships below, retired from the arena with Holden, and got out of the battle.

Now without any fighters to harass them, the Japanese circled the American ships (prudently out of antiaircraft gun range) and prepared to attack. The usual flares and float lights were dropped and then the Frans darted in. The *North Carolina* and *Washington* opened fire shortly after 1900, followed by the destroyers in the screen. At 1907 *Princeton* lookouts sighted seven planes low on the water dead ahead. But the Japanese fliers were not interested in the light carrier.

They were after bigger game, the *Lexington* and *Enterprise*. The task group began to maneuver drastically while at the same time firing radar-directed 5-inch and 40-mm shells that engulfed the enemy planes.

Five planes made runs on the *Lexington* to no avail. Four were quickly slammed into the water. The other was stopped in mid-air by the wall of fire, and fell into the sea without burning. The enemy pilots were brave. One Frances almost hit the *Lexington*'s bridge before falling in flames off the starboard quarter. Another "streaked like a fire ball, close aboard to port, flaming so hotly he warmed the faces as well as the hearts of the gunners."[7] This pilot desperately tried to crash his doomed aircraft into the planes parked aft on the flight deck. He almost succeeded. His right engine suddenly stopped and he crashed only a few yards from the stern.

Torpedoes were slicing through the water now, and all the ships were heeling over to miss them. At one point Captain Burke had to lean over the wing of the *Lexington*'s bridge to see one torpedo flash past. The *Enterprise* had two "fish" miss her by less than fifty yards.

The surviving enemy planes scuttled out of the area and by 2230 all radar scopes were clear. Only thirteen of the attackers were able to return to Yap. *Lexington* gunners claimed five planes, while the *Enterprise* claimed two and the *Princeton* one. No ships were lost but there had been casualties. Three sailors were killed and fifty-eight wounded, when antiaircraft shells were accidentally fired into other ships. The casualties had been caused by those almost inevitable (and unavoidable) incidents that had happened before in the fury of battle and would happen again.

D plus 1, the 16th, was a day of decision, planning and fighting for the Americans. Fueling took up part of the day as TG 58.2 fueled from TG 50.17's oilers in the morning and TG 58.3 did the same in the afternoon. The seemingly ever-present *Copahee* was again on hand to deliver replacement aircraft to some of the fast carriers and to receive their flyable "duds" in exchange.

The reports from the *Flying Fish* and *Seahorse* had finally reached Spruance and Mitscher, and they now knew the Japanese were coming out. The day before, Vice Admiral Richmond Kelly Turner (the Expeditionary Force commander) had recommended to Spruance that the landings on Guam be set for the 18th. (At this time it had seemed that the landings on Saipan were going fine, and there was as yet no firm word on the direction the Japanese Fleet was taking.)

When the reports of the Mobile Fleet's sortie into the Philippine Sea were received, it became obvious that some major decisions and replan-

ning were needed. On the morning of the 16th Spruance boarded
Turner's command ship, the *Rocky Mount*. In conference with Turner
and Lieutenant General Holland M. Smith, USMC, overall commander of the troops ashore, Spruance made several critical decisions. It was
decided to:

1. Land the 27th Division immediately. Since with this action there
   would be no reserve force, the Guam landings were cancelled and
   the Southern Attack Force was to stand by as a floating reserve.
2. Augment TF 58's screen by detaching some cruisers and destroyers
   from fire support TGs 52.10 and 52.17.
3. Unload supplies and troops until dark of the 17th, after which the
   transports would be sent 200-300 miles east for safety.
4. Send the old battleships and screens of TGs 52.10 and 52.17 about
   twenty-five miles west of Saipan to cover the island in case the
   Japanese got around TF 58.
5. Use the jeep carriers exclusively for close air support.[8]

The day before, Spruance had asked General MacArthur to have his
Wakde- and Los Negros-based PB4Ys stretch their searches to the
limit, about 1,200 miles. The Liberators did not pick up anything,
however. On the 14th Spruance had directed Vice Admiral John H.
Hoover at Eniwetok to send a patrol-plane tender forward and to
prepare a patrol squadron when ordered. Now Hoover was ordered to
send six radar-equipped PBMs of VP-16 from Eniwetok to Saipan. The
PBMs were to be used for long-range searches from Saipan.

Spruance returned to his flagship the *Indianapolis* and prepared to
join TF 58. Because the reports from the *Flying Fish* and *Seahorse*
seemed to indicate that two separate groups of enemy ships were out,
Spruance felt the Japanese would probably be following their usual
tactics of dividing their forces. This appreciation of the enemy's intentions, perhaps influenced by the Z Plan translation in his hands, was to
color Spruance's decisions throughout the battle.

Some very good advice reached Spruance on the 16th. Admiral
Nimitz, on the recommendation of Vice Admiral John H. Towers
(Nimitz's Deputy Commander-in-Chief), told Spruance and Mitscher
to watch out for the possibility that the Japanese might try to keep their
carriers out of range of TF 58's aircraft, and instead shuttle their
planes back and forth to Guam.[9]

From earlier reconnaissance and intelligence reports the Americans
had a pretty good idea of the composition of the Mobile Fleet. Admiral
Reeves, TG 58.3's commander, said in his operations plan: "Any resis-
tance to the operation by way of surface engagement or carrier attack
will probably be from part or all of the new Japanese First Striking

Fleet. This fleet is thought to contain five fast battleships and possibly the *Fuso* as well. Carrier Divisions One, Two, and Three (nine CV and CVLs with a total complement of 255 VF, 177 VSB, 99 VT and 9 VSO) and about eleven heavy cruisers, 35 DDs are believed assigned to this fleet."

Mitscher's appraisal was pretty much the same: "For the first time in more than 18 months the enemy has a large carrier force in fighting condition. His 3 CVs, 2 XCVs, and 4 CVLs which are ready for combat carry planes equivalent in number to those carried by 4 Essex and 3 Independence class carriers. . . . If the enemy uses all his carrier-based planes in conjunction with the land planes based in the Marianas, he will still have fewer aircraft available for attacking our ships than we will be able to employ against him. Enemy task force action will give our own task forces a chance to close the enemy, bring his force into action, and perhaps score a crippling victory."[11]

Mitscher's operation plan also considered three possible courses of action the Japanese could take if they sortied for battle: "(A) They could approach from the general direction of Davao under their air cover from the Philippines, Palau and Yap and strike the fleet from a southwesterly direction. (B) They could approach around northern Luzon and strike from a northwesterly direction. (C) They could approach easterly and strike from a position west of the Marianas."[12]

Mitscher and his staff thought (A) was most likely, though (C) was possible. The other possibility was considered very unlikely. While a southwest approach might be a diversion or a flanking route, Mitscher thought it not a "serious consideration so long as the major portion of the fleet could be engaged to the westward."[13] He also felt that as long as the new Japanese battleships (the *Yamato* and *Musashi*, in particular) were not in this attacking force, the old battleships, escort carriers, and screening vessels of the U.S support force could handle them.

On the morning of 16 June Mitscher informed his ships of the possibilities, saying, "Believe Japanese will approach from southerly direction under their shore-based air cover close to Yap and Ulithi to attempt to operate in vicinity of Guam. However, they may come from the west. Our searches must cover both possibilities. Will ask Harrill and Clark to search north and west of us tomorrow."[14] As related earlier, Clark's and Harrill's groups searched to the southwest of their position and found nothing. Clark's imaginative plan to "trap" the Japanese was stillborn, and the two forces raced south to join the rest of TF 58.

Mitscher was taking no chances and ordered his planes to hit the airfields on Guam and Tinian in an attempt to neutralize them. A total of 332 sorties were flown during the day and most of them met heavy and accurate antiaircraft fire. Six planes were shot down, including one by friendly antiaircraft fire, but only one pilot and two crewmen were lost. One of the luckier pilots, who was not without a sense of adventure, was Ensign W.R. Mooney. This *San Jacinto* flier was hit by flak over Guam but was able to set his plane down in the water and climb into his raft. Though about fourteen miles offshore, Mooney paddled his raft to Guam where he scrambled ashore undetected by the enemy. At night he would hide in the undergrowth, and just before dawn he would take his raft back down to the shore and paddle out to sea, hoping some friendly search plane would spot him and bring rescue. Mooney followed this ritual for over two weeks before finally being picked up on 3 July.

Another pilot shot down on the 16th was Commander William R. "Killer" Kane, CO of Air Group 10. Kane was to be air coordinator for the first strikes of the day. As he and his wingman approached Saipan shortly before 0600, the sea below was still dark. Only a few ships could be seen. Nervously, both pilots rechecked their IFF transmitters.

Not wanting to fly over the invasion forces, Kane began a turn back to the west. Suddenly, a big burst of flak exploded under the left wing of his Hellcat. The plane pitched over violently and Kane's goggles flew off his head. The Hellcat's engine began smoking and Kane started thinking about bailing out. More bursts appeared nearby and tracers were weaving around the plane.

Kane opened his canopy and released his seat belt. As he prepared to go over the side, he discovered his fighter was not on fire and the engine was ticking over smoothly. He settled back into his seat—forgetting to refasten his seat belt—and led his wingman out of the antiaircraft fire. But as he tried to climb back to his original altitude, the black puffs cracked around the two planes again.

As Kane called angrily over the radio for the ships to knock off the shooting, he saw his oil pressure drop to zero. He decided to ditch near some transports. The antiaircraft fire followed him down but stopped as he put the Hellcat into the water. The big fighter skipped once, then dug its nose into the water. Without his seat belt fastened, Kane slammed forward against the gunsight. Groggy and with blood streaming from his head, Kane pulled himself out of his sinking plane and clambered into his raft. Before the destroyer *Newcomb* picked him up, Kane had a few choice words—and many ugly thoughts—about gunners who did not know aircraft recognition and sailors who could not read IFF signals. That afternoon, with a splitting headache, he was returned to the *Enterprise*.

Mitscher kept his planes pounding Guam and Tinian throughout the day, but as soon as the attackers departed, the Japanese rushed to work and quickly had the airfields back in service. Following a day of bombing, Tinian reported to Tokyo that the field was back in operation as of 1800.

Another disturbing observation was made by Commander Ernest M. Snowden, skipper of Air Group 16. During a strafing pass of the Ushi Point field on Tinian, Snowden noticed quite a few enemy planes parked around the field. Many appeared to be untouched by bullets or shrapnel. Although twenty-four planes were claimed destroyed on the ground and many others damaged, there were too many untouched planes left for comfort.

In the meantime, after Admiral Mitscher told TF 58 that it appeared the Japanese were coming their way, Gus Widhelm had been having a hard time getting takers for his $1,000 wager that the Japanese would be heading out for a carrier duel.[15]

Far to the west of Saipan, Ozawa's forces were plowing deeper into the Philippine Sea. At 1000 on the 16th, Admiral Ugaki's battleship force rendezvoused with the 1st Supply Force at 11°00'N, 130°00'E. Fueling began immediately while the two units headed north toward the rest of the Mobile Fleet. At 1650 Ugaki joined Ozawa and the entire Mobile Fleet was finally assembled.

After the rendezvous, 1st Supply Force began fueling the rest of the Mobile Fleet in preparation for the coming action. Fueling was leisurely, not being completed until 1300 the next day, at which time the Mobile Fleet was at 12°15'N, 132°45'E. The oilers then broke off to join with the 2nd Supply Force which had left Guimaras on the 15th and had since been bringing up the rear of the Mobile Fleet. When the two provisioning units met, they turned northeast and headed for a position at 14°40'N, 134°20'E, where they were to stand by for further use. Ozawa was now a little over 750 nautical miles from Saipan.

Ozawa was biding his time. He and most of his other top commanders had great faith—misplaced, as it turned out—in the operations of their land-based planes in the battle. These planes would severely damage the U.S. forces, thus facilitating the Mobile Fleet's later attacks. Ozawa also knew that he could stay out of range of TF 58's planes because his planes had a much greater radius of action than the Americans. (Generally, they had an advantage of 350–560 miles in the search role, and 200–300 miles in the attack role.)[16] One other advantage fell Ozawa's way. The prevailing wind was from the east, which meant that he could launch and recover planes while heading toward the enemy. Mitscher, on the other hand, would have to keep turning

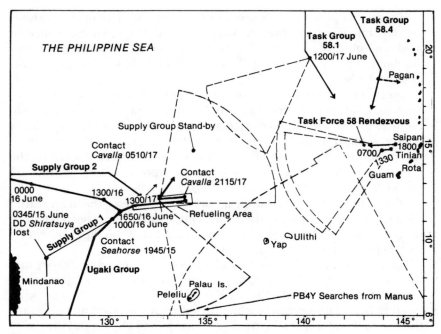

Movement of opposing forces, 16–17 June 1944.

east while air operations were in progress and would not be able to make much headway to the west.

A canny sailor, Ozawa was also pretty sure he knew the psychological makeup of his opponent, Spruance. The Japanese admiral figured that Spruance was a conservative and deliberate commander—one not inclined to take risks. He fully expected Spruance to sit close to Saipan and take no offensive action unless he had to.

Even though he was outnumbered fifteen carriers to nine, and two to one in planes, because of the "advantages" mentioned above Ozawa felt he had a fighting chance to destroy the Americans. The one factor that limited Ozawa was fuel. He had only enough to come straight at the enemy (a fact of which the Americans were, naturally, unaware), and the elaborate and complicated plans the Japanese loved to use could not be employed this time.

It appeared to the Japanese that part of their plans was already working, for on the 16th a Betty from the 755th Naval Air Group and four Jills of the 551st Group (all based at Truk) reported attacking U.S. vessels off Saipan. One cruiser was claimed sunk and two others damaged. Fifth Fleet kept operating, though, not even knowing it had been attacked.

Another of the ubiquitous U.S. submarines came across the Japanese on the 16th. The *Cavalla* (a new sub commanded by Commander Herman J. Kossler) was patrolling 360 miles east of San Bernardino Strait in company with the *Pipefish*. Although intelligence reports had presumably put them right on the track of the Mobile Fleet, a fruitless day of searching had turned up nothing. That evening Kossler headed for San Bernardino Strait to relieve the *Flying Fish*.

Shortly after 2300, while proceeding on the surface, Kossler got a radar contact. It was a small force, only four ships. Kossler brought the *Cavalla* in for a closer look. It was two oilers escorted by a pair of destroyers. He had stumbled on the 2nd Supply Force! Kossler ran ahead of the enemy ships and dived about 0340. Submerged, the *Cavalla* sneaked in for an attack. Just as Kossler was about to fire at an oiler, one of the destroyers charged. Kossler went deep to evade the attack. When he brought the *Cavalla* back up at about 0500, the enemy was nowhere in sight.

Kossler decided not to chase the oilers. His orders were to relieve the *Flying Fish*, and he had already wasted a day and a lot of fuel in the fruitless attack on the supply group. However, when he radioed his decision to Vice Admiral Charles A. Lockwood, ComSubPac and also commander TF 17, a quick change of orders came flashing back: "Destruction these tankers of great importance. Trail, attack, report."[17]

Kossler turned around and took his submarine back down the supply force's estimated track. It took some time, but at 2000 on 17 June Kossler hit the jackpot. While the *Cavalla* was proceeding on the surface, her radar picked up seven large "blips" about twenty thousand yards away. Kossler dove and closed with the target.

The Mobile Fleet steamed by the *Cavalla* as Kossler took in the parade with interest. Although he could have attacked, Kossler knew he had to get the information out first. After surfacing at 2245, he reported fifteen or more ships doing 19 knots and heading due east. Their position was reported as 12°23′N, 132°26′E. (Actually, the Mobile Fleet was about sixty miles northeast of that position.)[18] Because it was dark, Kossler missed many of the ships as they ran past, but the number of ships he did report—fifteen—would worry Spruance.

Although Lockwood appreciated the information Kossler had sent, he thought it was now time for action. He told Kossler and all the other submarine skippers in the area to shoot first and talk later. For his skippers' further edification another message said, "The above list of enemy ships does not frighten our varsity. We have all that and plenty more ready and waiting and they are all rough, tough and nasty."[19] Lockwood further ordered Kossler to, "Hang on and trail as long as possible regardless of fuel expenditure. . . . You may have a chance to get in an attack."[20] Kossler had lost the Mobile Fleet by the time he got Lockwood's message, but he determinedly took his boat toward where he thought the Japanese would be. He would be rewarded for his chase and the *Cavalla*'s crew would yet see some action.

Both sides were busy making final plans on the 17th. Operating under radio silence, Ozawa sent a Judy to Peleliu just before noon with a request for land-based air operations. Ozawa told Combined Fleet Headquarters and Fifth Base Air Force:

> The First Mobile Force, being at location 'E' on the evening of the 17th and having finished supplying operations, will advance to a general location west of Saipan by dawn of the 19th, going via point 'O' [possibly a translation error for 'C'] at 15.0 N latitude, 136.0 E longitude. In the meantime, this fleet shall guard against westerly advances of the enemy and their movements from the north. The objective is first to shell regular aircraft carrier groups and then, by employing all fighting power, to annihilate the enemy task forces and their invading forces. The following are the requests made of land-based air units:
>
> 1. It is requested that, from the evening preceding the decisive battle, you shall maintain a constant reconnaissance of the regular aircraft carriers of the enemy in the vicinity of the Mariana Islands. If this is impossible, notify us immediately of the condition and deployment of regular aircraft carriers as of noon.
>
> 2. We request intensified patrolling of the area west of the Marianas by each base on the day previous to the decisive battle. Special attention shall be paid to carry on reconnaissance in the sector from 160 degrees to 210 degrees from Iwo Jima. [Ozawa was figuring on the possibility of just the sort of end-run Jocko Clark had in mind.]
>
> 3. If the forces of the Yawata unit are not deployed on time, it is believed we shall be forced to delay the decisive battle by one day. Please notify us of such a probability.[21]

Ozawa was as yet unaware that the land-based phase of A-GO had gone seriously awry. Kakuta certainly was not telling him.

Off Saipan, Reeves's and Montgomery's task groups finished fueling shortly after midnight. The two groups wound up much farther east than planned, and Mitscher ordered them to make 23 knots to the west. Task Force 58 had to get as far west as possible because launching and recovering its planes meant the carriers would have to turn back into the easterly wind and, consequently, would not make good much distance toward the enemy.

Because of their distance to the east, TGs 58.2 and 58.3 sent night searches out 270–350 miles at 0200, half an hour later than planned. The two groups kept heading west until 0430. At 0700 the searchers were recovered. They had not seen anything. As the first searchers returned, another group of Helldivers and Avengers were launched to search to the west and southwest, to a distance of 325–350 miles. A third search, launched at 1330 by the *Bunker Hill* and *Lexington*, was as unsuccessful as the earlier attempts. Clark and Harrill, meanwhile, were ordered to search as far west as possible and to keep the area east of 138 degrees and south of 12 degrees covered.

Admiral Spruance ordered a minimum of air operations for the day, primarily search missions, but Mitscher thought it necessary to send in more strikes over Guam. About seventy-five sorties were flown in the afternoon. The strike "temporarily" closed Agana, but was costly to the Americans; several planes and pilots were lost to the deadly flak. The fliers were somewhat bitter, feeling that TF 58's battleships (at this time only preparing to form TG 58.7) should have been used to knock out the antiaircraft guns before the planes went in.

In the afternoon Mitscher radioed Spruance giving him the present and planned dispositions and movements of TF 58,

1. Present status:
    (a) Task Group 58.2 is 12 miles south of Task Group 58.3
    (b) Task Group 58.3 will be in Lat. 15°N, Long. 144°30'E at 1600 today.
    (c) A search was launched at 1330 distance 325 miles, betweeen bearings 215–285. This search is to be recovered about 1830 in vicinity Lat. 15°N, Long. 144°30'E.

2. Recommended disposition upon the joining of forces from Task Force 51:
    (a) Task Group 58.2 composed of carriers, CruDiv 13, DesRon 52, DesDiv 1; 12 miles south of Task Group 58.3.
    (b) Composition of Task Group 58.3: carriers, CruDiv 12, DesRon 50 and DesDiv 90.
    (c) Task Group 58.7 composed of battleships, CruDiv 6, DesDiv 12 (16 torpedoes each), DesDiv 89, and DesDiv 106; stationed 15 miles west of Task Group 58.3.

3. (a) If battle is joined before Task Groups 58.1 and 58.4 join us, Task Group 58.2 will be designated battle line carriers.
    (b) When Task Groups 58.1 and 58.4 join, propose to put Task Group 58.1 12 miles north of Task Group 58.3, and Task Group 58.3 and Task Group 58.4 12 miles south of Task Group 58.2.
    (c) As soon as Task Groups 58.1 and 58.4 join, propose to have *San Juan* join Task Group 58.2 and *Reno* join Task Group 58.3 so that one CL(AA) will be with each carrier group.
    (d) If battle is joined after Task Groups 58.1 and 58.4 join us, Task Group 58.4 will become battle line carrier group.
    (e) After first air battles have been fought and we have control of the

       air, recommend CruDivs 10, 13 and 12 and DesDivs 11, 1 and 90 be
       released from carrier groups to join Task Group 58.7.

  (f) After initial air battle, or before if it becomes feasible, recommend
       Task Group 58.1 take station about 50 miles to the northwest of
       Task Group 58.3 in order to hit Japs from northern flank and cut
       them off from escaping to the north.

4.   Recommended movement tonight; at 1800 course 310° until
       reaching Lat. 16°N, then course 270° until after daylight launch. It
       is hoped this will permit us to flank the enemy, keep outside of 400
       miles range of Yap and keep as far from other shore-based air
       flown in to Rota and Guam as practicable, and still be in position to
       hit enemy carrier groups (downwind from us).

5.   As soon as things quiet down a bit, one Task Group at a time should
       be refueled in vicinity of Marianas, during which time it can assist
       Task Force 51 on Guam, Rota, or Saipan as directed.[22]

Spruance initially approved Mitscher's plan, but late the next day
would change his mind and hold TF 58 close to Saipan. Mitscher, in the
meantime, was going ahead with his preparations: "Proposed plan for
strike on enemy surface forces," he signaled his carriers. "Make deck
load launch from CVs consisting of 16 VF, 12 VB and 9 VT. Second
deck load prepared for launch as second wave unless situation indicates delay advisable. Augment VT from CVLs as practicable. Arming
VT half torpedoes, VB half GP, half SAP. Later strikes include AP as
targets indicate."[23]

Admiral Spruance issued his battle plan at 1415, saying, "Our air will
first knock out enemy carriers as operating carriers, then will attack
enemy battleships and cruisers to slow or disable them. Task Group
58.7 will destroy enemy fleet either by fleet action if enemy elects to
fight or by sinking slowed or crippled ships if enemy retreats. Action
against the retreating enemy must be pushed vigorously by all hands to
insure complete destruction of his fleet. Destroyers running short of
fuel may be returned to Saipan if necessary for refueling."[24]

This "bare bones" plan sounded aggressive enough—but, like so
many good plans, it never bore fruit. Also striking, given Spruance's
concern about such a tactic, is the fact that this plan makes no mention
of a Japanese end run.[25] A message to Spruance from Admiral Nimitz
in the afternoon should, nevertheless, have given the Fifth Fleet commander some thoughts about sticking with his battle plan. "On the eve
of a possible fleet action," Nimitz radioed, "you and the officers and
men under your command have the confidence of the naval services
and the country. We count on you to make the victory decisive."[26]

At 1741 Spruance in the *Indianapolis*, plus CruDiv 12 (the *Cleveland,
Montpelier, Birmingham*), joined TG 58.3. After joining, Spruance sig-

naled Mitscher, "Desire you proceed at your discretion, selecting dispositions and movements best calculated to meet the enemy under the
most advantageous condition. I shall issue general directives when
necessary and leave details to you and Admiral Lee."[27]

This message left Mitscher in a quandary. It had been sent by
Spruance in reply to a query by Mitscher regarding the tactical command of TF 58. The tenor of the message, however, suggested to
Mitscher that he would not have complete control over TF 58.
Spruance would be continually hovering nearby to approve or dis-
approve any orders. To preclude any conflict between Mitscher and
Spruance, the TF 58 commander "preferred to submit his proposed
courses of action to Admiral Spruance before they were put out of
order, which meant that Admiral Spruance, although not taking OTC,
was actually operating as OTC."[28]

During the afternoon Mitscher sent word to the two task groups at
hand to prepare to dispatch their battleships and some escorting vessels to form the battle line, TG 58.7. Mitscher figured that with the
usual confusion when ships move in and out of formation, it would be
better to form TG 58.7 early, rather than wait until the Japanese were
nearby to interfere with this movement. At 1730 the seven fast battleships (the *Washington, North Carolina, Iowa, New Jersey, South Dakota,
Alabama,* and *Indiana*), along with four heavy cruisers and thirteen
destroyers, left the carrier groups and formed the battle line. Able and
aggressive Vice Admiral Willis A. "Ching" Lee commanded the task
group. After all the ships had rendezvoused, they took up station
fifteen miles west of TG 58.3. Mitscher had made his final dispositions
and was now awaiting the return of his two other groups the next day.

The searches during the day had turned up no ships, but the afternoon search had run into several enemy planes which had soon been
shot down. Surprisingly, it appears that the American commanders
took little note of these planes. The positions of the air actions and the
apparent direction the Japanese planes had come from did not lead
anyone to guess the line of advance of the Mobile Fleet. Captain Burke
said only, "those enemy planes probably did report our position."[29]

While the Americans were still vague about the position of the
Mobile Fleet, Japanese land-based air knew full well where the action
was. On the evening of the 17th, several heavy attacks were launched
by the Japanese Base Air Force against U.S. forces off Saipan. At 1750
five Jills and an Irving night fighter from Truk attacked an "enemy
transport convoy." What they actually found was Captain G. B. Carter's
tractor group (TG 53.16) of sixteen LSTs, seven LCI(G)s, nine sub
chasers, and the destroyer *Stembel*. The group was part of the Southern

Attack Force and was killing time waiting for the expected Guam invasion. The Japanese fliers claimed that they sank "thirteen transports and left one destroyer listing heavily."[30] What they actually got in return for the loss of three planes was a torpedo hit on LCI(G)-468. The explosion killed fifteen men and wounded three. The gunboat was severely damaged and eventually had to be scuttled.

A second, larger attack hit the Americans unloading at Saipan around dusk. This attack was apparently picked up by TG 58.2 radars about 1735, heading toward Guam. Because the estimated twenty to thirty planes were over one hundred miles away, no interception was attempted. But there were more than thirty planes. Thirty-one Zekes, seventeen Judys, and two Frans from Yap ignored the fire-support group and went for the ships unloading off Charan Kanoa. An LST was hit and caught fire, but the blaze was put out and the vessel salvaged. Turning back from this attack, the enemy planes ran across the jeep carriers maneuvering offshore. Although radar picked up the incoming planes, the fighter direction was inaccurate, and forty-six Wildcats went off on a wild goose chase.

Now, with only the ships' antiaircraft fire to confront them, the Japanese attacked. In the dim light many of the pilots thought they were attacking the fast carriers of TF 58. Bombs just missed *Gambier Bay* and *Coral Sea*. But the *Fanshaw Bay* was not as lucky. A 550-pound bomb sliced through her after elevator and exploded on her hangar deck. Eleven men were killed. The fires caused by the explosion were quickly put out by her crew, but the *Fanshaw Bay* had to retire to Eniwetok for repairs.

Five of the Judys and several Zekes landed after dark on the "temporarily out of commission" field on Guam. The other planes retired to Yap. The Japanese fliers were jubilant, thinking they had sunk two or three fast carriers and had left another burning. To the Japanese, who were not yet aware of the miscarriage of the land-based phase of A-GO, it appeared that these planes were doing their job well.

The problems for the escort carriers were not over yet. As two *White Plains* Wildcats were returning to their carrier, they were fired on by "friendly" ships, then jumped by four other Wildcats of the CAP. Although neither of the two fighters was shot down, one was so badly damaged that on landing it crashed into five other aircraft and all six had to be written off.

Affairs around Saipan finally quieted down during the night, but tension was steadily building among the sailors of TF 58. Where were the Japanese? It was not too long before TF 58 found out where the Mobile Fleet had been. The *Cavalla*'s contact report reached Spruance

The fast carriers weren't the only ones to receive the attention of enemy planes. Here the Gambier Bay is missed by a blazing Japanese bomber on 18 June 1944, while the carrier was supporting operations on Saipan. (U.S. Navy)

at 0321 on the morning of the 18th, and Mitscher had it twenty-four minutes later. But now a divergence of viewpoints between the two commanders emerged.

Mitscher and his two "braintrusters," Burke and Hedding, did some quick figuring. If the Japanese kept coming at 19 knots, they would be about 660 miles from Saipan at dawn and 500 miles from TF 58's proposed 0530 position. That was still too far for any attack on the enemy, but by steaming directly for the enemy's estimated 1500 position, TF 58 might be able to get in one strike in the late afternoon. But TF 58 was then widely separated, with TGs 58.1 and 58.4 far to the north of the other two groups. A noon rendezvous was planned and Clark and Harrill were ordered to link up with the rest of TF 58 as soon as possible. Mitscher could have headed west with the two groups he had on hand, letting the other groups catch up as best they could, but he preferred to be sure all his forces were concentrated for the coming action. When all his ships were together Mitscher would take TF 58 westward for the attack on the Mobile Fleet.[31]

Admiral Spruance had other plans. By the evening of 17 June he was worrying about a flank attack. He later commented, "At dark on 17 June the situation appeared to be as follows: Enemy forces probably consisting of 5 BB, 9 CV, 8 CA and a number of destroyers were at sea east of the Philippines for the purpose of attacking our amphibious forces engaged in the capture of Saipan. The task of Task Force 58 was to cover our amphibious forces and to prevent such an attack. The enemy attack would probably involve a strike by carrier-based aircraft, supported and followed up by heavy fleet units. The possibility existed that the enemy fleet might be divided with a portion of it involving carriers coming in around one of our flanks. If Task Force 58 were moved too far from Saipan before the location of the enemy was definitely determined, such a flank attack could inflict heavy damage on our amphibious forces at Saipan. Routes of withdrawal to the northward and to the southwestward would remain open to such a flanking force. The use of enemy airfields on Guam and Rota were available to the enemy except as our carrier-based aircraft were able to keep these fields neutralized."[32]

The fifteen ships that the *Cavalla* had reported also worried him. "It appeared from the *Cavalla* reports, however, that the entire enemy force was not concentrated in one disposition; that if the force sighted by the *Cavalla* was the same as that sighted by the *Flying Fish* in San Bernardino Strait, a speed of less than 10 knots had been made good; and that the position of the *Cavalla* contact indicated a possible approach to the Marianas by this task group via the southern flank."[33]

Spruance apparently did not consider that in the darkness the *Cavalla* could have missed many of the ships (which she had). Forty ships spread over a wide expanse of ocean cannot be easily seen by a submarine at periscope depth. He also reasoned that if the force the *Cavalla* sighted was the same one the *Flying Fish* had reported, it had made only a very slow advance. Even with the sighting of oilers nearby, it apparently did not occur to Spruance's staff that this slow advance could have been because the Japanese were fueling (which they were). And always there was Spruance's extreme concern, almost obsession, with the possibility of a flank attack. Yet this concern did not cause him to modify his battle plan, which never mentioned that possibility. Despite his aggressive battle plan of the day before, Spruance was beginning to settle into a defensive posture.

In the meantime, both sides were busily preparing for an action which appeared likely the next day. With the *Cavalla*'s report in hand, Admiral Lockwood shifted the four submarines of his Pentathalon Group (then scouting northwest of Saipan) one hundred miles south. He told them, "Indications at this end that the big show may be taking place at the present time. Exact location unknown but possibly *Finback, Bang, Stingray* and *Albacore* may be the corner post of the boxing ring. . . . Do not miss any opportunity to get in a shot at the enemy. This may be the chance of a lifetime."[34] Working a "square" scouting line, these subs would be athwart the track of the Japanese force. It turned out to be an excellent move and would indeed provide one of the subs with the "chance of a lifetime."

The 18th saw a miminum of air activity on the Americans' part. PBMs from the Saipan roadstead flew searches 600 miles west, while PB4Ys from the Admiralties also flew missions 1,200 miles to the northwest—all with no success. Unfortunately, one of the Liberator's search patterns extended only 1,050 miles. As luck would have it, it was through this area that Ozawa led the Mobile Fleet on the evening of the 18th and the morning of the 19th. The carrier-launched searches fared no better. The first planes lifted off the decks at 0532. Narrow ten-degree legs were flown to a limit of 325-350 miles and covered an area between 195 degrees and 280 degrees. No ships were seen, but several enemy planes, obviously out scouting, were picked off.

Essex searchers scored two kills. At 0755 Lieutenant (jg) R. L. Turner, flying a Helldiver, spotted what he identified as a Jill but was probably a Kate. Turner and his fighter escort gave chase. The enemy pilot did not see the Americans until it was too late. After a pass by the Hellcat pilot which started a fire in the plane's left wing root, Turner punched home about a hundred rounds of 20-mm fire into the Kate's fuselage and wings. A large piece of the left wing suddenly ripped off, almost slamming into the "2C". As Turner passed over the Kate, he could see the gunner hanging out of the cockpit and the pilot desperately trying to get out. Flames surrounded them and their clothes were burning. Then the Kate's left wing dipped and the plane spun into the sea. About an hour and a half later, Ensign K. A. Flinn, escorting another SB2C, slammed a Betty into the water with his .50-calibers.

Meanwhile, Lieutenants (jg) Charles E. Henderson and Clifton R.

Largess, flying Torpedo 10 Avengers, sandwiched a twin-float Jake between them and dropped the burning floatplane into the sea. Another pair of Jakes were the victims of a *Yorktown* fighter pilot.

Obviously, the Japanese had been busy launching searches, and with better luck than the Americans. Ozawa's force was making 20 knots and heading 060 degrees when he sent his first reconnaissance missions out at 0600. Fourteen Kates and two Jakes were to cover an area between 350 and 110 degrees to a distance of 425 miles. (Note that this was almost one hundred miles farther than the American searchers.) By 0800 two of the planes had sighted enemy carrier planes. The first contacts between the two sides had been made.

When the Japanese planes returned to their ships, the two Jakes and a Kate did not come back. (There is a discrepency between the number of Jakes launched and those claimed shot down. Where the extra Jake came from is unknown.) At noon Ozawa sent off another search. This one consisted of thirteen Judys and two Jakes. Ozawa was sure this search would turn up something. At this time the Mobile Fleet was at 14°40′N, 135°40′E (about 120 miles northeast of its 0500 position). As soon as the search was launched the fleet changed course to 030 degrees.

It was not long before a number of contact reports came filtering back to Ozawa. The first few sightings were of enemy aircraft and served only to heighten the tension on Ozawa's flagship, the *Taiho*. One report was of a PB2Y Coronado flying-boat (more likely a PB4Y from the Admiralties). At 1445 eight fighters were, rather unusually, sent out in a vain attempt to catch it.

The really important sightings began reaching Ozawa shortly after the abortive try to find the "flying-boat." The pilot of Plane No. 15 had reached his search limit of 420 miles and was on the dog-leg portion of his pattern when he sighted TF 58. At 1514 he began transmitting to Admiral Ozawa "enemy task force, including carriers" at 14°50′N, 142°15′E. The Americans had been found.[35]

Forty-six minutes later Plane No. 13 also reported enemy ships, including carriers, heading west. The conclusive sighting came from the crew of Plane No. 17, searching the sector north of Plane No. 15. Shortly after 1600 they reported sighting TF 58, amplifying this at 1640 with

> "UI2CHI*—1st group—2 regular carriers, 10-15 destroyers.
> URA4E —2nd group—2 seemingly regular carriers, 10 others.
> URA1A —3rd group—2 seemingly carriers, 10 others.[36]

*Grid position on Japanese maps.

This sighting put TF 58 at 14°12′N, 141°55′E. Plane No. 17 also reported that the enemy ships were heading west, that there were cloud layers at 29,500 and 3,300 feet and the cloud cover was 7/10s, and the wind was from 100 degrees at 11 mph. It was a good, solid sighting and report.[37]

Ozawa received Plane No. 15's report at 1530 and began making his final plans for the battle. At 1540 he ordered course changed from 030 degrees to 200 degrees and for his forces to prepare to shift into battle disposition. At this time the Mobile Fleet was about 360 miles from the "15-I" position. Ozawa had no intention of getting any closer than necessary to TF 58. By remaining 400 miles away, he could stay out of range of enemy planes, yet his own planes would still be able to strike.

But while Ozawa was patiently awaiting the proper time to attack, a number of his subordinates were anxious to take action. Rear Admiral Sueo Obayashi, 3rd CarDiv commander with his flag in the *Chitose*, readied the planes of his three carriers for an attack on the ships seen by Plane No. 15. Sixty-seven planes were spotted for takeoff and launchings began at 1637. However, only three Jills, fifteen bomb-carrying Zekes, and four Zeke fighters from the *Chiyoda* were airborne

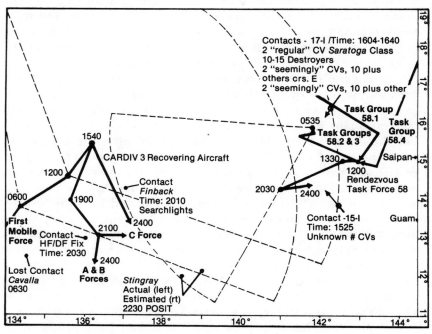

Movement of opposing forces, 18 June 1944.

when Obayashi received Admiral Ozawa's Operation Order No. 16, which had been sent at 1610. This order read: "1. At around 1500 enemy task forces believed to be, one, 350 miles bearing about 220° from Iwo Jima, and the other, 160 miles west of Saipan. 2. Mobile Fleet will retire temporarily, after which it will proceed north and tomorrow morning contact and destroy the enemy to the north, after which it will attack and destroy the enemy to the northeast."[38]

The north sighting was a phantom. Admiral Toyoda, in Tokyo, had sent Ozawa a land-based search plane's garbled transmission. A short time later Ozawa received a corrected report that showed there was nothing in that direction. At 1817 Ozawa issued Operations Order No. 19 which announced that the only target for the next day would be the enemy force west of the Marianas.[39]

When Admiral Obayashi received Operations Order No. 16, he immediately recalled his strike force. All the *Chiyoda* planes landed safely except one of the bomb-carrying Zekes, which crashed. Not everyone was happy with the recall. Although most of the senior officers believed that a late-afternoon or early-evening attack followed by a night landing on Guam (required because of the late takeoff) would be asking too much of the green aircrews, many of the junior officers thought otherwise. In their enthusiasm and zeal—and rashness—they were sure they could destroy the enemy that day.

The "Impressions and Battle Lessons (Air) in the 'A' Operation" written after the battle conveys the feelings of these younger officers. Regarding the recalled strike, it says: "On the 18th the 3rd flying squadron was determined to attack the enemy as soon as sighted and prepared to return to the carrier, if it was not later than 1400, and to land on Guam, if it was after 1500. But by order from the operational unit the attack was cancelled. Although the outcome of the attack could not be predicted, a surprise was planned before sunset. If it had been carried out, it could certainly have been a surprise attack, as compared with the attack carried out next morning. Under these conditions it would be better to be prepared for an attack immediately after discovery of the enemy. And in case there is a risk of our operation being already known to the enemy on the day of the attack, it is admittedly necessary to launch a night flanking movement on a large scale in order to administer the first blow on the enemy. If the 3rd flying squadron under the circumstance had reported its plan of attack to the flag commander of the fleet, there would not have been any blunder [on Ozawa's part, presumably]. And in receiving the order of cancelling, if it had any confidence in itself at all, it should have proposed its opinion."[40]

These statements are to the point. However, the top commanders from Toyoda on down disagreed with the conclusions. First, because of the fuel problem a flanking attack was out of the question. Then, surprise might have been achieved, but this is very doubtful; United States radar techniques were too good by this time. The raid would have been discovered even if the Japanese had attacked out of the sun. Mitscher was not going to let his guard down just because his planes had not yet spotted the Japanese. Finally, the Japanese fliers of June 1944 were generally not the same caliber as those of June 1942. Would a surprise attack on the evening of the 18th have been better handled than the disorganized mess of the next day? This is extremely doubtful. Ozawa was probably right in saving his aircraft for one big blow. It was no fault of his that although he got in the first strike on the 19th, it turned into a disaster.

While Obayashi's carriers trailed behind recovering planes, the rest of the Mobile Fleet headed 200 degrees. At 1900 course was changed to 140 degrees and speed was reduced to 16 knots. At 2020 Ozawa took a calculated risk and broke radio silence to inform Admiral Kakuta on Tinian of his proposed plans for the next day. It was a risk, but one that Ozawa thought necessary to gain the proper coordination with his land-based air for the next day's fighting. Unfortunately, Base Air Force was in no condition to provide much help, and Kakuta remained reluctant to tell Ozawa and Toyoda the truth of his situation.

This transmission, probably of just a few minutes duration, could have led to the destruction of Ozawa's fleet. A U.S. naval "Huff-Duff" (HF/DF—high frequency direction-finding) shore station picked up the message and identified the sender as Ozawa. The station also pinpointed the Mobile Fleet's position as 13°N, 136°E.[41] This was good sharpshooting; Ozawa's ships were only about forty miles away from that spot, and about three hundred miles from TF 58. The fix was passed on to Spruance.

Ozawa split his forces at 2100. Vice Admiral Takeo Kurita's powerful Van or C Force headed due east, while the other two units changed course to 190 degrees. Eventually Kurita's force would be stationed one hundred miles ahead of the rest of the Mobile Fleet and therefore closest to the enemy. With this formation Ozawa figured that any attacker would have to fly through a wall of fire thrown up by C Force and would thus probably be decimated before reaching his large carriers. C Force was the largest of the three units Ozawa utilized during the battle. Along with the light carriers *Chitose, Chiyoda,* and *Zuiho* were four battleships (including the monsters *Yamato* and *Musashi*), eight cruisers, and eight destroyers.

Vice Admiral Takeo Kurita, commander of "C" Force during the Battle of the Philippine Sea. (U.S. Navy)

At 0300 on the morning of the 19th, the Mobile Fleet turned to a course of 050 degrees and speed was upped to 20 knots. The three forces shifted into their battle formation, and by 0415 all was in readiness. Following behind C Force was Admiral Ozawa and A Force. (Besides commanding the Mobile Fleet, Ozawa was in tactical command of all the carriers and also commander of A Force.) A Force consisted of the big carriers *Taiho, Shokaku* and *Zuikaku*, three cruisers, and seven destroyers. Nine miles north of A Force was B Force, commanded by Rear Admiral Takaji Joshima. It was made up of the carriers *Junyo, Hiyo* and *Ryuho*, battleship *Nagato*, heavy cruiser *Mogami*, and eight destroyers.

Ozawa sadly lacked destroyers for screening and antisubmarine work. And this shortage would cost the Japanese dearly. The *Harder* (and other U.S. subs throughout the war) had hurt the Japanese greatly with their attacks on destroyers.

Back with TF 58, the 18th would be a day of momentous and controversial decisions. After huddling with his staff over the *Cavalla's* contact report and a later one which Admiral Spruance thought added "little to the information previously received,"[42] Mitscher decided a late afternoon air strike would be possible and a night surface action a very good possibility. Mitscher signaled Admiral Lee, "Do you desire night engagement? It may be we can make air contact late this afternoon and attack tonight. Otherwise we should retire to the eastward for tonight."[43]

"Do not (repeat, *not*) believe we should seek night engagement," was Lee's disappointing reply. "Possible advantages of radar more than offset by difficulties of communications and lack of training in fleet tactics at night. Would press pursuit of damaged or fleeing enemy, however, at any time."[44]

If there were any need for confirmation that the battleship was no longer the ruler of the sea, Lee's statement certainly provided it. In no way was Lee afraid of the Japanese; he had shown that at Guadalcanal. But he respected them as fighters, particularly in night battles. By this stage of the war also, the battleships had been reduced to spear carriers

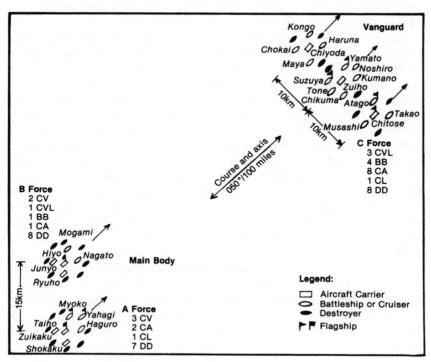

Disposition of the Mobile Fleet, 19 June 1944.

for the flattops. Their primary job was to protect the carriers with their awesome array of antiaircraft weapons. The fast battleships had not had the time to perfect tactics for a surface action; they had been too busy escorting the carriers. However, Lee must surely have been aware that in a hostile air environment, a night battle would be the *only* way his battleships could ever fight a purely surface action.[45]

The battleships would stay tied to TF 58.

Shortly after 0700 *Bataan* pilots sighted a life raft a short distance from TG 58.1. The raft appeared to be populated with dead men. The destroyers *Bell* and *Conner* were sent to investigate and discovered the men, eighteen in all, were alive. They had been members of a small Japanese cargo ship sunk enroute from Woleai to Guam on 13 June. They were later transferred to the *Hornet* to enjoy the amenities of the brig.

At noon the four task groups rendezvoused, with the antiaircraft cruisers *San Juan* and *Reno* joining TGs 58.2 and 58.3 respectively. For the impending action TGs 58.1, 58.3, and 58.2 were placed twelve miles apart on a north-south line. Fifteen miles west of the *Lexington* was Admiral Lee's TG 58.7. About twelve miles north and slightly east of TG 58.7 was TG 58.4.

Before the rendezvous Spruance made one of the most important decisions of the battle. "Task Force 58 must cover Saipan and our forces engaged in that operation," he told Mitscher and Lee. "I still feel that main enemy attack will come from westward but it might be diverted to come in from southwestward. Diversionary attacks may come in from either flank or reinforcements might come in from Empire. Consider that we can best cover Saipan by advancing to westward during daylight and retiring to eastward at night so as to reduce possibility of enemy passing us during darkness. Distance which you can make to westward during day will naturally be restricted by your air operations and by necessity to conserve fuel. We should however remain in air supporting position of Saipan until information of enemy requires other action. . . . Consider seeking night action undesirable initially in view of our superior strength in all types, but earliest possible strike on enemy carriers is necessary."[46]

The decision had been made. Instead of pursuing an offensive course as his battle plan had stated, Spruance was pulling back into a basically static defensive position. There would really be no possibility of "earliest possible strikes" now, and TF 58's "superior strength" was being wasted. Spruance was doing exactly what Ozawa thought he would.

Mitscher and his staff were dismayed. They "could not understand why the Commander Fifth Fleet would throw away the tremendous advantages of surprise and initiative and aggressiveness."[47] But Spruance was a "Big Gun" man (as was most of his staff). His experience in carrier warfare was primarily on a lofty plane. When Lee said he would not fight at night, Spruance was left, figuratively, at sea. Now without his beloved battleships to fight the battle, Spruance was unsure how to use his carriers. His choice—wait and let the enemy attack him.

More searches were flown at 1330. Though ranging out 325 miles, the planes again missed the Mobile Fleet, but this time by only sixty miles. Confrontations between opposing search planes again took place. *Hornet* planes bagged another of the vulnerable Jakes 240 miles out, and another Jake and a Judy were downed by aircraft from TG 58.3. Only thirty miles from TF 58, a number of Hellcats on CAP were run ragged by a single Judy.

This Judy first ran afoul of a division of *Monterey* Hellcats. Although the Americans were able to hole the enemy plane a few times, the Japanese pilot evaded them by the judicious use of cloud cover. Then, four more F6Fs from the *Cowpens* and six from the *Langley* began queuing up. Still, the Judy "evaded no less than twelve passes by doing a startling and expert series of maneuvers, including snap rolls, spins, split 'S's, falling leafs, and one snap loop that would have pulled the wings off a less sturdy plane."[48] VF-25's Lieutenant (jg) Frederick R. Stieglitz finally popped out of a cloud directly behind the Judy. Firing almost continuously, he poured 750 rounds into the dive bomber. The Judy caught fire and fell into the sea.

Flight operations continued until dusk. Mitscher then headed TF 58 into the setting sun so any enemy planes trying to sneak in would show up easily. This was just the time that Obayashi's planes would have been attacking if they had not been recalled.

The Japanese had been attacking throughout the day, but not with carrier-based planes. A number of the aircraft that had gotten into Guam the night before went out again on the morning of the 18th. This day they were unsuccessful in their attacks and suffered additional losses. One of the pilots was picked up by the Americans, to become one of the few Japanese aviators to survive the air battles around the Marianas. Enemy aircraft flying from Yap and Palau were also still active. An early-morning reconnaissance by nine Bettys found the jeep carriers southeast of Saipan. A large strike of six Franceses and eleven Zekes from Yap, and one Judy and thirty-eight Zekes from Palau, was directed against the carriers, but the pilots could not find their targets.

Some, however, did run across some oilers of TG 50.17, the Fueling Group.

The oilers *Saranac*, *Neshanic*, and *Saugatuck* were fueling four destroyers and destroyer escorts about forty miles southeast of Saipan when they were attacked by five planes shortly after 1630. The attackers did quite well, hitting all three of the oilers. The *Saranac* had eight seamen killed and twenty-two wounded and was so badly damaged she had to head back to the rear areas for repairs. The *Neshanic* was hit by a bomb that exploded drums of gasoline stowed on deck. Flames boiled up to the top of the mast, but the ship's damage-control party had the fire out in seven minutes. She and the *Saugatuck* were repaired at Eniwetok.

Events began speeding up on the evening of the 18th. Far to the west of TF 58 the submarines *Finback* and *Stingray* were patrolling. Shortly after 2000 the *Finback* was traveling on the surface at 14°19′N, 137°05′E, when her lookouts saw a pair of searchlights stab the sky to the south. Full speed ahead was ordered, but the sub was unable to close fast enough to pick up any targets on her radar. The lights had apparently come from one of Admiral Obayashi's carriers as it recovered some late returning planes. (The Japanese analysis of the battle later showed great concern with this and other breaches of security in the Mobile Fleet.)[49] There was some delay in sending a contact report, and it was not until 0150 on 19 June that Spruance received it. By that time he had already made the important decisions.

While the *Finback* was watching the lights, the *Stingray* had been having problems. A small fire had broken out in the conning tower but had soon been extinguished. The fire apparently affected the submarine's radio equipment, for a routine incident report to ComSubPac was badly distorted. Admiral Lockwood thought the Japanese had jammed the transmission. While Lockwood was trying to figure out what the *Stingray* was saying, the Huff-Duff stations had picked up the Mobile Fleet.

At 2030 TF 58 heeled around according to Spruance's plan and took up a course of 080 degrees and a speed of 18 knots. In the eight and one-half hours since the rendezvous, the ships had made only 115 miles to the west-southwest. At 2200 more bits of intelligence began reaching Spruance and Mitscher. The first interesting tidbit was the HF/DF fix. Mitscher got this report at 2245 and thought it good enough to take action on. Spruance, on the other hand, was unimpressed, taking the fix to be a Japanese trick. Mitscher, however, put his staff to work on the fix to see what they could come up with.

After several minutes' work they calculated that Ozawa's ships were 355 miles away and would probably remain there until daylight. It was still too great a distance for a strike by U.S. planes. However, by reversing course at 0130 on the 19th, TF 58 would be in an ideal striking range of 150 to 200 miles from the enemy by 0500.

At 2325, after many calculations and recalculations, Mitscher radioed Spruance, "Propose coming to course 270 degrees at 0130 in order to commence treatment at 0500. Advise."[50]

Spruance and his staff mulled over Mitscher's message. Even before Mitscher had submitted his plan Spruance had in his hand another piece of the intelligence puzzle; a piece that actually fit nowhere. About 2230 a message from Admiral Lockwood to the *Stingray* concerning the submarine's earlier garbled transmission was intercepted.[51] This message was not addressed to ComFifthFleet and was not intended for him!

Yet, surprisingly, Spruance became very interested in the *Stingray*. Figuring the *Stingray*'s patrol station as about 175 miles *east-southeast* of the Huff/Duff fix, Spruance concluded that the submarine had found the Mobile Fleet and her radio transmissions had been jammed for her troubles. It appears that by this time Spruance already had his mind made up, and this message to the *Stingray* merely confirmed his impressions of what the Japanese would do—come in two or three forces, employing diversionary tactics. After discussing Mitscher's plan for over an hour with his staff, Spruance replied to the TF 58 commander at 0038 on the 19th.

"Change proposed does not appear advisable," he told Mitscher. "Believe indications given by *Stingray* more accurate than that determined by direction-finder. If that is so continuation as at present seems preferable. End run by other carrier groups remains possibility and must not be overlooked."[52]

When this message reached Mitscher, both he and his staff were stunned. They were not then aware of the *Stingray* messages and when they did learn of them they could not believe Admiral Spruance would put such faith in a garbled transmission not even addressed to him. Disappointment pervaded the ships of TF 58. On board the *Enterprise* Captain Matt Gardner threw his hat on the deck and stomped on it.[53]

Task Force 58 continued eastbound.

By shortly after midnight on 19 June the decisions had been made on both sides. No matter what new information might surface in the next few hours, no matter how many calculations could be made, the die had been cast. The 19th of June would be the day of battle and TF 58 most likely would have to take the first blow.

chapter 5

"Like an Old Time Turkey Shoot"

IN THE DARKNESS of the early hours of 19 June, the ships of TF 58 sliced through the waters of the Philippine Sea, heading east. Trailing some 350 miles to the west was Admiral Ozawa's Mobile Fleet.

Though it was dark, on both sides there was activity on the ships and in the air. Aboard the carriers, aircraft were being gassed and ammunition loaded. Mechanics were carefully checking over the planes. Below decks, pilots and seamen alike tossed fitfully as they thought of what daylight might bring. Others less concerned or more able to control their fears were asleep almost as soon as their heads hit the pillows. On all ships, lookouts carefully searched the sky for that blob that was a little blacker than the darkness, carefully scoured the water for a small ripple that might be the wake of a periscope. Up on the bridges and in the "flag countries" of the ships, admirals and ensigns, captains and seamen were discussing the possibilities of action on this day.

Bogeys were on the scopes for some time after midnight, but few closed. Then, at 0100 a snooper (probably from Guam) began dropping flares near TG 58.1. The destroyer *Cowell* fired on the plane and a night fighter was sent after the intruder, but neither had any success. Equally unsuccessful was the destroyer *Burns*'s attempt to put out the flares by the unconventional method of depth-charging them.

Far to the west, Lieutenant H. F. Arle and his crew had been out in their PBM for over two hours when the radar operator picked up something on his scope. It was 0115. Forty glowing blips concentrated in two groups could be seen on the scope. Arle had hit the jackpot—the Japanese Fleet! (Actually, only Kurita's C Force had been picked up, but that was good enough.) The ships were only seventy-five miles northeast of the Huff/Duff fix.

Arle immediately began sending his contact report. There was no reply from any station. Again and again the message was sent, and again and again there was no answer. Arle's report had been heard, but not by those to whom he was sending it. A plane from another command some distance away heard the message but did not offer to relay it. At Eniwetok the seaplane tender *Casco* also heard the message but then sat on it.

Arle continued scouting and did not return to the Garapan roadstead until shortly before 0900. By then the information was useless. Thus, an atmospheric "glitch," and some poor judgment by those who did receive the report, combined to keep the Americans from using one of the most potentially valuable sighting reports of the entire battle.

The *Enterprise* began sending fifteen Avengers off on a search mission at 0218. Every forty-four seconds one of the big planes was catapulted from the "Big E's" deck. Finally, Bill Martin (back in the cockpit following his sojourn in the waters off Saipan) led the radar-equipped Avengers westward. Martin's VT-10 was one of the few U.S. squadrons proficient in night flying. In February they had shown their capabilities with an outstanding night attack during TG 58's raid on Truk.

Now the Avengers were flying to find the Japanese. For one hundred miles they flew on a course of 255 degrees until they reached an arbitrary fix called Point Fox. At 0319 they reached Point Fox and separated to search individually. For another 225 miles, narrow five-degree sectors were flown between 240 and 270 degrees. But again the Americans missed the Japanese by a hair's breadth. Kurita's C Force was still about forty-five miles away. Only a couple of obvious aircraft targets and a submarine contact marred the blankness of the radarscopes.

Ozawa, meanwhile, was forming the Mobile Fleet into its battle disposition. By 0415 the movement was completed and Ozawa's force was ready for action. Between 0430 and 0445 Ozawa sent out sixteen Jakes (of which ten would not return) from C Force, which was now at about 13°15'N, 138°05'E. The floatplanes were to search between 315 and 135 degrees and range out to 350 miles. A second-phase search of thirteen Kates and one Jake from CarDiv 3 and the cruiser *Chikuma* was launched between 0515 and 0520. Seven of these planes were lost during the searches. These planes were to search between 000 and 180 degrees to a distance of 300 miles. Ten minutes after the last Kate had taken off, the *Shokaku* began launching eleven Judys, with two Jakes from the *Mogami* tagging along. They were to scout an incredible 560 miles.[1]

Thus, by 0600 Ozawa had forty-three planes out searching for the Americans. One of these planes was forced back by engine trouble, but it was searching a sector where there were no U.S. ships. With this number of planes on search missions and most of the rest being readied for the impending strikes, the number of planes available for other tasks was very limited. Only small CAPs were flown over the Mobile Fleet, and antisubmarine patrols had to be called off altogether—a decision that would hurt the Japanese a few hours later.

Snoopers began appearing near TF 58 (now heading east by north) shortly after 0500. All escaped interception. By 0530 Mitscher's flagship *Lexington* had reached 14°40′N, 143°40′E, about 115 miles west-southwest of Tinian. At this time the ships turned to the northeast to begin launching the dawn search, CAP and antisubmarine patrols.

Although enemy ships again were not seen, the searchers (especially those from the *Essex*) had a profitable morning shooting down enemy aircraft. Two Jakes, two Kates, and a Jill were picked off by the pilots of Fighting and Bombing 15. Hellcat driver Lieutenant J. R. Strane got the first two kills. Strane was escorting a "2C" when the bomber pilot pointed out a Jake about ten miles away, heading northeast. The Americans passed over and behind the blue-black painted Jake, then Strane whipped his Hellcat around and got a perfect full deflection shot at the enemy's left side. Six .50-caliber guns poured slugs into the Jake's left wing and cockpit. The wing began to burn as the floatplane pulled up sharply. At 500 feet the Jake suddenly began spinning and corkscrewed into the water. Nothing remained on the surface but one pontoon.

A few minutes later Strane latched on to what he identified as a dark brown Jill. This time the enemy crew was more observant and tried to run for it. The Jill disappeared into a cloud and Strane followed it in. When he broke out the Jill was off his port beam. Before the Jill could duck into another cloud, Strane had gotten good hits on its wing and fuselage. As the enemy plane melted into a nearby cloud, it was burning. Strane kept after it. A few seconds later both planes popped out of the cloud. The Jill was dead ahead. Strane got in another good burst and the Jill's rear gunner, who had been firing, was silenced. Strane overshot the dive bomber, and as he passed he could see its pilot slumped forward. With flames pouring from the left wing, the Jill slowly began to climb. Then it stalled out, began to spin and went straight in from 3,000 feet.

Another *Essex* search team was also doing quite well against Japanese aircraft. A blue-black colored Jake was spotted low under a cloud by the dive-bomber gunner and pointed out to Ensign J. D. Bare in his Hellcat. Bare climbed to 500 feet to get above the Jake and began to close. The floatplane turned away, then turned back toward him. Bare got off a short burst that peppered the tail of the enemy plane. Realizing his predicament, the Japanese pilot hauled his plane around sharply and began a wingover. The Hellcat pilot stayed on his tail and fired only twenty rounds when the Jake exploded and dove into the sea.

About thirty minutes later, the pilot of the Helldiver, Lieutenant (jg) Clifford Jordan, saw a Kate heading west-southwest at 1,500 feet. Jordan waggled his wings at Bare and they began climbing up to the Kate's altitude. As Bare was having difficulty picking up the torpedo plane, Jordan made the attack. The Japanese crew apparently spotted their attackers for they turned toward them and headed for the water. Jordan made one pass, firing a long burst with his 20-mm guns. Flames spouted around the Kate's cowling and cockpit. It staggered, fell off on a wing and slammed into the water. The Kate's rear gunner was firing even as his plane hit.

Bare and Jordan were not through yet. At 0935 the two ran into another Kate, this one heading northwest at high speed. The two pilots swung around and took up the chase. After five minutes at military power, Bare was able to get in range. The Kate was faster than he thought and Bare missed astern with his first burst. With only one gun firing, Bare was able to start the Kate smoking with a second burst. Jordan took over as Bare dropped back to recharge his guns. The Helldiver roared in with both its fixed and free guns firing, but no damage was seen. Guns recharged, Ensign Bare came back into the fray and set the Kate ablaze with a good solid burst. The Kate pulled up and its pilot jumped out, but he was too low. His chute was just starting to open when he hit the water.

The American commanders were now getting somewhat jumpy, not having found the Japanese Fleet. Spruance ordered Rear Admiral Harry W. Hill off Saipan to get more long-range patrol planes into the air and to extend their range to 700 miles. The Americans figured they were "going to have the hell slugged out of [them]" and were "making sure that [they] were ready to take it."[2]

On Tinian Admiral Kakuta called up fifteen Zekes and four bombers from Truk to reinforce the few planes still flyable on Guam. With this

support, the Japanese could count on only fifty planes available at
Orote field. It was a far cry from what had been planned, yet Kakuta
was still sending Ozawa and Toyoda glowing reports about the successes of the land-based planes and the masses of them still available.
Kakuta's reports would not be helpful to the Japanese cause.

Enemy air activity increased around the task force as the carriers
were launching planes for the morning searches and CAPs. At 0549 a
lookout on the destroyer *Stockham* suddenly saw an enemy plane diving
out of a low cloud directly at the ship. "It was a complete surprise and
the first Jap plane that most of [the] ship's personnel had ever seen."[3]
The ship a made a hard swing to starboard. The plane's bomb landed
in the *Stockham*'s wake and failed to explode. The destroyer *Yarnall*
then shot the plane down.

About the same time as the attack on the *Stockham*, TF 58 radars
picked up bogeys near Guam. Four *Monterey* Hellcats were vectored
over to take a look. They found two Judys, one of which was sent into
the sea in an inverted spin.

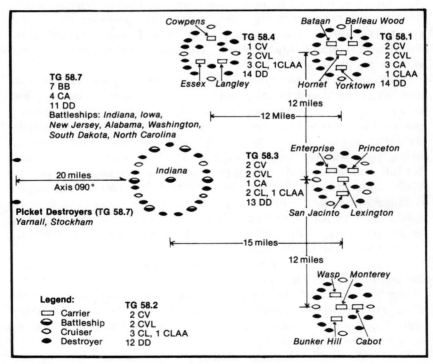

Disposition of TF 58 at start of action, 19 June 1944.

The sun began peering over the eastern horizon at 0542. With just a few clouds in the area, it looked like it was going to be another fine day. It also appeared that the rest of the day would probably be exciting. The situation was becoming "definitely tense."[4]

With Japanese air activity around Guam increasing, Admiral Spruance rightly became concerned with the possibility of enemy attacks from there. He suggested to Mitscher that if the dawn searches were again unsuccessful, a strike against Guam and Rota might not be a bad idea. Mitscher was not too keen on the suggestion; he told Spruance that he did not have enough bombs to neutralize both islands, and that all he could do was watch the situation with fighters until the Japanese tired of the game.[5]

Spruance's suggestion was sound; it would have been well for Mitscher's planes to plant a few bombs on the runways, to keep the Japanese planes out of action. Though the number of planes on Guam were not enough to be considered a decisive factor, the island was to remain a hot spot throughout the day. The carrier commanders, however, were more interested in their opposite numbers and attacks on Guam were considered purely secondary. Admiral Montgomery sent a message addressed to Mitscher, but really intended for Spruance, saying, "I consider that maximum effort of this force should be directed toward enemy force at sea; minor strikes should not be diverted to support the Guam–Saipan area. If necessary to continue divided effort, recommend detachment of sufficient force for this purpose."[6] No division of TF 58 took place, however.

About 0600 destroyers of TG 58.7 knocked down a Val which had probably come from Guam. Another snooper went down to the guns of the Cabot's CAP. At 0619 TF 58 changed course to the west-southwest. It was hoped that the task force could get close enough to the enemy to be able to launch strikes. But four launches between 0706 and 0830 slowed the advance considerably. At 0930 TF 58 was only about eighty-five miles northwest of Guam and by 1023 it was not much farther west than when it had started the morning.

At 0540 several ships had picked up signs of activity over Guam on their radars. At this time Guam was ninety miles distant. A division of Hellcats from the Belleau Wood was vectored over to take a look. When the four fighters arrived over Orote at 0600, they found the field a beehive of activity. Orote was certainly not out of action.

Lieutenant C.I. Oveland, leading the quartet, was studying the situation when puffs of flak blossomed a couple of thousand feet below. As he led his planes away from the flak, Oveland (like any good fighter pilot) kept his head on a swivel and saw four Zekes trying to bounce the

Belleau Wood planes from above and behind. Yelling "Skunks!" over the radio, Oveland at the same time racked his F6F around in a tight turn. The other three pilots followed suit and the Hellcats came roaring head-on into the Zekes. Oveland fired and his victim snapped over into an aileron roll that continued until the fighter smacked into the water. At the same time Lieutenant (jg) R. C. Tabler got another Zeke that went straight in.

The action was just beginning. More Zekes jumped into the fight before the Americans could reform. Oveland evaded one attacker by diving out of the action at over 400 knots indicated. When he climbed back to 15,000 feet and saw more enemy planes jumping into the fight, Oveland decided to call for help from TF 58. Meanwhile, a Zeke tried to pick off Tabler but was picked off himself when Tabler's wingman sawed off half the attacker's right wing with his six "fifties." Tabler took shots at two Zekes but had to break away when four other fighters started edging in from behind. One of the enemy pilots Tabler was chasing threw what looked like a coiled band of metal over the side of his aircraft. Though it flashed close to Tabler's plane, the coil caused no damage. The fourth member of the division, Ensign Carl J. Bennett, lost the other three pilots during the battle and had been shot up in the process. One shell came whistling through his canopy, showering plexiglass that cut the back of his head. Bennett still had time to smoke a "Tony" for a damaged claim. Oveland finally got his group reformed. Though enemy planes remained nearby, they had gotten wary and made no more attacks.

Following Oveland's call for help, Admiral Clark sent twenty-four more fighters to Orote and advised Mitscher of the situation. Meanwhile, TG 58.2 radars noted another group of enemy planes near Guam. *Cabot* fighters were sent to intercept and were about ten miles northwest of Guam when they heard Oveland's report. Within minutes they were mixing it with a group of Zekes. Six of the enemy fighters fell under the guns of the Hellcats, with Lieutenant C. W. Turner leading the way with three Zekes.

Following this action, things calmed down over Orote for a short while; the Japanese planes had either been shot down, left the area for safer climes or, more likely, landed and taxied to carefully camouflaged parking areas for refueling and rearming. On the latter point the *Yorktown* air group commander later commented, "Pilots were unanimous in the opinion that the field was practically deserted while photographs showed a considerable number of planes."[7] Mitscher was probably now wishing he had sent planes to Guam and Rota at dawn to keep the fields unserviceable; it was obvious TF 58 would be in for a hard time today.

The lull over Guam was short, as action heated up again shortly after 0800. Another group of enemy planes in the vicinity of Guam was detected at 0807. Fifteen *Hornet* and *Yorktown* fighters were already on the scene and quite a few more from other carriers were sent to help out. At 0824 the enemy was tallyhoed and an hour-long series of fights around Guam began. *Belleau Wood* fighters were again in the thick of the action.

Eight of the VF-24 F6Fs were jumped by about fifteen Zekes at 0845 near Orote. Big scorer for the Americans was Lieutenant (jg) R. H. Thelen, who downed three of the enemy fighters. Thelen bagged his first by following the Zeke through a slow roll and twisting dive. The Zeke blazed and went in. Two more Zekes came in on Thelen and his wingman, Lieutenant (jg) E. R. Hardin, from 12 o'clock low. Thelen flamed one but the other Zeke, though smoking, broke around to get on Hardin's tail. Hardin led the Zeke in front of Thelen, who proceeded to stop the attack by sending the enemy plane down in flames. As Thelen led his division home, one more enemy pilot attacked, but Lieutenant (jg) L. R. Graham got this one from dead astern. The Zeke exploded, throwing its pilot out. The Japanese flier was able to pull his ripcord and floated down under his chute, landing just offshore. The Fighting 24 pilots claimed seven Zekes destroyed and six others as probables or damaged.

The *Bunker Hill* had sent twelve Hellcats to Guam, arriving over Orote at 0920. Planes were taking off and landing at the field, and there were many enemy aircraft in the area. The VF-8 pilots began engaging Zekes and Hamps almost immediately. Combat extended from 16,000 feet down to sea level. Lieutenant (jg) H. T. Brownscombe's plane was hit several times in the first moments of the battle and he scurried for the safety of a cloud to assess the damage. When he discovered that, aside from a knocked-out gun, his damage was minor, he tried to rejoin his division. However, whenever he popped out of the cloud, he discovered a bunch of angry Japanese pilots buzzing around. Twice he came out of the cloud to find an enemy fighter in his sights. Both were blasted out of the sky. Finally, Brownscombe was able to edge away and rejoin his teammates.

The four planes led by Lieutenant (jg) L. P. Heinzen dropped down to strafe the airfield. One Zeke was hit as it was taking off and it ground-looped in a cloud of dust and smoke. Heinzen and his wingman, Lieutenant (jg) E. J. Dooner, dropped on a Topsy and a Zeke trying to land, and shot them both down. Dooner's Zeke smashed into a group of parked aircraft. The two fliers then mixed it up with another pair of Zekes. Henzen got one, but Dooner's oil line and gas tank were hit in the exchange of fire. The pair headed back for the *Bunker Hill*, but before they reached her, Dooner had to set his plane down in the water. Just as the Hellcat touched down, it exploded. Dooner did not get out. Though the loss of Dooner had taken some of the joy out of the victories, the thirteen planes the VF-8 pilots had shot down partially made up for his loss.

When some VF-16 fighters arrived over Orote most of the air battles had dwindled, but several Zekes could be seen taxiing on the field, along with a number of other planes parked around the field. The Americans immediately dropped down through moderate antiaircraft fire to strafe the runways. In repeated strafings, five or six of the parked aircraft were probably destroyed and several others damaged. None of the planes would burn, however, and it was thought they might have been degassed.

By the time the fighting around Orote was over the TF 58 pilots had claimed thirty Zekes and five other planes. This accounting is perhaps suspect (as were so many aerial claims by both sides during the war), but it is an indication of the intensity of the fighting. While some of the planes shot down had come from Guam, many were from Truk and Yap. Even though the enemy had lost heavily in the fights, Orote was far from being out of the battle. As the Americans rushed back to the task force in response to an urgent "Hey, Rube!", a great deal of activity could still be seen on the airfield.

While the battles were going on over Guam, Japanese scouting efforts had paid off. At 0730 a Jake crew returning from the limit of their search spotted their quarry. They picked out two carriers, four battleships, and ten other vessels—apparently Lee's and Harrill's groups. A contact report was immediately transmitted to Ozawa. This report was designated the "7I" contact. It placed the Americans 160 miles almost due west of Saipan. Four minutes later another Japanese plane verified the previous report, sighting fourteen ships including four battleships. The pilot of this Jake soon saw four more carriers. Ozawa now had the information he needed to launch his attack.

Ozawa figured he was about 380 miles from the Americans, with his van force about eighty miles closer to the enemy. He was just where he wanted to be. His planes could hit the Americans easily, but the enemy could not hit back. But Ozawa was now operating under a badly flawed premise. Buoyed, but tragically misled, by the overly optimistic reports by Kakuta of smashing victories by the land-based planes and of a safe haven on Guam, Ozawa was ready for the decisive battle.

At 0807, shortly after receiving the "7I" report, Ozawa brought his A and B Forces around to due south to keep his range at about 380 miles from the enemy. C Force turned southwest to close slightly with the rest of the Mobile Fleet.

Aboard the Japanese ships everyone was eager for action—and none more so than Admiral Obayashi. Impatient to get at the enemy and wondering why Ozawa had not yet given the order to launch, Obayashi began launching his own strike at 0825. Preceded by two Kates from the *Chitose* (sent out at 0800 as pathfinders), sixteen Zeke fighters, forty-five Zeke fighter-bombers, each carrying a 550-pound bomb, and eight torpedo-laden Jills left the *Chitose*, *Chiyoda*, and *Zuiho*. Not waiting for the planes of the other carriers to join them, the pilots of the 653rd Air Group flew east—to destruction.[8]

Ozawa had not been timid about launching his planes. He had merely been awaiting more contact reports. When no further updates reached him, he began launching the planes of his carrier division. At 0856 the first Zeke left the deck of the *Taiho*. The *Shokaku* and *Zuikaku* also began launching planes. This strike of the 601st Air Group, led by Lieutenant Commander Akira Tarui, was Ozawa's big punch—twenty-seven Jills carrying torpedoes; fifty-three Judys, each with a 1,000-pound bomb; and forty-eight Zekes providing escort. Two more Jills were sent ahead as pathfinders. Finally, the *Taiho* launched a Judy equipped with packages of "Window" to be used to create confusion on the American radar screens.[9]

The strike Ozawa launched from his own group of carriers was larger than that Admiral Nagumo had sent against Midway. But the year was 1944, not 1942; the Japanese were the underdogs now. In addition, Ozawa made a serious error in not coordinating his attacks. Instead of one massive blow that might have had a chance of breaking through the defending fighters, the two groups were spaced out far enough in time for the Americans to attack each in overwhelming numbers. (Given Obayashi's impetuosity, a coordinated attack may have been impossible, anyway.) The planes from Admiral Joshima's carriers, which could have proved useful, were also held back for the time being. Perhaps Ozawa was reserving Joshima's planes for cleanup work.

As the planes of the 653rd Air Group thundered east, the Hellcats of TF 58's CAP were already busy. At 0927 three *Essex* planes were vectored to investigate one of the bogeys that were beginning to speckle the task force's radars. This one turned out to be a returning Avenger with an inoperative IFF. Four minutes later an unfriendly contact was picked up by the *Hornet* some 40 miles to the north. A *Bataan* division sighted the bogey, a Zeke, shortly and dropped it in the water. Several other bogeys escaped the CAP a short time later.

It was 0930 when Admiral Mitscher finally received the 0115 PBM sighting. His comments upon receipt of the message are unrecorded, but they must have come right from the heart.

While the CAP was swatting down a few enemy planes, one snooper was flitting about its job unmolested. Plane No. 15, which had been launched from CarDiv 1 about 0530, was on the inbound leg of its search pattern when it ran across a group of American ships at 0945. The pilot immediately reported sighting three carriers and a number of other vessels at 12 22'N, 143 43'E. This report was called the "15 Ri" contact by the Japanese. Unfortunately, the pilot of this search plane forgot to correct for compass deviation, and the reported point was miles south of TF 58's actual position.

Fifteen minutes later another searcher had better luck in plotting the position of TF 58 units when he observed several vessels, including carriers, at 15 33'N, 143 15'E. This position was about 50 miles north of the "7I" point and was designated the "3 Ri" contact. As these searchers sent back their reports and Ozawa readied more strikes, the first two waves of attackers swept in toward TF 58.[10]

At 0957 the *Alabama* picked up the planes of Obayashi's 653rd Air Group at a distance of 140 miles. The *Iowa*, *Cabot*, and *Enterprise* quickly verified the contact. A few minutes later the task force flagship *Lexington* also had contact. The bogeys were bearing 260 degrees from the task force and were in two groups at 121 and 124 miles. Their altitude was estimated as 20,000 feet.

All ships not already at General Quarters quickly set the condition. Lookouts strained their eyes staring through binoculars, trying to pick out the speck of an enemy aircraft before it got too close. All 5-inch mounts that could rotated to face west. The 40-mm guns whined as their barrels weaved about in anticipation of the battle.

At 1005 Mitscher ordered the task groups, "Give your VF over Guam, 'Hey Rube!'"[11] Lieutenant Joe Eggert, TF 58's fighter director, sent out the old circus cry for help and then settled down for a busy few hours. Eggert, along with the five task group fighter directors (TG 58.1—Lieutenant C. D. Ridgeway; TG 58.2—Lieutenant R. F. Myers; TG 58.3—Lieutenant J. H. Trousdale; TG 58.4—Lieutenant Commander F. L. Winston; TG 58.7—Lieutenant E. F. Kendall) had a big responsibility during the battle. It was their job to see that enough

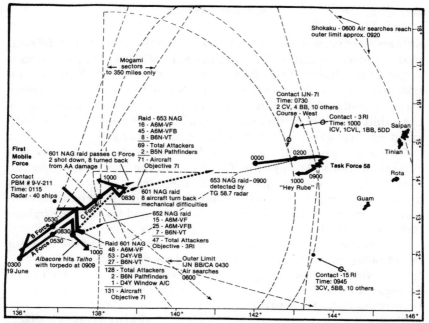

Shokaku - 0600 Air searches reach
outer limit approx. 0920

Mogami
sectors
to 350 miles only

Contact IJN- 7I
Time: 0730
2 CV, 4 BB, 10 others
Course - West

Contact - 3 RI
Time: 1000
ICV, 1CVL, 1BB, 5DD

Saipan

Raid - 653 NAG
16 - A6M-VF
45 - A6M-VFB
 8 - B6N-VT
69 - Total Attackers
 2 - B5N Pathfinders
71 - Aircraft
Objective 7I

Tinian

**First
Mobile
Force**

601 NAG raid passes C Force
2 shot down, 8 turned back
from AA damage

Contact
PBM # 9-V-211
Time: 0115
Radar - 40 ships

1000

0830

653 NAG raid - 0900
detected by
TG 58.7 radar

0000

0200

0900

Task Force 58

Rota

1000
"Hey Rube"

601 NAG raid
8 aircraft turn back
mechanical difficulties

Guam

C Force

652 NAG raid
15 - A6M-VF
25 - A6M-VFB
 7 - B6N-VT
47 - Total Attackers
Objective - 3RI

B Force

0530

0830

A Force

0530

1000

Albacore hits *Taiho*
with torpedo at 0909

Raid 601 NAG
48 - A6M-VF
53 - D4Y-VB
27 - B6N-VT
128 - Total Attackers
 2 - B6N Pathfinders
 1 - D4Y Window A/C
131 - Aircraft
Objective 7I

Outer Limit
IJN BB/CA 0430
Air searches
0600

Contact - 15 RI
Time: 0945
3CV, 5BB, 10 others

0300
19 June

Movements of opposing forces 0000-1130, 19 June.

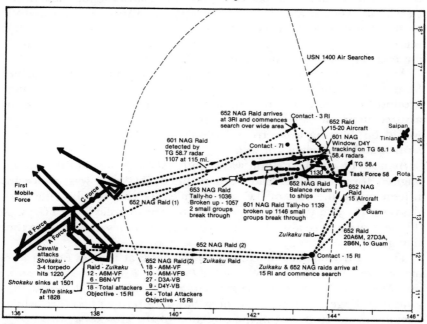

USN 1400 Air Searches

652 NAG Raid arrives
at 3RI and commences
search over wide area

Contact - 3 RI

652 Raid
15-20 Aircraft

Saipan

Contact - 7I

601 NAG
Window D4Y
tracking on TG 58.1 &
58.4 radars

Tinian

601 NAG Raid
detected by
TG 58.7 radar
1107 at 115 mi.

TG 58.4

1130

Task Force 58

Rota

**First
Mobile
Force**

C Force

653 NAG Raid
Tally-ho - 1036
Broken up - 1057
2 small groups
break through

652 NAG Raid (1)

601 NAG Tally-ho 1139
broken up 1146 small
groups break through

652 NAG Raid
Balance return
to ships

652 NAG
Raid
15 Aircraft

Guam

B Force

A Force

Zuikaku raid

Cavalla
attacks
Shokaku -
3-4 torpedo
hits 1220

Shokaku sinks at 1501

652 NAG Raid (2)

652 NAG Raid (2)
18 - A6M-VF
10 - A6M-VFB
27 - D3A-VB
 9 - D4Y-VB
64 - Total Attackers
Objective - 15 RI

Zuikaku Raid

652 Raid
20A6M, 27D3A,
2B6N, to Guam

Contact - 15 RI

Zuikaku & 652 NAG raids arrive at
15 RI and commence search

Raid - *Zuikaku*
12 - A6M-VF
 6 - B6N-VT
18 - Total attackers
Objective - 15 RI

Taiho sinks
at 1828

Movements of opposing forces 0900-2400, 19 June.

fighters were vectored to the right spot at the right time to handle each raid, while seeing that sufficient planes were held back for later attacks. While Eggert handled fighter direction for the entire task force, each task-group controller handled the planes of his group. Any fighter director could allot aircraft to the director on an individual ship or even shift planes between task groups. It was an enormously complicated job that was handled superbly by all concerned.

One area that could have caused problems during the day was communications. At this time TF 58 was in the process of changing over to newer radio equipment, and there were only two channels available that were common to all ships. Although these channels were badly overworked throughout the day, they held up, and the fighter directors were able to keep in touch with their planes.

Besides the excellent work of the fighter directors and the efficient use of radar, this day the Americans had an ace in the hole. Lieutenant (jg) Charles A. Sims, a Japanese language expert, was aboard the *Lexington* and was able to monitor the enemy fliers' radio chatter, thereby learning their plans in advance.

Most of the carriers were not in an ideal position to receive an attack, for their decks had been spotted for a strike against the Japanese fleet. Decks had to be cleared for use by the fighters, so Mitscher launched all his dive bombers and torpedo planes to orbit to the east until the battle was over. Any planes on the hangar decks that could not be launched immediately were dearmed and defueled.

At 1010 TF 58 was ordered to prepare to launch all available fighters. Nine minutes later came the "execute." Task Force 58 swung around to the east and into the wind. Mitscher ordered his ships to assume their air defense formation.[12] By heading eastward TF 58 would be drawing away from Ozawa's ships, but would be able to launch and land planes at will.

By now TF 58's formation was slightly askew. Instead of the nicely aligned formation that had been planned, TG 58.1 was twelve to fifteen miles due east of TG 58.3, while TG 58.4 was bearing 340 degrees, TG 58.2 160 degrees and TG 58.7 260 degrees from TG 58.3. These groups were also about twelve to fifteen miles distant from the flag group.

The first fighters began leaping off the decks at 1023 as Eggert was already vectoring the CAP's from the *Princeton*, *Essex*, *Hornet*, *Cowpens*, and *Monterey*. Not wanting to get caught with his Hellcats below the attackers, Eggert sent most of them clawing up to 24,000 feet, while keeping some down low in the direction of the attackers.

VF-1 Hellcats on the Yorktown *prepare to launch on 19 June 1944. The* Hornet *is in the background.*

Within fifteen minutes, about 140 Hellcats had been launched, while 82 others already airborne streaked west. The launch was swift, but now the Americans were helped by the Japanese. When the enemy planes (now designated as Raid I) closed to 72 miles they began to orbit. Their lack of training had begun to tell, and it would eventually prove immensely costly to them. Instead of diving in and closing with the enemy—knowing their targets and tactics like veterans would—they were being told by their group commander just what they were supposed to do. This briefing took almost fifteen minutes and provided the Hellcats with the time to gain valuable altitude and distance toward the enemy. It also provided the task force with that extra time to launch the last of the fighters. As the last F6Fs took off, the planes that had been over Guam began returning for refueling and rearming. Lieutenant (jg) Sims had now found the attacker's radio frequency and was relaying the gist of the Japanese leader's briefing to Eggert.

Their briefing over, the enemy fliers broke out of their orbit to start their run-in toward their targets. They were met by a wall of Hellcats ranging from 17,000 to 24,000 feet. More fighters were waiting lower, ready to pounce on any enemy plane that might try to sneak through at low altitude.

Fifty-five miles from the task force, Commander Charles W. Brewer, skipper of the *Essex*'s Fighting 15, spotted the enemy. It was 1025. Brewer estimated the raid as twenty-four "Rats" (bombers), sixteen "Hawks" (fighters) and no "Fish" (torpedo planes). Brewer had missed some of the planes. Eight torpedo planes had been sent, along with sixteen fighters and forty-five fighter-bombers. The enemy planes were at 18,000 feet. Sixteen of the planes (identified as Judys; actually Zeke fighter-bombers) were bunched together. Two four-plane divisions of Zeke fighters were at the same altitude; one division on each flank. Bringing up the rear, between 1,000 and 2,000 feet higher, were sixteen more Zekes. These were in "no apparent pattern of sections or divisions." Behind the onrushing enemy planes streamed thick contrails. (The atmospheric conditions causing the contrails would give the ships' crews a view of the battle few had seen before.)[13]

Brewer's planes were in a perfect position for a "bounce." Brewer rolled over from 24,000 feet and led his four planes in for an overhead pass. Lieutenant (jg) J. R. Carr took his four fighters in from the other side and the enemy formation was thus bracketed. The eight *Essex* fighters slashed into the enemy and the formation disintegrated.

Brewer picked out the formation leader as his first target. When he closed to 800 feet he opened fire and the Zeke blew up. Passing through the debris of the plane, he pulled up shooting at another Zeke. Half a wing gone, the enemy plane plunged flaming into the sea. Brewer picked off another fighter with a no-deflection shot from about 400 feet and the plane spun into the water in flames. Clearing his tail, Brewer saw a fourth Zeke diving on him. Racking his big Hellcat around, Brewer was quickly embroiled in a hot fight with the Zeke.

Commander Brewer was able to get on the Zeke's tail and began snapping short bursts at the violently maneuvering fighter. The Zeke pilot "half-rolled, then after staying on his back briefly pulled through sharply, followed by barrel rolls and wingovers."[14] The maneuvers did not save him. His plane caught fire and spiraled into the ocean. After this kill, Brewer found the raid had been broken up. He had had an excellent interception—four for four.

Brewer's wingman, Ensign Richard E. Fowler, Jr., also had a good day. On the first pass Fowler sent a Zeke smoking into the water. Diving through to 6,000 feet, Fowler jumped a couple of circling Zekes but overshot and found them, plus one more, glued to his tail. Another Hellcat distracted the enemy, and Fowler pulled around after them. He tried a 60-degree deflection shot at one and was amazed to see the plane suddenly snap roll in the opposite direction. Then he noticed that ten feet of the Zeke's wing was missing. The enemy pilot bailed out, but his parachute did not open.

Fowler turned toward another Zeke off his right side. When he opened fire the Zeke began to "skid violently from left to right, and then started to whip even more violently sideways."[15] The Zeke's vertical stabilizer had been sawed off. Fowler kept pumping shells into the doomed plane until it burst into flames. He then joined two more Hellcats chasing a Zeke, but when the enemy plane reached a cloud the other pilots turned back. Fowler kept going and caught the Zeke on the other side of the cloud. Though firing at an extreme range of 1,500 feet and with only one gun working, he sent the fighter into the ocean. Fowler wound up this interception by damaging another Japanese plane with his one gun.

On the other side of the Japanese formation, Lieutenant (jg) Carr was doing quite well also. His first victim was a Zeke that blew up immediately. Carr pulled up in a wingover and found another fighter a "sitting duck."[16] His .50-caliber slugs torched the fighter and it spiraled in. Another Zeke then jumped him and he pushed his Hellcat over. The dive left both the enemy and his wingman behind, and Carr now climbed back into the battle alone. As he climbed he picked off another fighter-bomber with a short burst to the engine and wing root. The plane exploded. Carr's fourth and fifth victories were a pair of fighter-bombers he picked out 2,000 feet above him and paralleling his course. He pulled up on the right-hand Zeke and set its port wing on fire. Something left this plane which may have been the pilot, but Carr was too busy skidding onto the tail of the other plane to take much notice. Carr set this plane afire just aft of the engine and it started down. He split-essed to catch it, but it blew up before he could fire again. As he pulled out, he saw the first Zeke splash. No more enemy planes were visible as he climbed back up, so he headed for the *Essex*. On the way he tried to count the oil slicks and splashes in the water but stopped after seventeen. This first onslaught by the *Essex* pilots had been devastating.

Twenty enemy planes were claimed and the slaughter was only beginning.

Shortly after Commander Brewer led VF-15 into the Japanese planes, more Hellcats waded into the fight. From the *Cowpens* came eight Fighting 25 F6Fs; a number of fighters from the *Hornet, Princeton, Cabot,* and *Monterey* followed, plus a few eager beavers from other flattops. The *Cabot* and *Monterey* pilots piled into the battle with vigor and claimed twenty-six more Japanese planes between themselves. The VF-31 pilots were especially effective, with five of the "Flying Meataxers" cleaving fifteen planes from the enemy formations. Lieutenant J. S. Stewart splashed three Zekes, as did Lieutenants (jg) F. R. Hayde and A. R. Hawkins, but the top scorer for the squadron was Lieutenant (jg) J. L. Wirth, with four planes.

As the *Monterey* fliers closed the attackers, a number of aircraft could be seen falling in flames. The VF-28 pilots added to the number in the next few minutes. Lieutenant D. C. Clements hit one Zeke with a high-speed pass from astern and the plane went down burning. As Clements rolled out, he saw two Zekes at his nine o'clock position. He tried a 90-degree deflection shot at one but missed. The Zeke began a climbing slow roll. Clements followed him through, snapping short bursts throughout the roll. As the Zeke dished out, it burst into flames. Clements next took out after another fighter which led him through some violent maneuvers followed by a 7,000-foot dive. He had been getting hits in the cockpit and engine area, but the Zeke would not burn. Finally, he rolled over the Zeke and saw the pilot slumped over the stick. The plane then slammed into the water. Clements next met another Zeke in a head-on pass, but with only one gun working, could do little damage. Finding his adversary a little too tenacious, he called for help and his wingman blew the Zeke off his tail.

Fighting 28's high scorer was Lieutenant O. C. Bailey with four fighters. Bailey got his first Zeke with a full deflection shot from astern, and the plane left a corkscrew trail of smoke as it spun into the water. While attacking another fighter, Bailey overshot his intended target, but the enemy pilot turned toward Bailey's wingman, Ensign A. C. Persson, who got him with a 45-degree attack from the rear. Another Zeke was seen low to starboard and the two Americans dove to the attack. The Zeke pilot tried to outscissor him, but Bailey got on the fighter's tail and flamed it. The pilot bailed out.

By now no more enemy planes were evident and Bailey and Persson turned back toward the task force. As they neared TG 58.7, they were fired on by "friendly" ships and Persson's F6F was hit. His left wing was badly damaged and his radio knocked out. Bailey shepherded his wingman back to the *Monterey* where Persson made a no-flap landing. Though the landing was good, the plane had been so damaged by the antiaircraft fire that it was unceremoniously stripped of all usable items and shoved overboard.

After seeing Persson safely home, Bailey headed back to where the action was. Flying at 20,000 feet, he saw a pair of Zekes about 4,000 feet below him. He rolled over and came in from astern. Bailey began firing at 400 yards at the trailing Zeke and continued until about 250 yards away. At this point the fighter burst into flames, flopped over on its back and went straight in. Bailey recovered underneath the other Zeke, pulled up and raked the plane with a burst. The Zeke dived away but after a short chase, Bailey nailed his fourth plane.

Commander William A. Dean, of the *Hornet*'s VF-2, saw twenty to twenty-five parachutes and "several dye markers in the water" during the course of the battle. The eight *Hornet* pilots claimed twelve enemy aircraft. Lieutenant (jg) Daniel A. Carmichael, Jr. led the Fighting 2 pilots with two Jills and a Zeke. A significant observation was made by Lieutenant (jg) John T. Wolf during a pass on a Zeke. With only one gun working and low on ammunition, Wolf scared one of the enemy pilots into dropping his belly tank and "what appeared to be a bomb." During his debriefing Wolf told his intelligence officer about the incident and the I.O., correctly assessing the report, underscored Wolf's remarks when passing the word along. For the next few hours the American fliers would be considering Zekes as possible threats to the ships, not just in fighter combat.[17]

The eight *Cowpens* pilots came into the attack at 20,000 feet and only about 20 miles from the task force. The Americans knocked down five Jills and four Zekes, but it cost them. Lieutenant (jg) Frederick R. Stieglitz was heard over the radio to say "scratch one fish" and was last seen in the air giving hand signals to indicate that he shot down two planes, but he never returned to the "Mighty Moo" to confirm his score. Ensign George A. Massenburg was plagued by a "rough" engine and was pursued for a time by a Zeke, but a fellow pilot chased the enemy plane away. However, Massenburg's engine finally seized and he had to set down in the water. Though he was seen to get into his life raft, he was not recovered.

In spite of the vicious onslaughts by the defending fighters, about forty of the Japanese planes broke through. Their formation had been cut up, however, and the survivors pressed on in small gaggles. Once again they were met by Hellcats, and once again smoke trails smudged the sky. Six pilots of the *San Jacinto*'s VF-51 found ten of the enemy fighting it out with about thirty U.S. planes several miles west of the task force. They shouldered their way into the brawl and claimed six enemy aircraft.

By this time the remaining Japanese planes were drawing close to the battleships of TG 58.7. Aboard the *Stockham* the sailors watched the enemy planes dropping out of the sky "like plums."[18] A few of the enemy fliers were also watching the *Stockham*, and they attacked the ship and the other "tin cans" of DesDiv 106. (The destroyers probably looked like easier targets than the bristling battlewagons.) These attacks, however, were no more successful than most for the day, and the destroyers escaped unscathed.

In a last-gasp effort, several planes broke through to attack the battleships. At 1048 the ships of TG 58.7 began firing. Gunfire from the *Indiana* tore the wing off a plane attacking her, and it crashed just 200 yards ahead of the battleship. Another plane went after the *South Dakota* and scored the only bomb hit of the day on a U.S. ship at 1049. Twenty-seven men were killed and twenty-four wounded, but the explosion didn't slow the tough battleship even one knot. The *South Dakota* gunners claimed their attacker, but their fellow gunners on the *Alabama* (steaming close by) said the plane got away.

Two more Japanese planes glided in on the *Minneapolis* from astern. One of them dropped a 500-pound bomb that landed only a few feet off the ship's starboard side. Several gas, oil, and water lines were ruptured and a small fire started. Three seamen were injured. One of the planes was shot down and the other retired from the area in obvious difficulty. Another dive bomber attacked the *Wichita* but only got two near-misses before it was shot down. Forty-millimeter fire from the *Indiana* punctured a smoke generator on the *San Francisco*, causing the ship to lay down a large trail of smoke. It was some time before her crew was able to jettison the generator.

By 1057 the hard-working fighter director Eggert could report that the radar screens were clear. Raid I was over. Only eight fighters, thirteen fighter-bombers, and six Jills were able to return to their carriers. Though antiaircraft fire had knocked down some of the attackers, it had been the fighters that had done most of the damage. At one point during the action Admiral Reeves had even signaled his ships, "Try to avoid shooting down our own planes. They are our best protection."[19]

The American losses, though light in comparison to those suffered by the Japanese, were nevertheless tragic to the men of TF 58. Besides the twenty-seven men killed on the *South Dakota*, four pilots were listed as missing in action, including the *Princeton*'s air group skipper, Lieu-

Another Japanese plane goes down under the fire of the TF 58 ships.

tenant Commander Ernest W. Wood. A number of Hellcats had been shot up and several had to be pushed over the side.

During the respite, TF 58 was landing, servicing, and rearming as many fighters as it could. Most of the bombers and torpedo planes were still orbiting to the east, waiting for some word on what to do. Admiral Reeves had an idea. At 1103 he asked Mitscher, "Desire issue following instructions my airborne deckloads before fuel depletion: *Enterprise* VT search ten-degree sectors to 250 miles median line 260 true. Attack groups follow along median line thirty miles behind. Search planes retire on contact, concentrate and attack in coordination other planes.[20]

"Approved, approved. Wish we could go with you," Mitscher replied.[21] But Reeves's plan was stillborn, as it proved impossible to break through the confusion on the radio channels to issue the necessary orders. The bombers continued their merry-go-rounds to the east.

A Hellcat lands on the Lexington *to rearm during the 19 June 1944 air battle.*
(National Archives)

Though he was willing to release some of his planes to go after the enemy, Mitscher was expecting more attacks; and he would not be disappointed. Just ten minutes after reporting his screens clear, Eggert had picked up another bogey on the *Lexington*'s radar at the incredible distance of 160 miles, bearing 250 degrees from the ship. This was Ozawa's big punch from the *Shokaku, Zuikaku,* and *Taiho.*

This raid by the 601st Air Group was cursed by bad luck from the beginning. As the *Taiho* was launching her planes, Commander James W. Blanchard was at the periscope of the *Albacore* watching the activity. Blanchard had been patrolling the southwest corner of the new square Admiral Lockwood had set up when Ozawa's own A Force stumbled across the sub's path.

Blanchard submerged and watched the targets steam past. The *Albacore*'s position was about 12 20'N, 137 00'E. A large carrier, a cruiser and several other ships could be seen seven miles away, 70 degrees off the port bow. Blanchard brought his crew to battle stations.

The submarine built up speed and closed the enemy. As Blanchard watched a second carrier was seen. Although he did not know it, the large eight-rayed flag he could see flying from this carrier was Ozawa's own flag. Unlucky *Taiho*. She was in a better position for an attack than the flattop Blanchard had originally seen.

Blanchard had a beautiful setup for a right-angle shot at the *Taiho*. The big carrier was 9,000 yards away and the torpedo run would be 2,300 yards. Just then a destroyer got in the way, and Blanchard decided to close in for a torpedo run of under 2,000 yards. He took another quick look. It appeared to be a perfect setup for a spread of six "fish." Then his luck changed. After all the information was fed into the *Albacore's* torpedo data computer, the TDC refused to come up with a solution. Wrong information had been fed into it and it would not supply an answer.

Blanchard was beside himself. The *Taiho* was making 27 knots and the range would soon start to open rapidly. He decided to shoot a spread of six torpedoes by eye and hope for the best. At 0909:32 the torpedoes were sent on their way. A minute later, Blanchard noted three pugnacious-looking destroyers headed his way, so he went deep.[22]

Warrant Officer Sakio Komatsu had just lifted his Jill off the *Taiho's* armored deck when saw one of the *Albacore's* torpedoes bubbling toward the ship. Without hesitation he wheeled his plane around and dove it into the torpedo. A geyser of water, smoke, and debris marked his passing. It was a brave, but ultimately futile effort. Two minutes after it had been fired another torpedo slammed into the *Taiho's* hull.[23]

This torpedo, the only one to hit, struck the *Taiho's* starboard side near the forward gasoline tanks. The ship's forward elevator jammed and gasoline and oil lines ruptured. But the carrier's speed slackened only one knot and no fires broke out. To the ship's damage-control officer the damage was only minor and repairs would quickly be accomplished. The *Taiho* raced on. The *Albacore* underwent a rather unenthusiastic depth-charging, and afterwards Blanchard would only claim possible damage to the carrier. It would be months before the truth would be learned.

Unaware of what was going on below, Lieutenant Commander Tarui led his planes toward TF 58. Eight soon dropped out because of various mechanical problems and returned to their carriers. Tarui then made the mistake of leading his planes over C Force. The ships' gunners were trigger-happy and, on the bizarre reasoning that enemy planes would appear at high altitude and from the west—not the east—they opened fire. Two planes were shot down and eight others damaged badly enough to have to turn back.[24] It must have been a disconcerting experience for the young Japanese crews to undergo this completely surprising encounter before getting anywhere near the enemy.

Lieutenant Commander Tarui regrouped his force and they plunged ahead. Shortly after 1100 they were close to TF 58. Tarui now made the same error his predecessor had made on Raid I—he began to brief his inexperienced crews on their part in the attack. Naturally this took time, and the Japanese planes circled and crossed over each other as the briefing went on. And Lieutenant (jg) Sims was again near the radio listening to Tarui's instructions and passing them on to Eggert. Once more a pause by the enemy had enabled the Americans to climb above the attackers and to fly far enough west so that the enemy would be under constant air attack before getting anywhere near the U.S. ships.

Ten *Essex* Hellcats, led by the air group skipper, Commander David McCampbell, were waiting at 25,000 feet when they received instructions to intercept the enemy. The pilots poured the coal to their fighters and took out after the bogeys. At 1139 McCampbell spotted Raid II. It appeared there were about fifty Zekes and Judys. (Actually there were almost twice as many.) The Japanese planes, now about 45 miles from the task force, looked like they were in one big formation of three-plane sections and nine-plane divisions and were stacked about 1,500 feet deep. At the time of the sighting, the Hellcats had almost a 5,000-foot altitude advantage.

Leaving four planes as high cover, McCampbell took the rest down for a fast pass from the side. McCampbell's first target was a Judy on the left side of the formation about halfway back. He had intended to cut his victim out of the pack, dive below him and continue under the enemy formation to the other side. However, McCampbell's plans changed abruptly when his 'fifties blew the Judy up in his face. McCampbell pulled up and charged across the formation "feeling as though every rear gunner had his fire directed at (him)."[25]

On the other side he picked off another Judy which burned and fell out of control. Working toward the front of the formation, McCampbell claimed a probable on a Judy that fell away smoking. He was now in position to attack the formation leader and his two wingmen. As he jockeyed for position on the leader, McCampbell noticed that what he had thought to be one large formation was actually two; one group was 600 feet lower and about 1,000 yards off to the side. His first pass on the leading plane seemed to have no effect. Breaking down and to the left, McCampbell swung around for another pass. This time he attacked the leader's left wingman from 7 o'clock above. The Judy exploded in a ball of fire.

McCampbell again broke down and to the left which placed him to the left and below the leading Judy. He pumped a continuous stream of bullets into the Judy until it "burned furiously and spiralled downward out of control."[26] By this time the guns of his fighter were suffering stoppages and McCampbell pulled away to recharge them. He then returned to the battle. The Japanese formation had been hacked to pieces, but the remaining enemy pilots doggedly pressed ahead. Another Judy, apparently the leader of the lower formation, came into view. McCampbell immediately began a high-side run on him. Only the Hellcat's starboard guns fired and McCampbell was thrown into a wild skid. The Judy took advantage of this unplanned maneuver and began a fast dive. McCampbell took up the chase, firing short bursts with his operative guns. Finally the impact of the 'fifties took effect. The Judy pulled up and over and dove into the sea.

The fighting during the "Turkey Shoot" was not all one-sided. Here an Essex *flier is helped from his Hellcat after being wounded during the battle. (U.S. Navy)*

McCampbell was now out of action and returned to the *Essex*. Destined to become the Navy's leading ace of the war with thirty-four aerial victories and a number of ground kills, he had shot down five Judys and claimed one probable in this one action. During the fight he noted that the enemy fliers took very little evasive action when they were attacked, except for some violent fishtailing which only slowed their planes down.

The rest of the VF-15 pilots claimed fifteen and one-half Zekes and Judys. (One pilot shared a Zeke with a pilot from another squadron.) While most of the Japanese planes were dispatched rather easily, some of the *Essex* fliers found the enemy could fight back. Ensign G.H. Rader did not return from the battle and Ensign J.W. Power, Jr., was wounded by a Zeke pilot whose plane he destroyed. Ensign C.W. Plant had knocked down four Zekes, but his next encounter was not too pleasant. While chasing a Zeke, Plant had another fighter lock onto his tail. Unable to shake the Zeke, he could hear the 20-mm and 7.7-mm shells "splattering off the armor plate."[27] Another F6F came by, finally, and shot the Zeke off his tail. When Plant got back to the *Essex*, 150 bullet holes (including one in each prop blade) were counted in his fighter. Another Fighting 15 pilot reported a "not unpleasant" experience when the container for his plane's water injection fluid broke, filling the cockpit with alcohol fumes.[28]

For six minutes VF-15 had the Japanese all to themselves. Then the hapless enemy fliers were pounded from all sides by newly arriving Hellcats. Fighters from most of the carriers piled into the confusing melee. One of the pilots just entering the battle was Lieutenant (jg) Alexander Vraciu, who already had thirteen victory flags painted on his Hellcat. Six more would be added at the end of the day.

Vraciu's first kill was a Judy that he exploded from only about 200 feet away. Two more Judys were then seen. Vraciu eased his fighter in behind the two planes and began to fire. His fire was returned by the rear gunner of the right-hand Judy. But the power of the six machine guns in the Hellcat's wings proved too much. The dive bomber belched a puff of smoke, immediately followed by a continuous stream of black smoke. The plane began its final dive. The rear gunner continued firing until his plane sliced into the water.

Vraciu was quickly onto the other Judy. Several short bursts produced the desired results. Fire and smoke suddenly appeared and the Judy fell out of control. Vraciu had shot down three enemy planes in almost as many minutes. The mass of planes made him apprehensive, however; it seemed there were too many attackers for the defending fighters to handle. A fourth Judy pulled slightly out of formation and

Vraciu plunged back into the fight. From dead astern he fired a long burst. The dive bomber burst into flames and fell awkwardly out of the sky.

He gave a quick glance to the tumbling Judy, but was more interested in a trio of dive bombers rapidly approaching their pushover points. With the engine of his F6F straining, Vraciu crept up on the trailing Judy. Flak bursts were beginning to blacken the sky, but Vraciu kept after his quarry. Finally he was within range and squeezed the trigger. The stream of shells literally disintegrated his target.

Vraciu did not waste time admiring his handiwork. The other Judys were now in their dives. He screamed down after the leading plane. Black puffs speckled the sky around him as he closed his target. When he got close enough he began to fire. For a few seconds nothing seemed to be happening and then—a bright flash! The Judy vanished, apparently undone by the explosion of its bomb.

Vraciu looked around. The enemy formation was gone; wiped out by the constantly attacking Hellcats and the deadly flak. He headed back to the *Lexington*, detouring around some "friendly" flak on the way, and was soon aboard his carrier. As he taxied up the deck, he looked up at the bridge. Admiral Mitscher was looking down at him. Grinning, Vraciu held up six fingers. As he climbed out of his cockpit after parking, Vraciu was greeted by a flock of well-wishers, including Mitscher. After the congratulations were over, Mitscher asked a pho-

Lieutenant (jg) Alex Vraciu happily signals his score for the interception.

tographer to take a picture of Vraciu and himself, "not for publication, to keep for myself."[29]

The VF-16 pilots had good shooting, claiming four Jills, nine Judys, two Kates, and seven Zekes without loss. Before the day was over they claimed twenty-two more planes downed, with only one plane lost in an operational ditching.

As the battle swirled overhead, Admiral Reeves recommended to Mitscher that TF 58 head west "turning into the wind only as necessary to land aircraft or takeoff." Mitscher approved this suggestion, and at 1134 told his task group commanders to "make as little to the easterly as practicable but land planes at discretion."[30]

The *Essex* and *Lexington* fliers were not the only ones to be scoring against the enemy planes. Lieutenant Commander R.W. Hoel led twelve *Bunker Hill* fighters into the action around 1130. Unfortunately, most of the VF-8 fighters were unable to intercept the attack. However, Hoel was able to lead his division into a group of twelve Zekes that had so far escaped attack. He shot down one fighter immediately and almost got another.

Hoel next made an attack on a Judy which spiraled into the water. A Zeke tried to break up his attack, peppering Hoel's Hellcat with 20-mm and 7.7-mm shells that caused his own guns to go into automatic fire and burn themselves out. Though his wingman finally chased the Zeke away, Hoel's plane was in bad shape. Hoel tried to make it back to the *Bunker Hill*, but at 4,000 feet the stick slammed all the way forward and his Hellcat went into an inverted spin. Hoel bailed out, receiving two fractured ribs in the process, and was shortly picked up by a destroyer.

The VF-8 pilots had not had a good interception, claiming only four Zekes and a Judy, but that was still five less planes to worry about later. The pilots told their debriefing officers, "No new information. Zekes continue to burn."[31]

Pilots of the *Bataan*'s VF-50 had better luck in their interception, claiming five Zekes, four Judys, and a Jill plus two others as probables. Lieutenant (jg) P.C. Thomas, Jr., chased a Zeke for some time before dunking him. The enemy pilot was very good, staying below 1,000 feet and timing his evasive maneuvers expertly. "It was like catching a flea on a hot griddle."[32] Unfortunately for the enemy pilot, he was boxed in by five F6Fs and was committed to a reasonably straight course. Finally the Zeke pilot stayed in one place too long and Thomas's shells exploded his plane.

As he turned for home, Thomas saw another Zeke putting on an "amazing exhibition" of aerobatics for four other Hellcats. "At about 300 feet he started slow rolling and completed some fifteen in succession. He would dive to about 50 feet and then jink up and down between there and a matter of five to ten feet above the waves. Probably he hoped to entice some F6 into following his maneuver and mushing into the water. Several times he pulled into a half loop, flew on his back for a few seconds fishtailing, and then pulled up in an outside loop. Finally he completed a full loop under 500 feet and was caught by a burst that flamed him as he started to level out."[33]

Ensign E. R. Tarleton had already downed a Judy when he spotted a Jill being stalked by another Hellcat. The American was out of range, but the Jill's rear gunner kept firing a few short bursts at him. With the attention of the enemy crew on the other F6F, Tarleton was able to sneak in from 8 o'clock and explode the plane. As he pulled up Tarleton saw the other Hellcat, its prop windmilling, crash into the water. The pilot never got out of his sinking plane.

Planes from the two light carriers in TG 58.2, the *Monterey* and *Cabot*, were also active against the Japanese attackers in Raid II. In a series of battles ranging from 23,000 feet down to below 10,000 feet the *Monterey* pilots claimed six Jills and a Zeke, and the *Cabot* fliers scored with four Zekes and a Judy plus two Zekes damaged. One of the Fighting 28 Hellcats was hit by "friendly" flak, but the pilot nursed his plane back to the *Monterey*, where it was stripped then pushed overboard.

Yorktown planes also gave the Japanese troubles. Before the day was over, the VF-1 fliers would claim thirty-four fighters and three bombers downed and five other planes as probables. Four more enemy aircraft were destroyed on the ground at Guam. Commander "Smoke" Strean led ten Hellcats into the battle at 24,000 feet. About 60 miles from the *Yorktown* the fliers encountered about fifty planes 4,000 feet lower, with an equal number of enemy planes at about 14,000 feet. As the lower group was already being set upon, Strean led his planes against the top cover. Strean and his wingman had good results, each picking off a Zeke and a "Tony." (More likely a Judy. The *Yorktown* pilots consistently reported Tonys during the day.)

The fight was now becoming more and more furious and confused, with battles from above 20,000 feet down to sea level. Lieutenant R. T. Eastmond knocked off one Zeke. As he pulled out, he counted seventeen aircraft falling out of the sky in flames. Eastmond saw another Zeke nearby and walked a burst across the enemy's cockpit. The Zeke suddenly spun, almost hitting Eastmond, and smashed into the water. Eastmond next saw a Zeke closing on an F6F. With his wingman he dove to the attack but was unable to close fast enough before the Zeke had sent the Hellcat into the sea. The Zeke got out of the area untouched.

A VF-1 Hellcat is signaled off from the Yorktown *on 19 June 1944 on an intercept mission. The target information is given the pilot via the blackboard. Note the "Top Hatter" insignia on the aircraft. (U.S. Navy)*

Lieutenant (jg) C. H. Ambellan had already exploded two fighters when he saw a third diving toward the task force. He took up the chase down to sea level but was unable to get in a good shot at the wildly maneuvering Zeke. Finally only one gun was firing. By kicking the hydraulic chargers, he got his three starboard guns to fire. They were enough. The Zeke broke into flames, disappearing in "one big orange puff" when it hit the water.[34] Ensign C. R. Garman had entered the fight with Ambellan but was not seen after the first pass and never returned to the *Yorktown.*

The Fighting 1 pilots were not finished tearing into the enemy aircraft. Lieutenant R. H. Shireman, Jr., led his division down from 20,000 feet into a mass dogfight at 10,000–13,000 feet. Shireman peppered a Zeke during a stern run, but his speed was so great he overshot his target. It did not matter. His victim was in an inverted spin and never pulled out. Lieutenant (jg) G. W. Staeheli sighted a Judy diving on a destroyer from 5,000 feet. He was able to blow the Judy's cowling off. The plane rolled over on its back and fell into the water.

The other two members of Shireman's division scored also. Lieutenant (jg) W. P. Tukey had already downed one Zeke when he caught another at 15,000 feet. This Zeke dove into the sea, leaving a large green stain spreading slowly over the sea. Ensign R. W. Matz met a Judy head on. His six 'fifties were too much for the dive bomber, which burst into a solid sheet of flame. Matz's canopy was partially open and when the Judy passed overhead he could feel the heat. Matz wound up the battle with another Zeke and two probables.

Although Commander McCampbell had believed that the Japanese planes would not break through the Hellcats, about twenty succeeded in breaching this defensive wall. The *Stockham*, still on picket duty in front of TG 58.7, had her hands full during a hectic twenty minute period as enemy planes came at her from every direction. She was not damaged by these attacks and shot down three of her attackers. Two more were claimed as probables. During these attacks the men on the *Stockham* watched as the "battleships, cruisers, and destroyers . . . put up a tremendous barrage which, together with the burning planes all around the horizon, created a most awesome spectacle."[35]

Many of the planes that broke through were knocked down by ship's fire, but some fell to the fighters. Lieutenant William B. Lamb from the *Princeton's* VF-27 found himself in the company of twelve Jills with only one of his six guns working. (As can be seen, the failure of several guns was not uncommon to U.S. fighters on this day.) For a time he flew formation with the Jills, staying just out of range of their fire. After radioing their course and altitude to the ships, Lamb waded into the enemy and destroyed three of them with his one gun.

Four pilots of the *Enterprise's* VF-10 "Grim Reapers" worked their way into the enemy planes nearing the ships. Lieutenant Donald Gordon and Lieutenant (jg) Richard W. Mason caught a Judy pushing over into its dive on a battleship. One pass by each pilot was all it took to ensure the Judy would never pull out of its dive. Less than a minute later Gordon and Mason saw another Judy low on the water. Both pilots later told their debriefing officer that they saw the Judy drop a torpedo. (Since a Judy was a dive bomber, it is doubtful this particular plane was carrying a torpedo.) The Judy flamed briefly as Gordon fired into it, then torched completely and crashed following Mason's pass.

Meanwhile, Lieutenant Marion O. Marks and Ensign Charles D. Farmer saw two Jills in their torpedo runs against the battleships. Marks latched onto one Jill, but was unable to bring it down on his pass. Farmer then took over, firing two long bursts from dead astern. The torpedo plane vanished in a violent explosion. The other Jill was not seen again.

From 1150 until about 1215 the battleship of TG 58.7 came under attack by dive and torpedo bombers. Two Jills thought the *South Dakota* looked like a juicy target but were chased off by antiaircraft fire from the *Alabama*. While the *Alabama* gunners were concentrating on the Jills, a Judy sneaked in on the battleship and dropped two small bombs which missed and caused no damage. The *Indiana*, in the meantime, was doing her share by shooting down five enemy planes and evading their attacks. One torpedo launched at the speeding ship mysteriously exploded only fifty yards from her. At 1214 another Jill attacked the *Indiana* from the "starboard side flying very low. It had no torpedo. . . . About 100 yards off it caught fire, swerved upward a short distance, and then glided down striking the ship at the waterline. . . . The plane bounced off the ship and immediately sank, leaving (a) swirl."[36] The *Indiana* rushed on with only minor damage. The *Iowa* was also attacked by a Jill, but its torpedo scored a clean miss.

A geyser of smoke and spray erupts from the premature explosion of a torpedo aimed at the Indiana. *The attacking plane also goes down in flames. Photo taken from the* Wichita. *(National Archives)*

Aboard the nearby cruiser *San Francisco* the ship's Automatic Weapons Officer received a superficial wound on a finger during the action, probably from friendly 40-mm fire. "To encourage his gun crews to greater effort he held up his bleeding finger and shouted, 'The bastards have drawn blood, shoot them down!'"[37]

Around noon enemy planes gave Admiral Reeves's TG 58.3 some exciting moments. A Judy and three Jills zeroed in on the *Enterprise* and *Princeton*, the latter steaming about 2,000 yards off the *Enterprise*'s starboard beam. Though the planes had been detected by radar, lookouts did not pick them up until they were only 6,000 yards away. The Judy was the first to attack, dropping down on the "Big E" in a shallow dive. Taken immediately under fire, the plane bored in to drop its bomb about 750 yards off the carrier's starboard quarter. Hit repeatedly by fire from many ships, the Judy wobbled away to crash about 4,000 yards ahead.

As the dive bomber crashed, the first Jill darted in aiming at the *Princeton*. Before the Jill was able to drop its torpedo it was shot down by the light carrier. The second Jill was also splashed by the combined gunfire of the carriers and their screen. The last Jill was aiming at the *Enterprise* and was able to drop its torpedo before its right wing was blown off (apparently by 5-inch fire from the *Enterprise*). The torpedo exploded in the carrier's wake. The Jill went into a spin, then plunged vertically into the sea 300 yards from the *Princeton*.

Holding down the southern end of TF 58's formation was Admiral Montgomery's TG 58.2. About 1145 lookouts on the *Wasp* spotted two planes 20,000 yards distant. They were thought to be "unfriendly" but there was no positive identification. The forward lookouts tracked the planes until they disappeared behind the ship's island and into some clouds. The aft lookouts were ordered to pick up the planes, which were now reported as "friendly," and keep an eye on them. Suddenly, one of these "friendlies" turned and made for the *Wasp*. The plane, now identified as a Judy, came in fast from the starboard quarter. The *Wasp*'s 40-mm and 20-mm guns were on it quickly, but the plane was able to drop its bomb. The 550-pound bomb landed just off the carrier's port beam, spraying the ship with shrapnel. One sailor was killed instantly by a fragment and several others wounded. The Judy, smoking and in apparent difficulty, finally crashed about 12,000 yards ahead of the ship.

The *Bunker Hill* was also undergoing her share of harassment. At 1203, lookouts on the carriers sighted two Judys emerging from a cloud at 12,000 feet and only four miles away. The planes were just pushing over into their dives. Though the forward 5-inch mounts

The Bunker Hill *has a close one. What appears to be the aft half of a Judy can be seen at the middle left. (National Archives)*

could not bear, eight other 5-inch guns were immediately firing, along with seven 40-mm quad mounts and fifty-three 20-mm guns.

Hits were made on the two planes almost immediately, but one pressed home his attack. The other Judy pilot apparently disliked the heavy fire and started to turn toward the *Cabot*. A direct hit blew it in half, with its nose landing off the *Bunker Hill's* starboard bow and its tail off the stern. The pilot was thrown from his plane, his parachute opening. The other attacker was able to drop his bomb before his aircraft was hit. Both bomb and plane landed close aboard the carrier's port elevator. The near-miss was surprisingly effective—two men killed and seventy-two wounded, the port elevator knocked out, fires in Ready Rooms 1 and 2, several fuel tanks and vents ruptured, and numerous small holes in the side of the ship. The *Bunker Hill* shook off these wounds, however, and remained in the battle.

By 1215 the task force radars were again clear of bogeys. The enemy had been dealt another savage blow. Of the 128 planes that had been launched in this raid, only 31 (16 Zekes, 11 Judys, and 4 Jills) returned. To the west of the task force, many fires still burned and many oil slicks fouled the water.

Miles away, Admiral Ozawa was unaware of the disaster that had befallen his first two attack waves. Even if he had known of the losses to his air groups there was little he could have done. And he was struggling with other problems. Around 1100 his force had been spotted by a Manus-based PB4Y.[38] Then he had run afoul of American submarines and was suddenly minus two carriers!

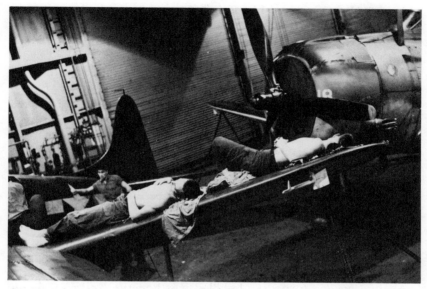

Crewmen aboard the Lexington *catch a few minutes' sleep on the hangar deck during a lull in the action.*

After the *Taiho* had been hit by the one torpedo from the *Albacore*'s tubes, she continued on without slackening speed. To her crew the damage was trifling. After all, wasn't this brand-new vessel virtually "unsinkable"? Air operations continued as the *Taiho* steamed at 26 knots. But now she was a time bomb waiting for the moment to go off.

Clumsy attempts to repair ruptured fuel and oil lines and to pump overboard the fuel in damaged tanks had been made by the ship's damage control parties. Large quantities of gas were spilled on the hangar deck as it was being pumped over the side. Then, an inexperienced damage control officer made a disastrous decision. In an effort to dissipate the fumes seeping from the tanks, he ordered the ventilating ducts opened. The effect was just the opposite of what he had planned; it only spread the volatile Tarakan petroleum fumes, and the equally dangerous avgas fumes, throughout the ship.

As the *Taiho* plowed ahead, her crew unmindful of the disaster to come, another of Ozawa's carriers suffered a fatal blow. Ozawa's A Force was about sixty miles away from the *Albacore*'s point of attack when it had the misfortune to stumble across another U.S. submarine, the *Cavalla*. Commander Kossler had followed Admiral Lockwood's order to trail the Mobile Fleet and now, many hours later, was ready for "a chance to get in an attack."

At 1152 Kossler raised his periscope to take a look around. "The picture was too good to be true!" he later wrote.[39] Off the *Cavalla*'s port bow was a large carrier and two cruisers. A destroyer, the *Urakaze*, was about 1,000 yards on the sub's port beam. The carrier was the *Shokaku* and she was busy launching and recovering planes. Kossler took the *Cavalla* in closer to make sure the flattop was not a "friendly."

Three times Kossler took a periscope sighting while the *Urakaze* steamed unsuspectingly close by. The Japanese screening forces, already weakened by their losses around Tawi Tawi, were now further hindered by their own lamentable showing in antisubmarine warfare. The *Cavalla* was able to get within the screen and make a good setup on the *Shokaku*. Kossler sneaked another peek at the carrier.

A big "Rising Sun" flag was visible. The *Cavalla*'s sailors readied their torpedoes. Kossler planned to fire six of them, figuring that at least four would hit. The first five torpedoes shot out of the tubes and streaked toward the *Shokaku*. Another quick glance was taken at the *Urakaze*. She was still apparently unconcerned with what was going on about her. Kossler fired his last torpedo as he took the *Cavalla* deep.[40]

As the *Cavalla*'s torpedoes bubbled past her, the *Urakaze* woke up and charged the sub. As he went deep, Kossler heard three solid hits, then the *Urakaze* and several other destroyers were upon him. Eight depth charges exploded fairly close to the *Cavalla* to start a three-hour working over of the sub. Over one hundred depth charges were eventually dropped, with at least fifty of them exploding very close. But the Japanese hunters didn't stay with their attacks and let the *Cavalla* escape.

Although Kossler had heard only three explosions, four torpedoes had actually slammed into the *Shokaku* at 1220. The big carrier slowed and fell out of formation. Flames raged through the ship and explosions tore her apart. The *Shokaku*'s damage control personnel were better than the *Taiho*'s and got many of the fires under control, but they could not contain them all. And all the while, the deadly fumes from ruptured gas tanks, and tanks carrying the Tarakan petroleum, were seeping throughout the ship.

The *Shokaku* was doomed. Her bow settled lower and lower in the water. Finally the water began to pour into the ship through her open forward elevator. Shortly after 1500 the fires cooked off a magazine and this explosion, intensified by volatile fumes, ripped the carrier apart. What was left of her turned over and sank at 12°00′N, 137°46′E. The *Shokaku* took with her 1,263 officers and men (out of a complement of about 2,000) and nine aircraft.

A short distance away the crew of the *Cavalla* heard and felt the tremendous explosions and breaking up sounds of the dying carrier. Kossler later radioed Admiral Lockwood, "Believe that baby sank."[41] Lockwood radioed back, "Beautiful work *Cavalla*. One carrier down, eight more to go."[42]

Also nearby was the *Taiho*. Her life was now being counted in minutes. Though Ozawa "radiated confidence and satisfaction,"[43] and had launched planes for Raids III and IV, his confidence was misplaced. Just one half-hour after the *Shokaku* had exploded, the *Taiho's* turn came. At 1532 a violent explosion shook her. Her armored flight deck split open and bulged up; the sides were blown out of the hangar deck; holes were torn in her hull bottom. Many of her crew were killed in this one monstrous blast. The *Taiho* began to settle. Ozawa wished to go down with his flagship but was finally dissuaded by his staff. A cruiser and a pair of destroyers were ordered to close for rescue attempts. Ozawa, his staff, and the Emperor's portrait were taken by lifeboat to the destroyer *Wakatsuki*. From there they were transferred to the cruiser *Haguro*, arriving on that vessel around 1706. By this time the *Taiho* was a raging cauldron. No ship could get close enough for rescue work. At 1828 another thunderous explosion rocked her. She heeled to port, kept going over and then went down stern first. Her losses were great—1,650 men out of a crew of 2,150, plus thirteen planes.

Ozawa's big problem now (besides the obvious and traumatic one caused by the loss of the two carriers) was communications. Although the *Haguro* was flagship of the 5th CruDiv, she was hardly equipped to handle the business of a Fleet flagship. Only the *Zuikaku* was properly equipped and she was not nearby at this time. To compound Ozawa's problems, the only set of codes for direct communication with Combined Fleet had gone down with the *Taiho*. It was only after a code common to all flag officers was used that contact was restored.

The Japanese had continued aerial operations, even through the submarine attacks. Between 1000 and 1015 Admiral Joshima's CarDiv 2 launched fifteen Zeke fighters, twenty-five Zeke fighter-bombers, and seven Jills of the 652nd Naval Air Group. These planes would make up what the Americans called Raid III.

These planes were heading for the "7I" contact when they were radioed new instructions at 1030. They were now to attack the enemy at position "3 Ri" which had been reported by a searcher at 1000. Plotted about fifty miles north of "7I", the "3 Ri" target was actually located farther south. Unfortunately, only twenty planes received

these instructions and headed for their new target. The rest of the
formation kept on for "7I". Upon reaching this position these planes
found nothing. After searching vainly for some time, the enemy aircraft returned to their carriers.

The twenty Zekes (both fighters and fighter-bombers) that went on
to "3 Ri" had better luck. Though north of TF 58, they saw some U.S.
ships. Initially sighting a pair of battleships, they passed these up to
search to the northeast for carriers. Unable to find anything else, the
attackers turned back toward the battleships at 1255.

These planes had been detected thirty minutes earlier by TG 58.4's
radars and tracked. Now as they began to close the task force, twelve
Hellcats from the *Hornet* and four night-fighter F6Fs from the *Yorktown*
were vectored against the attackers. Several more *Langley* fighters were
airborne to help if needed.

At 1304 the *Hornet* fliers tallyhoed the Japanese planes at 15,000–
16,000 feet. Between twelve and fifteen Zekes were counted. Each pilot
picked out a target and bored in. When the shooting was over the
Hornet pilots claimed nine Zekes, while the *Yorktown* group claimed five
more. Enemy records, however, indicate that only seven Zekes were
lost in the entire attack group.[44] While this *Hornet/Yorktown* team mixed
it up with the enemy, several other *Yorktown* fighters suffered through
a fruitless intercept, apparently chasing a heavy cloud that had registered on the task group's radars.

Only a few Zekes got through to attack Harrill's carriers, and only
one dropped a bomb. It landed about 600 yards from the *Essex* at 1320.
A division of *Langley* Hellcats saw the bomb splash and took out after
the attacker. They were helped in sighting the Zeke by the flak bursts
that trailed behind him. Finally the VF-32 planes bracketed the Zeke
and two solid bursts were fired into it. The fighter broke into flames in
the cockpit area and plunged into the sea.

Raid III was over. The Japanese had been very lucky this time. Only
seven of the forty-seven planes launched did not return.

While the American fighters had been having a field day with the
Japanese, the other two parts of TF 58's offensive punch had been
boring holes in the sky. When the first enemy planes had started
appearing on TF 58's radars around 1000, Mitscher had sent most of
his dive and torpedo bombers to the east to stay clear of the action.
There they had remained, engines throttled back to conserve fuel.
Occasionally a braver soul would edge in toward the task force to see
what was going on, only to be chased back by a wary fighter ready to
shoot first and check identification later. To the bomber pilots the
endless droning was more than just (literally to some) a pain in the

rear—it was extremely frustrating. Finally they decided to do something about it.

Jocko Clark had sent seventeen *Hornet* and fifteen *Yorktown* SB2Cs to attack Guam before noon. The planes bombed and strafed (seven *Hornet* aircraft carried no bombs) the Agana and Orote areas at 1145 with reasonable success. The *Yorktown* planes were hard hit by the flak, however. Lieutenant S. W. Roberts's Helldiver crashed as he made a strafing run on Orote. Lieutenant (jg) O. W. Diem's dive bomber was badly damaged by the antiaircraft fire, and he found he could not get his tail hook down. Diem's radioman, ARM2c J. D. Stevens, though suffering painful leg wounds, crawled into the aft fuselage and succeeded in lowering the hook. Diem's landing on the *Yorktown* was good, but his plane was so battered it had to be surveyed.

Farther south Lieutenant Commander Ralph Weymouth, Bombing 16's skipper, realized that if he wanted his planes to remain airborne much longer, they would have to get rid of their bombs. What better place to get rid of them than over Orote field? Shortly before 1300 Weymouth took his Dauntlesses to Orote, about sixty miles away. He was joined by eleven more SBDs and nine Avengers from the *Enterprise*. Ten F6Fs came along for escort.

The *Lexington/Enterprise* group arrived over Orote about 1330. The 1,000-pound armor-piercing bombs the Dauntlesses carried (in anticipation of a carrier battle) did little damage to the runways, but did help keep the defenders' heads down. The 500-pounders with four-to-five-second delay fuses that the Avengers carried worked much better and left several craters in the coral surface of the runways. Antiaircraft fire was still heavy around the field and a number of planes were bounced around by it.

Lieutenant G. L. Marsh's plane took a fatal hit in the engine during the dive, but he was able to make his drop and stagger four miles out to sea before ditching. Marsh and his gunner got into their raft and, covered by four *Bunker Hill* fighters, made themselves reasonably comfortable. In a short time two SOC Seagull floatplanes from the cruiser *Montpelier* plucked the men from the water. However, the two planes could not take off carrying the extra weight. Eventually a destroyer was summoned to pick everyone up. The two SOCs were so battered by the sea that they had to be destroyed.

Weymouth's unauthorized action did not draw the wrath of his superiors; rather, they were impressed by his initiative. Admiral Montgomery also suggested that the Guam and Rota airfields be worked over by the rest of the bombers. For the rest of the day the fields were kept under attack, with the loss of only one *Yorktown* bomber in the afternoon. These attacks could not have come at a worse time for the Japanese. The runways were cratered, and much-needed fuel went up in flames just as the last big raid of the day began coming in. And still Kakuta was telling Toyoda and Ozawa that Guam was safe.

Following Raid III's abortive attack, there was a short lull in the action. (There was a brief flurry at 1310 as four F6Fs jumped six Bettys and four Judys 40 miles south of the task force. This was probably the only land-based attack the Japanese were able to scrape up on the 19th, and it cost them several planes.) A number of ships took the opportunity to secure from General Quarters and go to Condition "One-Easy." Those Avengers that had been carrying torpedoes, and were thus unable to attack Guam, were taken aboard their carriers. Down in the noisy ready rooms, happy pilots told of their battles to the Intelligence Officers or compared notes with each other. Aboard the *Lexington* Lieutenant Commander Paul D. Buie, VF-16's CO, heard one of his pilots tell another, "Why, hell. It was just like an old-time turkey shoot down home!"[45] The phrase got around and it wasn't long before the action on 19 June 1944 became known as the "Great Marianas Turkey Shoot."

Ozawa still had one more punch left for the day. This would be Raid IV. At 1030 Kurita's C Force had turned to the southeast to parallel the rest of the Mobile Fleet's course. While heading in this direction Ozawa launched his last planes. Admiral Joshima's 2nd CarDiv (*Junyo, Hiyo,* and *Ryuho*) sent out the main force, while the *Zuikaku* added four Zekes and four Jills. Although Admiral Obayashi's 3rd CarDiv was tied up with recovering survivors of the earlier strikes and could not send any planes, the thirty Zekes, ten Zeke fighter-bombers, nine Judys, six Jills, and twenty-seven Vals that did go still comprised a formidable force.

The launch of Raid IV was completed by 1130. Thirty minutes later C Force turned to the northeast to clear the area and head for the refueling point. The other two forces changed course to the east to get closer to the "15 Ri" contact.

Unfortunately for the Japanese, Raid IV would have no more effect on the Americans than the three previous attacks. And Raid IV would not be helped by the fact that it was sent against a phantom target—the "15 Ri" contact.

Understandably, when the Japanese reached the supposed position of TF 58, they found nothing. After searching around without success, the formation broke up. Some of the planes, including all the Judys, headed for Rota. The eight *Zuikaku* aircraft and the ten fighter-bombers headed back to their carriers. The largest group—twenty

Zekes, twenty-seven Vals, and two Jills—set course for Guam. All the enemy planes ran afoul of the Americans.

Around 1330 the radars on the American ships began picking up the enemy planes. The *Monterey* reported a large bogey (estimated by the *Bunker Hill* as fifteen to twenty planes at 20,000 feet) bearing 214 degrees and 134 miles. At 1405 more bogeys (or possibly the same) were reported bearing 187 degrees, 68 miles at 24,000 feet. It was not for another eight minutes that the rapidly closing planes were positively identified as enemy. They were only fifty-three miles from TG 58.2. The *Monterey*, who had had the best look at this raid, was told to control the intercept with *Wasp* fighters, but communications were so bad the *Wasp* FDO had to take over the intercept.

The *Monterey* fighters were held a short distance out toward the enemy, while the *Wasp* Hellcats clawed their way to altitude. At 1417 the *Cabot* was ordered to launch eight additional fighters. Three minutes later the *Wasp* fighters intercepted the raid and shot down three planes. But, in a bad mistake, these pilots passed on no information about the altitude of the .enemy (about 12,000 feet then) and the remaining CAP fighters stayed at 25,000 feet.

At 1422 the task group began a left turn to 280 degrees. Just then a lookout on the cruiser *Mobile* spotted two Judys racing in for glide bombing attacks. The cruiser quickly opened fire and all the ships began maneuvering. Eight or nine Judys had come in under the CAP and were at about 6,000 feet and already in their dives when first seen. The *Cabot* was still launching her fighters.

The *Wasp* was doing 22 knots and in a 15-degree left turn when the Judys zeroed in on her. Captain C. A. F. Sprague immediately swung her around in a hard right turn. These gyrations did not bother the *Wasp*'s gunners; they kept tracking the Judys, and quickly splashed three. One of the Judys followed its bomb straight in about 200 feet off the *Wasp*'s port bow. Fragments of bomb and plane flew through the air and rattled off the carrier's skin. One large piece knocked down four men manning a 20-mm gun, but they scrambled back up to reman their gun. Two near-misses 250 feet off the starboard quarter wounded one man. An incendiary cluster burst about 300 feet above the ship, splattering the flight deck with pieces of phosphorus that ignited when stepped on but caused little damage.

The *Bunker Hill*, in the meantime, was receiving her own share of unwanted attention from the Judys. One plane dropped three bombs that missed the ship by 50 to 200 yards. These near-misses did no structural damage; however, the explosions and movement of the ship caused a parked Hellcat to bounce off into the water. The plane captain was in the cockpit of the fighter at the time and was taken for a wild ride; he was later rescued. The Judy crashed outside the formation. The *Cabot* also subtracted another Judy from Japanese stocks by blowing the plane's tail off. The attack on the two flattops had been fast and furious, but there had been few casualties and little damage.

The eighteen planes heading back for their carriers would not get home unscathed either. Shortly after 1500, when they were approximately 200 miles west of Guam, they ran into a *Lexington* search team of two Avengers and a Hellcat. What looked like an easy setup to the Japanese fliers turned into a hornet's nest for them.

The three American planes were bounced by eight or ten Zekes at 500 feet. Turning into his adversaries, the Hellcat pilot quickly racked up two fighters. One of the Avenger pilots apparently killed the pilot of another fighter, for the Zeke went in at a 45-degree angle without burning. The other Avenger pilot damaged yet another Zeke which fled from the area smoking heavily. A fourth fighter was also damaged by the Americans. By this time two more Avengers and their accompanying fighter escort had come over from the adjacent sector. Jumping into the fray, this Hellcat pilot brought down three more Zekes. This brought to six the number of enemy planes downed.

In comparison to the shooting of the *Lexington* fliers, the Japanese were able to put only one 20-mm shell through the vertical fin of one of the torpedo planes. Though badly in need of more instruction, the enemy pilots could still inflict damage and death. A *Bunker Hill* Helldiver/Hellcat search team found this out. The two planes encountered a group of enemy aircraft (possibly the same ones that had such a hard time with the *Lexington* teams) and were both shot down around 1530.

The largest group in Raid IV was in the meantime approaching Guam. These planes were to get a rude reception. Having seen nothing of TF 58, the pilots jettisoned their bombs. As they neared Guam they were probably relaxing in anticipation of their landing. But Guam was not to be a relaxing spot. At 1436 the *Hornet* had launched seven fighters, nine torpedo planes, and fourteen dive bombers for Guam. One *Yorktown* F6F and two *Lexington* Dauntlesses which had been aboard the *Hornet* also went along. These planes badly cratered Orote at 1530, making the field inhospitable for landing aircraft. One SB2C was shot down by the flak and another damaged. The gunner of the damaged dive bomber did not think his plane was going to make it, so he bailed out five miles offshore. He should have stayed with his plane. The Helldiver made it back to the *Hornet*, but the gunner was not recovered.

The incoming enemy planes had been picked up by TF 58's radars at 1449 and twelve *Cowpens* fighters were vectored to meet them. The *Cowpens* planes would be joined by twelve *Essex*, nineteen *Hornet*, eight *Enterprise*, four *San Jacinto*, and a few *Princeton* fighters in the slaughter to come.

The *Cowpens* fighters arrived about 1500, a little before the *Hornet* bombers tore up Orote field. Vals were just arriving over Orote in preparation for landing. Zekes, providing cover for the landing planes, were only 2,500 feet above the Vals. It could not have been a more vulnerable time for the Japanese fliers.

Commander Gaylord Brown, leading the *Cowpens* group, was first to spot the dive bombers. "Forty enemy planes circling Orote field at Angels 3, some with wheels down," he radioed.[46] The Hellcats fell on the enemy aircraft like hawks onto chickens and the enemy formation disintegrated.

Commander McCampbell joined the action with his *Essex* fliers. Diving through scattered clouds, the Fighting 15 pilots opened fire on the surprised enemy. McCampbell and his wingman, Ensign R. L. Nall, attacked the leading two fighters of a four-plane division. On the first pass Nall damaged the enemy wingman who dropped out of formation. On the next run McCampbell shot down his target. By now the Hellcats had slowed down considerably and were under attack by the remaining Zekes. Unable to break away, McCampbell and Nall turned into their attackers. The Japanese were good marksmen, shooting away Nall's elevator and severely damaging his plane.

The Americans finally broke away and went into a Thach Weave. The damage to his F6F caused Nall to drop slightly behind and the two Zekes began to stalk him. McCampbell scissored back to destroy the closest fighter in one pass. The other Zeke split-essed and ran for Orote. While Nall headed back to the *Essex*, McCampbell went after the Zeke. He caught the fighter and began firing from directly astern. "He attempted to evade by completing the most beautiful slow-roll I have ever seen," McCampbell later said. "It was so perfect that there was no necessity even for changing point of aim or discontinuance of fire."[47] The Zeke began to smoke and the pilot dove for the dubious safety of Orote. McCampbell did not follow, as he now found himself alone over Guam.

As McCampbell headed for the rendezvous point, he saw two SOCs on the water rescuing some downed pilots. Two *Enterprise* Corsairs were attempting to protect them from the attention of numerous Zekes. Joined by Lieutenant Commander G. C. Duncan, McCampbell joined the action and helped keep the Zekes off the floatplanes' backs

until they were able to taxi out of danger. While he was circling the
floatplanes McCampbell observed seventeen fires or oil slicks within a
one-mile radius of Apra Harbor. McCampbell had done his share
during the day to see that there were many plumes of smoke from
dying Japanese aircraft. To the two he bagged over Guam could be
added the five he shot down in the attacks on TF 58. His score of seven
planes for the day was excellent shooting in any league.

During the low-altitude fight Duncan had picked off three planes.
One had exploded in a big ball of fire and the other two had gone
down, like so many enemy planes, in flames. Ensign W. V. Twelves,
Duncan's wingman, also cut two Zekes out of the pack. At 200 feet
above the water Twelves got one fighter with a 30-degree deflection
shot. The plane "flamed and skipped on the water for hundreds of feet
before it went in for good, leaving a beautiful trail of flame on the water
behind it." Without changing altitude, Twelves hammered at another
Zeke from the side.[48] The plane hit the water, leaving a long plume of
black smoke.

Lieutenant Commander J. F. Rigg was bothered throughout the
fight by malfunctioning guns which necessitated getting to within
point-blank range to score any hits. Nevertheless, he downed one Val
which nosed up on Orote field and had four more Vals and a Zeke as
probables. Rigg's Hellcat was well holed by a good Zeke pilot and he
had to land on the *Enterprise*.

One of the easiest kills of the day was brought off by Lieutenant (jg)
Robert F. Kanze of VF-10. Kanze destroyed a Val on his first pass over
Guam. The pilot of a nearby Val must have seen what happened to his
companion, for as soon as Kanze headed in his direction, he bailed out
without a shot being fired.

The *Hornet* planes jumped into the fight at 1615. Many enemy planes
were still in the area. Two pilots joined the Val's landing circle and
proceeded to chew up the dive bombers. Ensign Wilbur B. Webb
slipped in behind a division of three Vals and, working left to right,
shot down all three. He then whipped over the field and got behind
another three-plane division. He flamed two of them and their pilots
bailed out. "Spider" Webb's sixth and last kill was yet another Val that
he knocked down with a head-on pass. Webb had also poured enough
shells into two other dive bombers to claim them as probables.

Lieutenant Russell L. Reiserer, commander of the *Hornet's* night-
fighter detachment, did almost as well as Webb. He had already made
two strafing runs on Orote, plus directing an SOC to a downed pilot,
when he saw five Vals coming south around Orote Point. In a stern
chase he picked off three of the vulnerable aircraft. Then he saw three

more of the dive bombers streaming around the southern tip of Guam at 100 feet. In a repetition of his earlier attacks, he bagged two more Vals. They had been flying so slowly that Reiserer had to lower his gear and flaps to stay behind them.

By the time the fight was over, thirty of the forty-nine planes that had tried to land at Orote had been destroyed. The rest of the planes were so badly damaged in the fight or cracked up on landing on the cratered strip that they were useless. It had been another disaster for the Japanese, but it had not been completely one-sided. Ensign T. E. Hallowell, from Fighting 51, had been lost, as well as Lieutenant Henry C. Clem, the executive officer of the *Enterprise*'s Fighting 10.

Clem and Lieutenant Commander Harmer, VF(N)-101's C.O., were escorting a pair of *Montpelier* SOCs a few miles off Orote Point when a Zeke jumped the floatplane Clem was covering. Clem tried to follow the agile Zeke but stalled out. Before he could recover, the Zeke whipped around and shot him into the sea. Harmer took out after the Zeke and was able to put a few shells into it but it escaped. When Harmer returned to where Clem had gone in, all he could see was a slowly spreading oil slick.

With the decimation of Raid IV, Ozawa's carrier force had spent itself. For the remainder of the day most of the action took place over Guam, though at 1750 a bogey was plotted 109 miles south of TG 58.2. Twelve *Bunker Hill* fighters were sent to intercept. At 1827 the enemy force was met and two Bettys shot down. In addition to the strikes on Guam, Rota had been visited several times during the day, but there had been little to report. Several late-afternoon sweeps found a few enemy aircraft on the ground, however—evidently stragglers or survivors of the fight over Guam, and these were promptly shot up.

The last big fight of 19 June occurred over Orote about 1825. Patrolling over Orote at this time were seven *Essex* Hellcats led by Commander Brewer, who had started the day's slaughter with Raid I. The *Essex* had reported bogeys closing on Guam, but the Fighting 15 pilots circling over the field didn't see anything until a lone Judy was sighted preparing to land.

The *Essex* planes took after the dive bomber. Lieutenant J. R. Strane got on the Judy's tail and his first burst caused flames to sprout from the left wing. A second burst started an engine fire. The Judy went into a tight right turn. The turn was too tight; the plane rolled over on its back just before it splattered all over the field. Just then Brewer tallyhoed at least sixteen Zekes dropping on the Americans from astern. (These were probably part of the group picked up earlier on radar.) The VF-15 pilots were in a bad position—strung out and low on airspeed—and only four Hellcats could turn into the attack. The Zekes were able to make coordinated attacks, with four to each Hellcat.

Brewer and his wingman, Ensign Thomas Tarr, Jr., both hit Zekes at the same time. The enemy planes continued their dives right into the ground. After this fight the two Americans were never seen again. Some time later a Hellcat was seen to pull up into either a loop or wingover, stall, and apparently crash. Whether it was Brewer or Tarr is unknown. The remaining *Essex* pilots kept whittling down the odds, and by the time the fight ended about 1845 they had shot down eight planes with three more as probables.

Of the day's activities, a Japanese soldier who had been watching wrote in his diary, "The enemy, circling overhead, bombed our airfield the whole day long. When evening came our carrier bombers returned, but the airfield had just been destroyed by the enemy and they could not land. Having neither fuel nor ammunition the fifteen or sixteen planes were unable to land and had to crash. . . . It was certainly a shame. I was unable to watch dry-eyed. 'The tragedy of war' was never so real."[49]

By dark the "Great Marianas Turkey Shoot" was over. Rarely had there been a more lopsided air battle than that fought on 19 June 1944. For over twelve hours (from 0600 to 1845) there had been almost continuous action over TF 58, Guam, and Rota. In the greatest carrier battle of the war, both carrier forces had launched more planes into action than had ever been done before, or ever would be again, during the war.

The bare statistics tell the story of this huge battle and its onesidedness. On 19 June Admiral Ozawa threw 374 (including floatplanes) of his 473 operational aircraft against TF 58. Only 130 of these returned to their ships. To the 244 planes that Ozawa lost should be added the 50 land-based planes of Admiral Kakuta. So the 294 planes the Japanese lost in combat, of which 19 were shot down by antiaircraft fire,[50] compare fairly well with the American claims of 353 aircraft destroyed. In addition, twenty-two more planes went down with the *Shokaku* and *Taiho*. And a number of those planes that made it back to their ships were so damaged they never flew again.

On the American side, considering the amount of action during the day, losses were remarkably light. Twenty-two planes had been shot down by fighters or the deadly flak around Orote. Three had been lost on search missions and six others lost operationally. Twenty pilots and seven aircrewmen had been killed. Four officers and twenty-seven sailors had been killed aboard ships.

It had been a fantastic day for the fighter pilots, and a great day for all parts of the TF 58 team. The exceptional work of the fighter directors had guided the fliers to their kills; the deck crews had worked quickly and efficiently to launch, recover, and relaunch their planes; the antiaircraft gun crews had performed a valuable role in splashing a number of enemy planes and chasing off others. However, one of the most important roles of the day had been played, not by an American, but by a Japanese. As related earlier, Lieutenant (jg) Sims had gotten into the enemy's airborne radio frequency and had been able to monitor orders of the Japanese attack coordinator, who was thus unknowingly furnishing the Americans with his plans. When the battle was almost over and the enemy pilot about to return to his base, Admiral Mitscher was asked if the CAP should go get him. "No indeed!" Mitscher replied. "He did us too much good!"[51]

chapter 6

Attack into the Setting Sun

As DUSK SETTLED over the Philippine Sea on 19 June, the air battles quickly tapered off and soon stopped. Aboard the American ships there was an air of jubilation. Pilots who had already landed waited for squadron mates to land, so as to swap stories. Sailors kept telling each other of the many Japanese planes they had seen diving into the ocean leaving greasy trails of smoke or the geysers of water thrown up by the few near-misses. From admiral to seaman, all hands were satisfied that the Japanese air units had suffered a shattering defeat.

What was less satisfying to Admiral Mitscher was TF 58's position during the day. When Raid I had come in around 1000 Mitscher's flagship the *Lexington* had been over 100 miles from Guam, but due to the constant launchings and recoveries throughout the day, the task force's course had been east by south. By 1500 the *Lexington* was only twenty miles from Guam's northwest tip.

At this time, however, Spruance ordered a change of course to the west, to close the Japanese fleet. But that was easier ordered than done. Mitscher first had to zigzag to the north and recover his aircraft. This took almost five hours. It would be 2000 before he could definitely head west.

About an hour after the *Lexington* had turned away from Guam, Spruance radioed Mitscher: "Desire to attack enemy tomorrow if we know his position with sufficient accuracy. If our patrol planes give us required information tonight no searches should be necessary. If not, we must continue searches tomorrow to ensure adequate protection for Saipan. Point Option should be advanced to the westward as much as air operations permit."[1]

(Point Option is a moving point based on a carrier's planned position for any given time. Therefore, theoretically, an aviator on a mission knows just where his carrier will be at a later time.)

At 2000 TF 58 took up a course of 270 degrees and all ships went to 20 knots. A half hour earlier Mitscher had detached Harrill's TG 58.4. It was to remain behind off Guam. On the 17th, while the other groups had topped off their destroyers, Harrill had supposedly dallied. Now he thought his destroyers needed fuel. Harrill asked to be left behind while he fueled.[2] Mitscher and Spruance conferred and decided TG 58.4 could cover Guam and Rota while the rest of TF 58 headed west. Though fifteen carriers used against an enemy force now woefully deficient in aircraft might seem to be a case of overkill, no one could foresee the outcome of the battle, and all the carriers might be needed. However, Harrill's force was now a burden and would slow the chase of the enemy.

Though supposedly in a similar fuel predicament as Harrill, Jocko Clark radioed Mitscher, "Would greatly appreciate remaining with you. We have plenty of fuel." Mitscher shot back, "You will remain with us all right until the battle is over."[3] Harrill's days as a task group commander were numbered.

Task Group 58.4 spent the next two days keeping Guam and Rota under surveillance. On the 20th the *Essex* launched four night fighters at 0208 to harass the two islands. Nothing happened over Rota, but the two F6Fs assigned to Guam discovered Tiyan airstrip (near Agana) to be lighted. They promptly shot up the field and the lights went out. The Japanese were not to be deterred, and at 0410 they turned the lights back on and began sending planes into the air. Four planes got off the ground, but three were quickly sent tumbling back in flames by the waiting Hellcats.[4]

A dawn fighter sweep found little of interest on the two islands. Harrill's group spent much of the day fueling from the *Lackawanna* and *Ashtabula* and receiving replacement aircraft from the escort carrier *Breton.* An afternoon sweep by twenty *Essex* planes encountered eight Zekes west of Orote Point. Ensign J. W. Power's plane was bracketed by a pair of fighters, and he was last seen heading for a cloud with a Zeke close behind. One Zeke was shot down and another damaged. The rest of the Zekes contented themselves with staying in the clouds.

Two strikes and an intruder mission the next day encountered little more than the usual heavy antiaircraft fire. One SB2C was lost in an afternoon strike on antiaircraft positions on Marpi Point. Harrill's force remained near Guam until the rest of TF 58 returned on the 23rd.

Meanwhile the remainder of TF 58 headed west. Enemy planes still pestered the task force. During the evening several small raids closed with TG 58.1 but did not get within gun range. Admiral Lee again had his battle line twenty-five miles ahead of TG 58.3. Mitscher and Spruance badly needed information on the Mobile Fleet's whereabouts. All they had were the *Albacore*'s and *Cavalla*'s attack reports (the latter's report having been received at 2132) and a PB4Y contact report made at 1120. Additionally, at 1957 Spruance received an HF/DF fix that put the enemy somewhere around 10°30'N, 136°30'W at 1800. By then the Japanese were moving far north of that fix.

A plan to send out a long-range search by night fighters and the *Enterprise*'s radar-equipped Avengers had been considered by Mitscher but rejected. He did not want to lose any more distance than absolutely necessary in this downwind chase; a launch now would lose some of that precious distance. Also, Mitscher (and a number of other top-ranking carrier officers of that time) had a deep-seated dislike of any form of night operations. A further consideration was that most of Mitscher's night fighters had been used in the Turkey Shoot, while the torpedo pilots had spent several hours counting RPMs as they orbited outside the battle area. The crews needed sleep if they were to be in good shape for a battle the next day. Mitscher decided he would have to rely on PBM searches from Saipan.

At 2207 TF 58 changed course to 260 degrees and picked up speed to 23 knots, the best speed for economical fuel use. (The restrictive factor here was the destroyers. They were fuel-limited and a faster speed would cause them to burn too much of the precious stuff.) Shortly after 2300 the task force entered the area of the afternoon air battle, and several U.S. airmen were picked up. The speed and course of TF 58 had been planned to close the distance with the Mobile Fleet—but it did not. The Americans did not know exactly where Ozawa's ships were, and were heading toward what they thought was the Japanese retirement track. Actually, Ozawa had already changed his course to the northwest and was beginning to open the distance.

For the Japanese, 19 June had not been a happy day. The loss of the *Taiho* and *Shokaku* was very apparent; the loss of so many aircraft was not yet so. A feeling of unease pervaded the Fleet, but the officers and men of the Mobile Fleet were not yet ready to give up.

Though only one hundred planes had returned to their ships, most of the Japanese commanders were still optimistic: Ozawa probably because he was isolated on the *Haguro*, the others because of the reports of the sinking of four carriers, the damaging of at least six others, and the shooting down of a fantastic number of the despised "Grummans." Tokyo even got into the act when it broadcast that eleven American carriers and many other ships had been sunk! Some of this information had come from pilot's reports, but much of it had been supplied by the incredibly sanguine Kakuta on Tinian. Why he would continue to send such patently false messages is still a mystery.

A and B Forces had changed course to the northwest at 1532 (just when the *Taiho* was being blown apart) to head for a rendezvous with C Force and the supply ships. Ozawa had arrived on the *Haguro* at 1706. It would not be until the next day, however, that he would learn just how many aircraft he had remaining. At 1900 Ozawa signaled his ships his intention to fuel the Mobile Fleet the next morning. This signal was followed shortly before midnight by another message ordering his ships to "proceed in a northwesterly direction and maneuver in such a way as to be able to receive supplies on the 21st."[5]

In Tokyo Admiral Toyoda had been following the battle (as much as he could since communications were temporarily lost when the *Taiho* went down) and early on the 20th he radioed Ozawa, "It has been planned to direct a running battle after reorganizing our forces and in accordance with the battle conditions. (1) On the 21st, Mobile Fleet shall reorganize its strength and take on supplies. Disabled vessels shall proceed to the homeland. Also, part of the aircraft carriers shall proceed to the training base. [This was Lingga.] (2) On the 22nd, according to the situation, you shall advance and direct your attack against the enemy task force, cooperating with the land-based air units. After this has been done, you shall dispatch your air units to land bases. Thereafter, operations shall be carried on under the commander of the 5th Base Air Force. The aircraft carriers shall proceed to their training base. (3) After the 22nd, according to the conditions, you shall manage most of your craft in mopping up operations around Saipan."[6]

At 0530 on the 20th, both sides began launching their first searches. Kurita's C Force launched nine Jakes to search 300 miles between 040 and 140 degrees. These floatplanes were followed a little over an hour later by six Kates from Admiral Obayashi's carriers, searching between 050 and 100 degrees. Neither group sighted any U.S. ships, though the Kates saw two enemy carrier planes at 0713. However, some of the searchers were seen by American pilots, for three Jakes and a Kate failed to return, victims of the Hellcats.

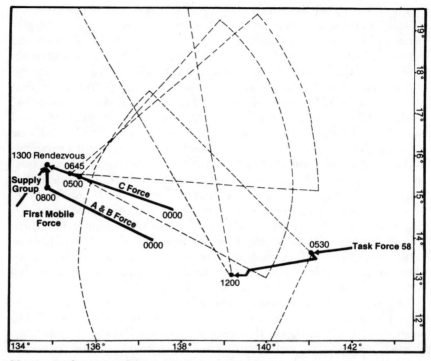

Movement of opposing forces 0000-1200, 20 June 1944.

When Kurita received the report of the sighting of U.S. planes, he wanted to retire west as quickly as possible. But Ozawa, when finally given the sightings after a long delay, was more confident. He thought the sightings were false. The Mobile Fleet would still refuel on the 20th and prepare for another battle the next day.

As the Japanese were launching their first search planes, Mitscher was sending his own planes out. Incredibly, this was still a routine effort. At this time, there seemed to be no thought of sending Avengers or Hellcats off on long-range missions. The planes flew their normal 325-mile search patterns. With no word on the position of the Japanese Fleet since the submarine attacks and the HF/DF fix, this was an amazingly short-sighted use of the planes.

The American planes went out to their limit, covering an area between 250 and 355 degrees. Only a few enemy aircraft were seen. The *Enterprise*'s air group commander, "Killer" Kane, picked off two of them. The first plane, a Jake, went down quickly. Forty minutes later a plane identified as a Jill, probably a Kate, was seen heading directly for the formation of two Avengers and the fighter. One turret gunner got off a few rounds before his guns jammed, then Kane took over. With a three-second burst Kane set the enemy's belly tank on fire. The fire spread rapidly. The pilot pulled up to 700 feet, then dove for the water. At 200 feet he jumped from his plane, but his chute streamed. "Plane and pilot hit with a splash. The Jap's body could be seen underwater with a pool of blood forming above."[7]

Just some 50 to 75 miles farther west from the 325-mile limit were the Japanese ships. If Mitscher had sent his planes a bit farther the Japanese would have been seen and the dusk attack could have been avoided.

As the dawn search droned on without results, Spruance and Mitscher became increasingly concerned that the Japanese had escaped. Spruance signalled Mitscher, "Damaged *Zuikaku* may still be afloat. If so, believe she will be most likely heading northwest. Desire to push our searches today as far to westward as possible. If no contacts with enemy fleet result consider it indication fleet is withdrawing and further pursuit after today will be unprofitable. If you concur, retire tonight towards Saipan. Will order out tankers in vicinity Saipan. *Zuikaku* must be sunk if we can reach her."[8]

"*Zuikaku*" was actually the now sunken *Shokaku*.

As noon approached Mitscher was listening to his Air Officer Gus Widhelm propose a special search-strike by Hellcats. Widhelm had estimated that the Japanese were probably headed northwest at 15 knots while covering the "*Zuikaku*." His idea was to send twelve Hellcats, each carrying 500-pound bombs and belly tanks, out 475 miles to find the Japanese. These fighters would be escorted by eight other F6Fs. Mitscher reluctantly approved Widhelm's plan.

At noon the twelve fighter-bombers, flown by volunteers and led by Air Group 16's skipper, Commander Ernest M. Snowden, began rumbling down the *Lexington*'s deck. In the air they were joined by their escorts from the *San Jacinto*. All took up a heading of 340 degrees. After the fighters left, Mitscher brought TF 58 around from 261 degrees to a course of 330 degrees. At this time the task force was 315 miles west of Guam.

Once again the men of TF 58 settled down to wait.

Thirty minutes after the Hellcats had departed, the last ships of the Mobile Fleet reached the fueling rendezvous at 15°20'N, 134°40'E. The rendezvous could not be considered orderly or disciplined. In fact, it was a real mess. With Ozawa still unable fully to control his ships from the *Haguro*, the fleet milled around in a disorganized manner, making little headway in the important matter of fueling. Though the

Aboard the Lexington *Commander Ernest M. Snowden, Air Group 16's skipper, reports about the unsuccessful search for the Japanese Fleet that was led by him. (U.S. Navy)*

oilers had been in position and ready to deliver fuel since 0920, the combatant vessels had straggled in over the next few hours, and none had taken on fuel.

Tempers were short and the officers and men jumpy—afraid that U.S. planes would catch them during the vulnerable process of fueling. Ozawa finally ordered the fueling to begin at 1230, but this order was cancelled when a false sighting of enemy planes was reported. The Mobile Fleet continued to mark time as TF 58 gradually closed the distance.

At 1300 Admiral Ozawa was at last able to transfer to the *Zuikaku*. With communications now capable of handling the fleet staff, Ozawa finally learned how bad his losses had been the day before. But Ozawa, bolstered (and badly misled) by the disingenuous reports from Kakuta, was more than ready to carry the battle to the enemy the next day.

Also at 1300 the *Chitose* and *Zuiho* sent three Kates searching 300 miles to the east. One of these planes spotted two carriers and two battleships at 1715, but by the time the report reached Ozawa it was of no value. The Americans were already on their way.

At 1330 eight Avengers covered by four F6F's took off from the *Enterprise* to search between 275 and 315 degrees out to the usual 325 miles. The *Wasp* also contributed two fighters and two Helldivers. Scouting between 295 and 305 degrees were Lieutenant Robert S. Nelson and Lieutenant (jg) James S. Moore in their Turkeys, escorted by Lieutenant (jg) William E. Velte, Jr.

Aboard the *Lexington* and the other ships of TF 58 the waiting for a report—any report—on the whereabouts of the Japanese was becoming oppressive. Captain Burke was stalking back and forth in the *Lexington*'s flag plot, cursing softly to himself. Gus Widhelm was ready to sell for fifty dollars his thousand-dollar bet that TF 58 planes would bomb the enemy fleet. It was obvious that Snowden's fighters had not seen anything. The only hope of spotting the Japanese in time to launch a strike today now lay in the eight Avengers and two Helldivers.

Nelson's little group had taken up a course of 297 degrees for the outbound leg. The trio cruised at 150 knots for best range and flew between 700 and 1,500 feet because of some high haze. An hour and a

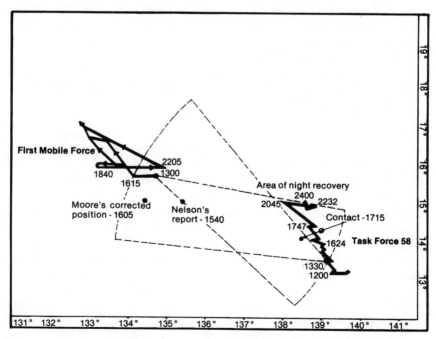

Movement of opposing forces 1200-2400, 20 June 1944.

half after takeoff, Nelson saw an enemy plane but decided to let it go and keep searching. At 1538, when he was getting close to the end of his outbound leg, Nelson saw something slightly to his left and about 30 miles ahead. It was a ripple on the horizon. Nelson led his group into a nearby rain shower in order to close in unseen and climbed to 3,000 feet. Two minutes after he had seen the ripple, Nelson was able to view what no man in TF 58 had yet seen—the Japanese Mobile Fleet.

"Enemy fleet sighted, time 1540, Long. 135-25E., Lat. 15-00N., course 270° and speed 20 knots," Nelson sent back to TF 58 by voice radio and morse code. "Two groups, one heading west and one heading east. Ten ships in northern group and twelve in southern. They seem to be fueling. Large CV in Northern Group."[9] The *Enterprise* fliers had seen Ozawa's A Force, with the *Zuikaku*, the cruisers *Myoko* and *Haguro*, and seven destroyers. Nelson could not make out the southern group of ships (probably B Force) clearly, but thought it contained two or three carriers, some oilers, and the usual screen.

For thirty minutes more Nelson, Moore, and Velte shadowed the Mobile Fleet, sending out more reports. Their report sent at 1606 was a very important one. When doublechecking Nelson's navigation plot, Moore found a longitudinal error. The new fix placed the Japanese ships 60 miles farther west at 15°35′N, 134°30′E. This was the correct position but placed the closest enemy vessels over 275 miles from TF 58. It was a long way to fly!

At 1610, when it appeared that several enemy planes were taking an interest in them, and the *Zuikaku* sent a burst of flak in their direction, the three fliers beat it for home. They had completed their job and done it well.

Meanwhile, another group of searchers had come upon the enemy ships at 1542. Ensign E.W. Laster was the first to see them. The three pilots watched the ships (apparently vessels of C Force) for a few minutes before turning for their carrier. A contact report was sent immediately, followed a short time later by the amplification, "Two groups, one group ten miles north of the other. 10-12 ships, one CV, four BB and six cruisers. 134-12E, 14-55N, course 000, speed 10 knots."[10]

Even before these reports had reached him, Mitscher was signalling his ships, "Indication that our birdmen have sighted something big. Speed 23."[11] This was at 1518, and where he got this report is unknown. But finally, shortly after 1540 when Nelson's message reached Mitscher, the gloom in the *Lexington*'s flag plot suddenly broke. The Japanese had been sighted for sure.

Nelson's report had been garbled, however, and it took a few minutes to get confirmation of Nelson's sighting from other ships that heard it. At 1548 Mitscher signalled his carriers to "Prepare to launch deckload strike".[12] On the *Lexington* the task force navigator had been plotting the enemy's position. Incredulous whistles broke the air when he came up with the plot. It *was* a long way to fly!

Mitscher huddled with his staff, deciding if the distance was too far for his fliers. In a few moments the decision was made. They would go, but it would be close.[13]

No one knew better than Marc Mitscher that this attack was going to be risky. A man with great compassion for his fliers, he also knew that the job must be done. After the battle he said: "The decision to launch strikes was based on so damaging and slowing enemy carriers and other ships that our battle line could close during the night and at daylight sink all ships that our battle line could reach. . . . It was believed that this would be the one last time that the Japanese could be brought to grips and their navy destroyed once and for all. . . . Taking advantage of this opportunity to destroy the Japanese Fleet was going to cost us a great deal in planes and pilots because we were launching at the maximum range of our aircraft at such a time that it would be necessary to recover them after dark. This meant that all carriers would be recovering daylight-trained air groups at night, with consequent loss of some pilots who were not familiar with night landings and who would be fatigued at the end of an extremely hazardous and long mission. Night landings after an attack are slow at best. There are always stragglers who have had to fight their way out of the enemy disposition, whose planes are damaged, or who get lost. It was estimated that it would require about four hours to recover planes, during which time the Carrier Task Groups would have to steam upwind or on an easterly course. This course would take us away from the position of the enemy at a high rate. It was realized also that this was a single-shot venture, for planes which were sent out on this late afternoon strike would probably not all be operational for a morning strike. Consequently, Commander Fifth Fleet was informed that the carriers were firing their bolt."[14]

"Launch first deckloads as soon as possible," Mitscher signaled his carriers. "Prepare to launch second deckload."[15] Mitscher also told Spruance, "Expect to launch everything we have. We will probably have to recover at night."[16]

Aboard the big carriers *Bunker Hill, Enterprise, Hornet, Lexington, Wasp,* and *Yorktown* and the light carriers *Bataan, Belleau Wood, Cabot, Monterey,* and *San Jacinto** pilots whistled too, as the target information flickered on the teletype screens in the ready rooms. But these were not happy whistles. The usual exuberance of the fliers was considerably

---

*The Princeton was to take part in the second strike.

dampened by this information. In many of the ready rooms Mitscher's final instructions were boldly chalked onto blackboards—"GET THE CARRIERS!"

Over the loudspeakers came the order, "Pilots, man your planes!" Pilots and crewmen raced for their aircraft. For this launch there was no bantering or good-natured ribbing among the fliers. They all knew this was going to be a rough mission. At their planes the pilots quickly strapped in with the help of their plane captains, and just as quickly glanced at their fuel gauges. All planes had been topped off, but with the exception of the Hellcats, they would be cutting it awfully close.

"Start engines!" came over the bullhorn, and a whine, followed by the pistol-shot bark of cartridge starters, cut through the air. A tentative chug sounded for a few seconds, then the engines settled into a throaty roar.

Immediately the deck signalmen began coaching the first aircraft into position. The carriers had begun to swing around to the east at 1621 and picked up speed to 23 knots. The order "Launch aircraft!" came, and at 1624 Lieutenant Henry Kosciusko lifted his Hellcat off the *Lexington*'s flight deck.

On the other flattops the deck crews were also sending their planes off as fast as possible. The hard-working deck crews performed wonders, and ten minutes after Kosciusko had taken off, the last plane had left its carrier. It had been a superbly executed (and for many carriers, a record low time) launch. At 1636 TF 58 came back northwestward.

As TF 58 was launching its planes, Admiral Ozawa was studying an interesting message from the cruiser *Atago*. The cruiser had picked up the report from Nelson's little group informing Mitscher of the revised position of the Mobile Fleet. It was obvious that his ships had been discovered, but it took Ozawa another thirty minutes to order all fueling stopped. He next ordered his ships to change course from west to northwest and increase speed to 24 knots.

While his planes were being launched, Mitscher received the depressing news that the enemy was some 60 miles farther west than had originally been thought. After consulting his staff, Mitscher decided to hold the second deckload for use the next day. "Have launched deckload strike," he informed Admiral Spruance at 1644. "Expect retain second deckload for tomorrow morning."[17]

The eleven carriers had dispatched 240 planes against the Mobile Fleet. Fourteen of these aborted for various reasons and returned to their ships. Of the planes that continued on, 95 were Hellcats (some carrying 500-pounders), 54 were Avengers (only a few of which were carrying torpedoes; the rest, four 500-pound bombs), 51 were Helldivers, and the remaining 26 planes were Dauntlesses flying out for their last carrier battle.

There was no organized rendezvous as usually practiced by the squadrons. Each unit set off to the northwest on its own, gradually joining up with other squadrons on the way. The pilots climbed their planes painfully slowly to altitude, then when reaching cruising altitude, they leaned their engines as much as possible to conserve fuel. The chase after the enemy was going to be a long, slow haul.

About thirty minutes after takeoff the fliers received the shocking information that the Japanese were about 60 miles farther west.

Bombing 16's Lieutenant Commander Weymouth got his information directly from Nelson. Nelson told Weymouth the "main body" was located at 15 30'N, 133 30'E and was heading west at 15 knots. The tanker force was about 20 miles southeast of the warships.[18]

Weymouth thanked Nelson and began plotting the new position. All around him the other pilots were also furiously figuring. The intercom chatter, today quite subdued, died away to almost nothing as the pilots realized the import of the new position report. It was an emotional moment in this dramatic flight.

In the cockpits of the droning planes the pilots and crewmen (some not yet out of their teens) silently figured their chances. They still had a long way to go, and it would be a long way back—to a night landing. The strain on these young fliers was tremendous. They couldn't relax their vigilance for a second, as they couldn't be sure when a Zeke might come screaming down to knock one of them blazing into the sea. They did not want to let their comrades down by flying all the way to the target and then not get a hit. The thought of a water landing also weighed heavily on them. But they continued west.

Commander Jackson D. Arnold, the skipper of the *Hornet's* Air Group 2, had already made his plans for a water landing. "I had decided," he later said, "that if the enemy fleet finally was discovered even farther west then originally plotted it would be best to pursue and attack, retire as far as possible before darkness set in, notify the ship by key, then have all planes in the group land in the water in the same vicinity so that rafts could be lashed together and mutual rescues could be effected."[19]

While the American planes were slowly closing the distance, Ozawa was busy getting the Mobile Fleet organized. The report of the sighting of two enemy carriers had reached him at 1715. Still undismayed by his losses, Ozawa had Admiral Obayashi launch a small raid of seven torpedo-carrying Kates led by three radar-equipped Jills. If caught by darkness after attacking TF 58, these planes were to continue on to

Guam and Rota. Shortly before 1800 Ozawa told Kurita to prepare his ships (the heavy vessels screening Obayashi's carriers) for use as a diversionary force in a possible night action. The Americans came on the scene before the order was executed, and it is probably just as well for the Japanese that it was never carried out, since the Mobile Fleet was then too strung out.

The Mobile Fleet was badly lopsided. Farthest to the north was A Force and the *Zuikaku*. Accompanying her were the cruisers *Myoko*, *Haguro*, and *Yahagi* and seven destroyers. A Force was heading 320 degrees and making 24 knots. About 18 miles to the southwest of the remains of CarDiv 1 was Admiral Joshima's B Force and CarDiv 2. The two big carriers *Junyo* and *Hiyo* and the light carrier *Ryuho* were screened by the battleship *Nagato*, the cruiser *Mogami* and eight destroyers. (The *Mogami* had been ordered to join C Force, but this had not been done when the attack came in; which was probably just as well since both A and B Forces had few screening vessels already.) Both B and C Forces were steaming a course divergent (300 degrees at 24 knots) from A Force. This did not help the antiaircraft defenses of the Mobile Fleet. Some eight miles farther south was Admiral Kurita's C Force, with Admiral Obayashi's CarDiv 3 in formation. Here was the firepower of the Mobile Fleet. Ostensibly the Van Force, Kurita's ships were now out of position to intercept attackers from the east, but they could still throw out a lot of steel. The force's three light carriers were fairly even with each other on a north-south line. Each was surrounded by an extremely close screen of heavy ships and destroyers. At the north end of the formation was the carrier *Chitose*, covered by the superbattleship *Musashi* and the cruisers *Takao* and *Atago*. The *Zuiho* was next in line, escorted by the second superbattleship *Yamato* and the cruisers *Chikuma*, *Kumano*, *Suzuya*, and *Tone*. On the south flank was the *Chiyoda*. Guarding her were the battleships *Kongo* and *Haruna* and the cruisers *Chokai* and *Maya*. Adding their weight to the firepower of C Force were seven destroyers and the light cruiser *Noshiro*. Finally, bringing up the rear about 40 miles to the east and slightly south were the vulnerable oilers of the 1st and 2nd Supply Forces. These six oilers were escorted by a like number of destroyers. Heading 270 degrees and unable to make the 24 knots the Mobile Fleet was doing, these vessels were rapidly being left behind.

Shortly after 1800, radars on C Force ships supposedly detected the incoming attack. The reported bearing (230 degrees relative) was in no way related to the actual bearing of the American planes. It is possible that the detection and/or bearing was either operator error or one of those "glitches" that confounded radar operators on both sides during the war.

The first accurate sighting of the attackers was made at 1825 by a scout plane searching just to the east. The Americans were reported splitting into four groups for the attack. It was another few minutes, however, before an American pilot saw any part of the Japanese fleet.

The scene as the Americans came upon the Mobile Fleet was one that Hollywood could not have staged any better. To the west the sun, a blood-red ball that reminded many pilots of the "meatballs" (slang for the national insignia or Hinomaru) on Japanese planes, was low on the horizon. Its rays dyed scattered clouds stacked from 3,000 to 10,000 feet, brilliant reds, oranges, and golds. Between A and B Forces lay a big cumulus buildup swelling to over 14,000 feet. Another large cloud formation lay northeast of A Force. To accompany this backdrop was a fireworks display like nothing the Americans had ever seen. Bursts of red, blue, black, pink, yellow, and lavender flak, with some spectacular white blossoms flinging out streamers of phosphorus, speckled the sky. It was magnificent—and very, very deadly.

The battle that now took place was a wild, incoherent melee. In the twenty to thirty minutes of daylight that were left to them, the Americans dove on the enemy ships in uncoordinated attacks from every direction. There was no time to join up, orbit looking for the right target, and make a textbook approach and attack. For most, there was just time to make one pass and get out. The action was so fast and furious, and spread out over so large an area, that many of the attackers never saw an enemy plane. In fact, it was believed and reported to Admiral Mitscher that not more than thirty-five fighters had attacked the Americans. Actually, Ozawa was able to clear his decks of forty Zeke fighters and twenty-eight fighter-bombers. No matter the actual number, those that did intercept seemed to be a veteran group which managed to escape the Turkey Shoot.

Most of the air groups zeroing in on the Mobile Fleet had either not seen the oiler group straggling along in the wake of the faster ships or had passed it up in favor of "bigger game." But these valuable ships were not to escape unscathed. The *Wasp*'s Air Group 14 saw to that.

Led by Lieutenant Commander Blitch, the *Wasp* group consisted of sixteen Hellcats without bombs, twelve SB2Cs carrying one 1,000-pound and two 250-pound GP bombs each, and seven Avengers, each with four 500-pound GP bombs. As he followed the *Bunker Hill*'s planes, Blitch saw the Supply Group. However, he did not see the rest of the Mobile Fleet. Relying on reports from another group's planes of two carriers to the south, Blitch led his force in that direction. This was a mistake, as he found out after flying south about 40 miles. He decided to do a "180" and attack the oilers.

His decision was based on two thoughts: his planes were getting low on fuel, and he figured that "this time [TF 58] would chase the Jap Fleet instead of running away from it [and he] decided to knock out the fleet oilers in order to prevent a speedy retirement, which would require refueling by them."[20]

As he neared the Supply Group, Blitch studied his target intently. Against four of the oilers he sent three "2Cs" each. A fifth oiler—the last in line—received the attention of four Turkeys. The last three torpedo planes were to attack whatever targets looked particularly inviting. Blitch divided his fighters into two groups, eight of which were to strafe the destroyers and the remainder to provide cover, then proceed to the rendezvous 10 miles west of the Supply Group.

As the planes dove to the attack, the two columns of three oilers each divided sharply. One column began a hard turn to port, while the other followed suit to starboard. The Americans discovered that the Supply Group was no patsy, as destroyers and oilers alike threw up a wall of flak. Many of the attackers took numerous 25-mm and 37-mm hits as they dropped down.

The Helldivers, followed closely by the Avengers, did a job on the slow-moving oilers. The *Seiyo Maru* took several bombs that started a large blaze. The *Genyo Maru* was ripped open by four near-misses and coasted to a stop. A third oiler, the *Hayasui Maru*, was hit by one bomb and near-missed by two others. The other oilers and a pair of destroyers also received considerable attention with near-misses and strafing. The *Hayasui Maru*'s damage control party was efficient and was able to put out the fire caused by the bomb. She reached safety. The other two oilers that were hit were not so lucky. The damage to the *Seiyo Maru* and the *Genyo Maru* was so extensive that they were scuttled that evening, the surviving crewmen being rescued by destroyers.

A group of Zekes jumped Air Group 14 as it headed for the rendezvous. Five Helldivers that had become separated from the rest of the planes encountered six fighters that knocked down one of the bombers. The enemy planes were finally driven off by Hellcats from another group. Another bunch of Zekes were waiting at the rendezvous, and for a few minutes a furious battle took place between the opposing fighters. Though Fighting 14 claimed five enemy fighters, the squadron lost Lieutenant E. E. Cotton. Cotton and a Zeke pilot disappeared in a brilliant flash as they flew head-on into each other. The remainder of the Air Group reformed and began the long flight back to the *Wasp*.

To the west of the Supply Group, all three parts of Ozawa's force were now coming under attack in a wild and confusing scene. With so little time left before darkness settled over the ocean and with fuel running low, the attackers did not take time to set up coordinated attacks, but made "every man for himself" runs from every possible direction. In fact, it appears that one group leader might have been a bit too eager to get in and get back out: "Pilots . . . reported being greatly disconcerted at hearing a transmission of the task group flight leader to the planes of his home carrier, telling them to make a quick attack so as to get back to base and into the traffic circle before other planes arrived."[21] However, Admiral Clark would later absolve the leader of any blame, saying, "The radio transmission to hurry home was made to the fighters with a view of getting them landed and out of the way before the heavier planes came back short of fuel."[22]

At the northern edge of the Mobile Fleet, the *Zuikaku* hurriedly launched nine fighters as the Americans approached. These nine Zekes, along with eight others already airborne, were all that the

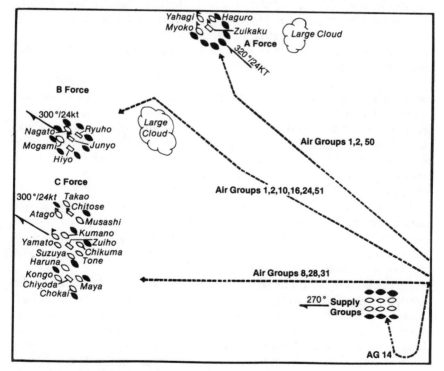

The attack on the Mobile Fleet, 20 June 1944.

Zuikaku could muster after the Turkey Shoot. The attackers now boring in on this force came from TG 58.1. Leading them was Air Group 2's skipper, Commander Arnold. As he drew near, Arnold saw Ozawa's A Force to the north and, separated by a big cumulus buildup, Joshima's ships 15 miles to the southwest. But what caught Arnold's eye was the big carrier alone to the north. He had seen the *Zuikaku* before in the Coral Sea and did not want to let this veteran escape again. Quickly Arnold ordered his planes to attack the *Zuikaku*.

The flattop was steaming northwest at 24 knots when the *Hornet* planes attacked. On each side of her bow, 1,600 yards away, were the *Myoko* and *Haguro*. In an approximately 2,200-yard circle around the carrier were the *Yahagi* and seven destroyers. Although not supposed to lead the attack, Lieutenant H. L. Buell's division was in the best position to make a run on the *Zuikaku*, and so he was given permission to lead the way. In an 80-degree dive, Buell led the first six Bombing 2 Helldivers down. The enemy ships opened up with a colorful pyrotechnic display. Into the fiery show the planes dove, releasing their thousand-pounders at about 2,500 feet. The flattop was slewing around in a hard starboard turn as Buell's group dropped on her and presented a "good lengthwise stem-to-stern target."[23] The fliers thought they had made two or three solid hits on the ship, for explosions and fires were seen to start on her.

Lieutenant Commander G. B. Campbell led a group of eight planes around a large cloud just north of A Force in order to dive into the wind and out of the setting sun. These planes pushed over from 12,000 feet and also released their 1,000-pound GP and SAP bombs at 2,500 feet. As Campbell attacked, he saw "one big hole with a fire down inside near the island."[24] Most of the crews noticed large fires raging from amidships forward. Like the pilots of the other division, these Helldiver fliers thought they had scored telling hits on the *Zuikaku*.

When he pulled out of his dive, Ensign E. D. Sonnenberg was jumped by a Zeke. His gunner pumped a stream of .30-caliber fire at the fighter, apparently damaging it, for it beat a quick retreat. Another Zeke made a run on Sonnenberg's Beast, but it was also chased off by his gunner's fire.

As the last *Hornet* plane pulled out of its dive and screamed over the escorting vessels (treating some of them to strafing), Lieutenant Commander J. W. Runyan led his thirteen *Yorktown* Helldivers down from 15,000 feet against the carrier. (The "*Yorktown* had been called upon to launch twelve VB in this attack. However, mindful of the unreliability of the SB2C aircraft, fifteen had been launched. Two had been forced to return to base due to minor operational difficulties.")[25] The antiair-

The Zuikaku *is surrounded by bomb bursts as she twists and turns to escape the attacks.*

craft fire was extremely intense, buffeting the planes all the way down and following their retirement. Runyan could see a "large hole rimmed with fire apparently emanating from the hangar deck below."[26] The Bombing 1 pilots all released their bombs between 1,000 and 2,000 feet. One hit was observed aft of the island, another on the port side opposite the island, and a third on the stern. Several more bombs were close near-misses. The *Zuikaku* was burning and smoking heavily now, and the last two *Yorktown* pilots broke out of their dives to attack (with unknown results) a nearby heavy cruiser.

Following close on the heels of the dive bombers were six *Hornet* torpedo planes—four of which carried torpedoes, the other two, four 500-pound bombs. The glide-bombing attacks were easily deflected by the violently maneuvering *Zuikaku*. But the VT-2 pilots certainly tried hard enough. Lieutenant (jg) K. P. Sullivan was boring in on the carrier and was just about to release his torpedo when he discovered a flak burst had jammed his bomb-bay doors. As he passed over the *Zuikaku*'s stern, Sullivan saw a heavy cruiser dead ahead and decided to try again. After a few jerks on the emergency release handle, his torpedo did drop. The cruiser turned toward Sullivan and his "fish" missed to the right.

Ensign V. G. Stauber also had his troubles. As he made his run-in, he found that he had forgotten to open his bomb-bay doors. Breaking to the right and down the *Zuikaku*'s starboard side, he proceeded to make a run on a heavy cruiser. Remembering to open his doors this time, Stauber dropped his torpedo which ran "hot and true." His turret gunner excitedly reported a spout of dirty water and smoke at the end of the torpedo's track. But it was not a hit. What it actually was will never be known. The Japanese reported no hits to any vessel in A Force other than the *Zuikaku*. Possibly the torpedo "prematured," or a near-miss from a dive bomber caused the apparent hit.

The last planes to attack the *Zuikaku* came from the light carrier *Bataan*. The ten VF-50 Hellcats carried 500-pound bombs. Lieutenant C. M. Hinn took six fighters to the east, and Lieutenant Clifford E. Fanning led his division west in order to bracket the carrier. Nearing the enemy ships, Hinn's group entered the cloud just north of A Force. Out of the cover of the cloud they dove on the ships from 8,000 feet. Two pilots circled west to dive on the *Zuikaku* from that direction, while Hinn led the rest of his planes against a heavy cruiser. The *Bataan* pilots did not notice what their bombs did, though they did see one bomb tumbling end-over-end, its tail fins missing.

Meanwhile, Lieutenant Fanning's division had run into a hornet's nest. As he led his team in a circle around the *Zuikaku*, Fanning saw two Zekes pouncing on a pair of unsuspecting Hellcats. Firewalling his fighter, Fanning was able to get on the tail of one of the Zekes, and gunned it down. The other enemy plane broke away and was not seen again. The division pulled up to 17,000 feet, dropped their belly tanks, and began spacing out in preparation for their attacks on the burning flattop. Just then about fifteen or twenty Zekes, painted up dirty green with shiny black cowls, jumped them. The division broke up and it became every man for himself.

Two Zekes zipped in front of Fanning and he broke sharply left to get behind them. Just as he lined up on one fighter, tracers arced over his wings. Fanning rolled right, but the enemy's fire apparently had parted his right rudder cable, for his Hellcat went into a flat spin. The Japanese pilot followed him down and gave him another burst. There was an explosion and his windshield was covered with oil. All his flight controls suddenly went free, and Fanning began thinking about leaving his plane. But since he still had plenty of altitude and did not want to bail out over the Japanese fleet, he stayed with his plane a bit longer.

His patience was rewarded, for he was finally able to pull out at 10,000 feet.

Although the "oil" that coated his windshield turned out to be hydraulic fluid, not oil, and although the big Pratt and Whitney R-2800 kept ticking over, Fanning's situation still was not bright. Besides his rudder problem, the right aileron cable and part of his left flap had been shot away; two-thirds of his right stabilizer had buckled and was hanging straight down; his radios were knocked out; and he had several shrapnel splinters in his left shoulder and one over his left eye. But Fanning decided to try for the *Bataan* anyway.

When the Zekes first jumped them, Lieutenant Wiley A. Stoner and Ensign Cyrus S. Beard had split-essed instead of scissoring. As he pulled out, Beard saw an F6F being attacked by an enemy fighter. He shot the Zeke off the American's tail, but not before the Hellcat staggered up in a climb, then fell off on a wing. (Beard thought the pilot was Stoner, who did not return from the fight.) He did not have time to follow the other Hellcat down because of all the Zekes around him. The next few minutes were just a blur to Beard as he twisted and turned to escape his assailants. He was able to destroy one more Zeke before he broke off the action. One incident in these chaotic minutes remained imprinted in Beard's memory: "He found himself in a spin and saw a Zeke shoot down over him and then pull up sharply above. As the Jap reached the top of his zoom, he seemed to flip right around on his tail and start down again without once swerving out of his original line of flight. Beard nosed down, picked up a little speed and then pulled up straight into the enemy plane, hoping to divert him from his dive. Placing his pipper squarely on the Jap's spinner, he held the trigger in a long no-deflection burst. Just as Beard's plane stalled out, the Jap whizzed past missing him by what seemed like about three feet."[27]

Beard was sure he had damaged the fighter, but could not follow the Zeke down. As he nosed over, another Zeke shot away his radio aerial. He headed for the safety of a cloud. Finally evading the Zekes, Beard joined three other F6Fs and headed for home. The fourth member of the division, Lieutenant (jg) William Y. Irwin, shot down one fighter and damaged two more before setting out to the east.

As the Americans left the area, they could see the *Zuikaku* burning furiously. The carrier was in serious trouble. Besides the bomb hits and near-misses, she had been strafed several times, causing some injuries topside. Fires on the hangar deck were getting out of control rapidly, and her damage control parties were being forced to use hand fire extinguishers, the *Zuikaku*'s water mains being knocked out. The order "Abandon Ship!" was given, only to be cancelled a few minutes later when the damage control personnel began to make headway against the fire. The fires were eventually brought under control, and the *Zuikaku* reported her "fighting and navigational capabilities not impaired."[28] Perhaps they weren't impaired, but she had precious little left of her main battery (her planes) to fight with. She eventually made it back to Japan and was repaired—in time to be sunk four months later.

While the *Zuikaku* was undergoing her ordeal, the main body of the U. S. planes were falling on Joshima's B Force. His ships were beating a healthy 24 knots to the northwest when they were first seen. Besides the antiaircraft fire put up by his ships, Joshima's B Force had the protection of the largest group of fighters left in the Mobile Fleet—about thirty-eight. He would need their help.

Among the first planes to drop on B Force were fourteen bomb-toting Hellcats led by Commander Arnold. After he had sent his dive and torpedo bombers toward the *Zuikaku*, Arnold had turned south-west toward the carriers of CarDiv 2. The *Hornet* fighters closed up behind him. Picking out a flattop to attack, Arnold chose what he identified as a light carrier. If he and the rest of the *Hornet* fliers were correct in their ship identification, then they attacked the *Ryuho*. (Ship identification was a field in which aviators on both sides were some-times not very precise. To compound the problem, during the battle the Americans consistently erred in calling Joshima's *Hiyo* and *Junyo*, the "*Hitaka*" and "*Hayataka*." This was caused by a misreading of the Japanese characters for the names of these two ships.) The "Rippers" dove on the carrier, claiming at least one hit, but Japanese records show only near-misses that caused minor damage.[29]

Following closely behind the *Hornet* planes were some more bomb-laden fighters, this group from the *Yorktown*. Air Group 1's CO, Com-mander Peters, and his division stayed at altitude to coordinate and observe the action. Peters later commented, "The AA fire from scat-tered ships and the wide area in which forces were involved made it comparable to watching a ten ring circus with a sniper shooting at you from behind the lions cage."[30]

While Peters's little group remained high, "Smoke" Strean led eleven "Top Hat" fighters to the west between A and B Forces looking for enemy fighters. When he found none, Strean turned back toward Joshima's ships. Strean saw a likely-looking target, identified as a "*Hitaka*-class carrier," in the southwestern part of the force. When he got within range, Strean took his pilots down from 10,000 feet in

60-degree dives. Most releases were made around 2,500 feet, with the pilots pulling out at 1,000 feet. The young fliers claimed three hits and five near-misses. One bomb was seen to go through the edge of the flight deck and explode in the water close aboard. One pilot who dove too steeply unloaded his bomb on a light cruiser instead, missing it by just a few yards.

Whether the ship the *Yorktown* fighter pilots attacked was the *Hiyo* or the *Junyo* is still unknown. Both ships were damaged during the confusion of the attacks, but by what groups is impossible to determine.

The next *Yorktown* planes to attack were five torpedo-carrying and three bomb-laden Avengers, all led by Lieutenant Charles W. Nelson. He took the five planes with torpedoes between the two enemy forces, then made a steep left-hand diving turn through some clouds toward B Force. Breaking out of the clouds at 2,500 feet, the Americans leveled off at 350 feet. The *Ryuho* was the target. Darting in at 220 knots, the Avenger pilots waited until 1,000 yards from the carrier before dropping their torpedoes. They claimed two hits on the flattop, as well as one more on a destroyer which "blew up and sank." Another "fish" was aimed at a cruiser which overlapped the light carrier, but it apparently missed. As Nelson pulled out, his Avenger was smashed by flak and it plunged burning into the sea. The other Avengers were attacked in their pullouts by Zekes, but these were driven off by the gunners and the timely arrival of an unidentified F6F.[31]

The three TBMs with bombs had initially turned toward A Force, but finding themselves alone, turned back against Joshima's ships. A glide-bombing attack from 10,000 to 2,500 feet was made on a large carrier. Lieutenant Robert L. Carlson's plane was hit by antiaircraft fire and it tumbled down in flames. The other three aircraft claimed three hits on the carrier.

Again, Japanese and American claims of hits do not reconcile. No destroyer was hit and, certainly, not all of the hits on the carriers of B Force can be attributed to any single unit. Commander Peters, high above the action, was skeptical about the claims of the attackers.

"Observations made by pilots of attacking planes are almost totally unreliable," he said later. "The camera is the only good observer. From the air, a bomb hit doesn't appear much different from the AA fire of the ship during the plane's approach. Hits can be estimated more by the lack of splashes in the water than by any other method. Naturally, if a fire is started it is readily visible."[32]

Meanwhile, four torpedo-armed *Belleau Wood* Avengers had been among the first planes over the Mobile Fleet. Lieutenant (jg) George P. Brown led the quartet. Initially the *Belleau Wood* aircraft had been part of the force targeted for the *Zuikaku*. But when the other TG 58.1 planes scooted north to attack that ship, Brown saw the *Hiyo*. It appeared that the flattop was not under attack at that time, and Brown wanted to get a hit on a carrier badly. Now he was going to get his chance.

The cloud between A and B Forces attracted his eye. He took his group down through it in a 50-degree dive from 12,000 feet. A 180-degree turn was made while descending so as to have the setting sun behind the planes when they made their runs. When they broke through some scattered clouds at 2,000 feet, the Avenger pilots found they still had about 5,000 yards to go before they would be able to drop their torpedoes. Nevertheless, they bored in, spreading out for an "anvil" attack on the carrier. Brown came in on the bow just off to port, while Lieutenant (jg) Benjamin C. Tate approached off the starboard bow and Lieutenant (jg) Warren R. Omark made his run from the starboard quarter. Ensign W. D. Luton, flying the fourth Avenger, got separated from the others during the turn and went searching for other game.

When the planes broke out of the clouds, intense antiaircraft fire began smudging the sky around them. Brown's big Avenger was hit several times as he descended for his final run. Parts of the left wing were ripped off, and a blaze broke out in the fuselage. Brown pulled up and his radioman, ARM2c Ellis C. Babcock, and gunner, AMM2c George H. Platz, immediately bailed out. They drifted down into the middle of the fleet where they had ringside seats for the remainder of the battle.

With his crewmen away, Brown stayed with his plane and returned to his attack altitude. Nothing was going to stop him from his attack, not even a terrible wound that must have made flying the big TBF extremely painful. The fire soon burned itself out. The *Hiyo* was heeling over in a sharp turn to port when Brown dropped his torpedo. It ran hot, and probably hit. After his drop, Brown flew the length of the carrier hoping to draw fire away from his comrades now making their runs.

Tate's torpedo also ran hot but might have missed. (The Japanese later claimed that only one aerial torpedo hit, but then said that a submarine torpedo also hit, causing a "large conflagration."[33] Since no sub was present then, it can be inferred that two aerial torpedoes hit or that an internal explosion occurred. Finally, bailed-out crewmen floating nearby say three torpedoes hit.)

In any event, Omark's torpedo ran hot and true. The *Hiyo* was fully in her turn when Omark came barreling in at 240 knots and 400 feet.

His torpedo smashed into the carrier's side about a quarter of a length from the bow. Water rushed through the hole and flooded the engine room. The carrier coasted to a stop near where Babcock, Platz, and a *Lexington* Avenger crew were observing the scene from water level. Ensign Luton had also attacked another carrier, but with no results, so far as he and his crew could tell.

As the *Belleau Wood* planes pulled away, defending fighters flashed in. Lieutenant Tate's plane had already been hit by antiaircraft fire several times. The top of his stick had been shot off, and he could not use his wing guns. The turret gun was also jammed and out of commission. Two Zekes positioned themselves on either side of him and took turns making passes on the Avenger. Tate bluffed them by turning into them on each attack, and the Zekes would break off. Tate was finally able to escape when he found a friendly cloud. After popping back out of the cloud, he joined with a TBF flying low on the water. It was Brown. His plane was a blackened, mangled mess. Brown was seriously injured, blood pouring from his wounds. Tate tried to shepherd him home, but Brown could not fly a straight course and Tate eventually lost him in the growing darkness.

Omark had also been jumped by the enemy—one Zeke and two Vals—but his turret gunner drove them off with accurate fire. After shaking off the enemy, he headed east and soon overtook Brown, still pressing doggedly for home. Omark led his shipmate toward the task force as darkness settled over the Philippine Sea. Brown's flying grew increasingly erratic, and Omark finally lost him when Brown flew into a cloud. Brown never returned to the *Belleau Wood*.

Antiaircraft fire had hit Luton's Avenger and jammed his bomb-bay doors in the open position. Luton went as far as he could before the drag of the doors exhausted his fuel supply, then set his plane in the water. He and his crew were rescued the next day.[34]

The *Belleau Wood* lost one more plane during the attack and in a rather unusual way. In the initial attack the Fighting 24 Hellcats, three of which were carrying 500-pounders, were jumped by several enemy fighters. The bomb-laden Hellcats quickly dove away to drop their bombs with unobserved results. The other fighters mixed it up with the Zekes. Lieutenant (jg) V. Christensen scored a probable but had his own plane shot up in the process.

Ensign M. H. Barr evaded one Zeke then saw a Hellcat being chased by a pair of enemy planes. As the trio flashed by, he exploded one Zeke and sent the other away smoking. Still another Zeke made a run on Barr but overshot and Barr was able to put some damaging bursts into it. Barr then saw Lieutenant (jg) R. C. Tabler being chased by a Zeke and dove down to chase the enemy away. Just then "all hell broke loose."[35]

Heavy shells had torn into his plane and fire broke out in the cockpit. Barr threw open his canopy, unbuckled his seat belt and began to climb out. More tracers whizzed by and the fire went out, so he decided to climb back in and try to get away from the Japanese fleet. His situation was grave. The blast of machine-gun fire had torn up his wings and fuselage. Two to three inches of gasoline were sloshing about the cockpit. His hydraulic system had been shot out, as well as most of his instruments, and his engine was barely running.

Finally, Barr decided to ditch. Despite a fire in his wing and the fact that his left wing "kept 'falling off' and looked as though it would crumble,"[36] he was able to make an easy water landing. He climbed into his raft and watched Tabler fly back toward TF 58. Barr was rescued the next day. Barr later claimed (and was backed up by Tabler, who had witnessed the incident) that it was an overeager Hellcat pilot who had brought him down. But he was lucky. The six .50-calibers in a Hellcat had devastating power.

The attacks on B Force were not over yet. Trailing behind the *Yorktown* and *Hornet* groups were the planes from the *Lexington*'s Air Group 16 and the *Enterprise*'s Air Group 10. The two groups were built around the aging but still well-liked Dauntless dive bomber. The *Lexington* had sent fourteen of them, accompanied by six Avengers and nine Hellcats. (Two fighters, one TBF, and one SBD had returned earlier with mechanical problems.) Actually, VB-16 still had fifteen SBDs in the attack for Lieutenant (jg) Jack L. Wright, having landed on the *Enterprise* with an emergency the day before, launched from that carrier and bombed with VB-10, then rejoined his own unit for the flight home. The *Enterprise* sent eleven dive bombers, five torpedo planes, and twelve fighters. None of the Avengers carried torpedoes. Tagging along with the big carriers' aircraft were two more bomb-toting Avengers—all that the *San Jacinto* could send.

Ralph Weymouth, leading the *Lexington* group, saw the large oil slick that many of the earlier attackers had seen, and changed course to 300 degrees to follow it. The other planes, bobbing and weaving gently in the air, followed. Shortly after changing course a pilot saw some ships ahead. As he neared them, Weymouth could see they were the oilers and escorts of the Supply Group. Weymouth kept going, ignoring the supply vessels. Other pilots, whose sharpness of eye was not up to that of their skipper's, took the oilers to be carriers and wondered what the hell he was up to. Weymouth knew his job, however, and had better targets in mind.

At 1845 he changed course ten degrees to the right to pass under the overhang of the huge thunderhead sitting to the east of Joshima's ships. As the *Lexington* planes came around the north side of the cumulus mass, what appeared to be the entire Japanese Navy was suddenly spread out before the Americans.[37]

Indeed, it was much of the Japanese Navy. To the northwest was the *Zuikaku*, burning and smoking and under attack by another group. Far to the west was another body of ships, too distant to be identified. Fifteen miles ahead, Weymouth saw what he guessed were two "*Haya-taka*"-class carriers, two or three *Kongo*-class battleships, two to four *Mogami* and *Tone*-class cruisers, and four to six destroyers or light cruisers. About four miles east-southeast of this formation was a *Chi-tose*-class light carrier with its screen. Weymouth's eyesight was not too bad, although only the battleship *Nagato* and the heavy cruiser *Mogami* were actually present, along with eight destroyers.

As the *Lexington* planes eased around the cloud, the pilots heard an urgent "Tallyho!" on the radio, and seven of the fighters zoomed up to engage the enemy. All they found were more Hellcats. Disgustedly, the VF-16 pilots reversed course. The *Lexington* bombers were nowhere in sight! They had seemingly vanished; the seven fighter pilots would not see the other planes until after the battle. The only fighters left to protect the bombers were the two flown by Alex Vraciu and Ensign Homer W. Brockmeyer.

The two F6F pilots and the rest of the *Lexington* fliers were surprised when eight Zekes from the *Zuikaku* suddenly slashed into them from out of the clouds. The enemy attack was well planned, and they blasted Lieutenant (jg) Warren E. McLellan's Avenger out of the sky on the first pass. McLellan did not know he was under attack until "about fifty tracers appeared to pass through (his) plane and go directly out ahead and slightly upwards."[38] He honked back on the stick and the plane shot upwards, but by now his cockpit and the center section of the plane were afire. McLellan was unable to reach the mike to tell his crewmen to bail out, but ARM2c Selbie Greenhalgh and AMM2c John S. Hutchinson needed no urging to abandon ship. With his cockpit becoming a blowtorch, McLellan leaned out of his plane as far as possible, placed his feet on the instrument panel and pushed himself out. Under the billowing silk of their chutes, the three men drifted down into the rapidly expanding darkness. In the meantime, the other Avengers were able to keep the Zekes at a distance with accurate fire.

When the Zekes appeared, Vraciu found himself with plenty of company. He and Brockmeyer were boxed in by the enemy planes. The two pilots began to scissor as the Zekes darted in. But there were too many of them, and one got in behind Brockmeyer. Before Vraciu was able to get a clear shot at the enemy plane, Brockmeyer's Hellcat was hit and spiraled down, leaving a heavy trail of smoke. Vraciu exploded his partner's assailant with two bursts. Vraciu then smoked another Zeke with a head-on pass, but did not see it crash. As quickly as the fight started, it was over. The remaining Zekes raced ahead to catch the SBDs, leaving Vraciu with the sky to himself.

The Dauntlesses were not to be easy pickings. The rear-seat men had seen the attacks on the TBFs and were waiting for the enemy to close. A fusillade of .30-caliber fire met the enemy planes, and they were unable to get close enough to do any damage. The Zekes pulled away as the fleet's fantastic antiaircraft fire display began reaching for the Dauntlesses. The dive bombers were now at 11,500 feet, having dropped slightly from their cruising altitude during the fighter attack. Weymouth had led his pilots to the west as he had studied the targets. Now he brought them around in a left-hand turn toward the pushover point. They would be making an upwind attack to the east. At his signal the SBDs lined up in their bombing order.

At 1904 Weymouth pushed over toward his target—the southern "*Hayataka*." (This should have been the *Hiyo*, but it appears the *Lexington* fliers attacked the *Junyo*.) At 1,500 feet he dropped his bomb and began his pullout. His gunner thought he saw a smoke billow up near the carrier's island. Following closely behind Weymouth—so closely that there were three or four bombs in the air simultaneously—were eleven other SBDs. The pilots thought they had hit their target at least six more times. After the battle the Japanese stated that the *Junyo* had received two hits near the stack and six near-misses.[39]

Three of the Bombing 16 pilots did dive on the *Hiyo*. Lieutenant (jg) George T. Glacken found himself out of position almost directly over the *Junyo*. He decided to drop his bomb on the carrier to the north. Just as he released, the *Hiyo* heeled over in a turn and his bomb hit just off the stern. Lieutenant Cook Cleland and Ensign John F. Caffey followed Glacken, claiming hits on the flattop's fantail and aft of the island. "The ship was smoking heavily and there was a fire on the flight deck as these planes retired."[40]

Coming in at the same time as the dive bombers were the Torpedo 16 Avengers, led by Lieutenant Norman A. Sterrie. The TBFs were each carrying four 500-pound SAP bombs. As with the other bomb-toting torpedo planes, they had to use the glide-bomb technique. Sterrie led his planes down from 9,000 feet. Airspeed quickly built up to over 300 knots, faster than the TBFs were supposedly stressed for, before the pilots pickled out their bombs between 1,800 and 3,000 feet. Their speed was so great that one plane had its right-hand bomb-bay door crushed; the bombs on that side skipping erratically into space when dropped. Another Avenger lost its center canopy when the speed proved too fast. The *Lexington* fliers thought they had hit their target—most likely the *Junyo*—at least three times.

The two *San Jacinto* Avengers came in as the *Lexington* fliers were making their attacks. The VT-51 pilots, Lieutenant Commander D. J. Melvin and Ensign J. O. Guy, thought they had actually made the first attacks on a carrier—probably the *Hiyo*—for they saw no dive bombers making any move toward the ship. Guy released his bombs from 5,000 feet and did not see any results, though Melvin was sure his wingman had scored two hits. Melvin, meanwhile, was having a problem. He had not noticed that his bombs had not released until he began his pullout. Pushing over again, he found he was in a good position for an attack on a destroyer. From 2,500 feet he manually released his bombs and watched one hit inside the ship's bow wave. "The other three did not hit the water but were all believed to be hits on board the starboard side near the base of the forward gun mount, for there was a violent explosion at this point that spread along a great portion of the ship's side."[41] Since the Japanese reported no damage to any destroyer in the action, it is probable that the explosions Melvin saw were actually the flashes of the ship's antiaircraft guns opening up on him.

The dive and torpedo bombers had not lost any of their number during the attack. But now they were going to have to fight their way out. Some very angry Japanese, employing a variety of guns, were trying their best to see that the Americans did not get home.

Weymouth decided the quickest way back was directly over several destroyers and cruisers. This turned out to be almost as exciting as the actual attack. Every ship within range opened up. By jinking and pulling every evasive maneuver they could think of (including ducking in their cockpits now and then when a shell burst too close), the *Lexington* fliers finally made it through the curtain of flak. But old enemies—the Zekes—were waiting for them.

Ten to twelve Zekes made passes on the Avengers as they headed for the rendezvous at 500 feet. Sterrie's plane drew the attention of four fighters. One Zeke made a level run from the rear and the gunners were unable to track him. The enemy pilot made a fatal error, however, by half-rolling and climbing away. The turret gunner had a perfect shot and stitched the Zeke's belly with forty rounds of .50-caliber fire. The fighter whipped over and dove into the sea.

As the TBFs fought off their attackers, the Dauntlesses were undergoing their own ordeal. When Cleland and Caffey pulled out from their attacks, a Zeke was waiting for them. The fighter came in from the right side on Cleland, but Cleland's gunner picked him off with several bursts into the belly. A puff of smoke belched from the Zeke, a wheel dropped down, and the fighter staggered off to land in the water near a destroyer. Before the Americans could enjoy their victory, a Val or Judy with its wheels down came in from the left side. Cleland could not turn into the attack, for a two-foot flak hole in his right wing made control a little touchy. Caffey took over, charging into the enemy plane with all guns firing. The Japanese pilot took off for a quieter area.

After the rest of the SBDs had run the gauntlet of ships' fire, eight Zekes ganged up on Weymouth's section of three planes. Their attacks were generally lackluster, with only three making determined passes. The Zeke's amazing maneuverability impressed the Americans even while they were under attack. The first two fighters were driven off by the combined fire of the three rear-seat men. The third Zeke pilot was more aggressive. This fighter started for Weymouth, then settled for Lieutenant (jg) Jay A. Shields's plane. Its wing and cowling guns twinkled as it bored in closer. The three gunners returned the fire, getting hits in the fighter's engine, but it kept coming. Lieutenant Thomas R. Sedell, Shields's longtime roommate, saw his friend suddenly shudder violently. His head snapped back and his goggles flew off; he appeared to be screaming. He slumped over his stick and his SBD plunged into the water. As the plane started down, Shields's gunner, ARM2c Leo O. LeMay, started to stand up in the rear cockpit with his guns spraying wildly. The guns kept firing until the ocean engulfed LeMay. The Zeke pilot had little time for elation. As he pulled up, his engine cut out and with its prop turning over slowly, his plane slammed into the sea.[42]

By now, Hellcats from various groups were dropping on the Zekes. Several enemy planes were shot down and the rest driven off. The *Lexington* planes, many damaged and one missing from each squadron, regrouped and pointed their noses east for the long flight back.

Air Group 10's attack came about the same time as Air Group 16's. "Killer" Kane, wearing a special helmet to protect his head still tender from his being shot down four days earlier, led the group. As he came straight in from the east, Kane saw that the *Ryuho* had drawn away from the other carriers by several miles. She was now in an excellent position for a dive-bombing attack.

Leaving four fighters for high cover, Kane took the remaining eight F6Fs down shortly after 1900 for strafing runs. Kane's division raked the light carrier from stern to bow with long bursts beginning at 5,000 feet and carrying through to 2,500 feet. The other division probably

strafed the *Junyo*. Behind the fighters came the SBDs under the command of Lieutenant Commander James D. "Jig Dog" Ramage. His
planes were carrying 1,000-pound bombs, and his pilots were hoping
to place them where they would do the most good.

Ramage led six Dauntlesses against the *Ryuho*. In their bombsights
the carrier's bulk seemed to jump at them as they drew closer. Ramage's bomb just missed astern, but close enough to probably do some
damage. Four of the next five SBDs also had near-misses, and one
plane could not get its bomb to release. The last pilot to dive was
Lieutenant (jg) Albert A. Schaal; his thousand-pounder sliced through
the aft port corner of the flight deck. Six Zekes had followed (but not
too closely) the Dauntlesses down, then sped ahead to catch the dive
bombers on their pullouts.

While Ramage went after the *Ryuho*, Lieutenant Louis L. Bangs had
taken his division of six SBDs farther west. He saw another carrier,
apparently the *Hiyo*, that appeared to be in trouble and this made a
tempting target. The *Hiyo* was damaged by the *Belleau Wood* attack.
Bangs pushed over with three planes from 9,000 feet. All three hit the
carrier. Bangs's bomb hit the fantail, knocking a group of aircraft clustered there into the water. Lieutenant (jg) Cecil R. Mester's
dropped just forward of the first hit, and Lieutenant (jg) Donald Lewis
followed up by planting his bomb just aft of the island on the starboard
side. "A sheet of flame enveloped the side of the ship."[43] The remaining
dive bombers, which included Lieutenant (jg) Wright from the *Lexington*, registered near-misses on an unidentified light carrier.

The *Enterprise*'s bomb-laden Avengers jumped the *Ryuho* the same
time the dive bombers did. Lieutenant Van V. Eason led five planes in
on the light carrier. Eason had initially spotted the *Zuikaku* and had
tentatively planned on attacking her. Then he had seen the *Ryuho* at a
closer distance and at that time not under attack. Though his planes
were at 12,000 feet and well above their normal starting altitude for a
glide-bombing attack, Eason decided the advantages of position in
relation to the *Ryuho* outweighed any disadvantages. So, at 1915 Eason
made a steep diving turn to the left, and the rest of the Avengers
dropped into trail behind him.

The dives were fairly steep (about 50 degrees) and, just like their
Lexington comrades, the VT-10 pilots were soon watching their airspeed needles flick past the redlines. Eason held his Avenger in the
dive to 3,500 feet, then toggled his bombs at the wildly careening
carrier. As he pulled out, Eason thought two of his bombs had ripped
into the *Ryuho*. Right behind came Lieutenant (jg) Joseph A. Doyle. He
released his bombs between 4,500 and 5,000 feet. As he pulled out,

"two red balls on a silver grey wing flashed by in front of (him) going straight down."[44] The Zeke disappeared. Doyle laid his bombs close to the carrier's bow and thought he also had gotten a pair of hits. As Lieutenant (jg) Ernest W. Lawton brought his big Avenger screaming down, the high speed and changing air pressure blew out his canopy glass with a crack that sounded like an AA-shell explosion. Lawton imagined he felt blood on his neck. By 5,500 feet his airspeed had built up to over 350 knots and he could not hold his sight on the carrier any longer. He released his bombs at 5,000 feet. One hung up and the other three fell off both sides of the *Ryuho's* bow. Lieutenant C. B. Collins was fourth to push over, and his bombs were laid neatly across the flattop's forward deck—one each in the water off both sides and two near the forward elevator.

Last to dive was Lieutenant (jg) Ralph W. Cummings. Like those before him, he was not happy about having to start his dive at such a high altitude, but resolved to do the best he could. As he later told his debriefing officer, at 8,000 feet he was "boresighted ahead and inside of a carrier turn that would do credit to a DD. We were set to release when Lindsey informed me that the bomb-bay doors weren't open. When had that *ever* happened to me? Bomb-bay doors not open over a Jap carrier!!

"So we snarled a little, I guess, roller-coastered into a second dive, opened bomb-bay doors and from then on it was dive-bombing from 7,000 feet. Just about as we released something seemed to tear all the glass out in my hatch port side. As we pulled on out I had time to worry about being hit and noticed also that something had kicked out a lot of glass in the second cockpit port side."[45] Only three of his bombs released and all apparently missed.

The *Enterprise* planes pulled out to the east and beat it for home. Zekes were waiting but were not very aggressive. One fighter made a stern pass on Eason's TBF. Due to fogging of his turret glass, Eason's turret gunner did not fire at the Zeke until it began to break away. A long burst sliced into the Zeke's belly. The plane slowrolled onto its back, broke into flames and crashed. Another fighter met Lawton's and Collins's Avengers and was badly holed before it limped off. A group of fighters jumped the SBDs of Bangs and Mester, putting 7.7- and 20-mm slugs into Mester's wing and engine. The Wright Cyclone kept chugging away and the Zekes were finally driven off.

"Killer" Kane's fighters waded into the Zekes harassing the *Enterprise* bombers. Kane and his wingman, Ensign J. L. Wolf, finished off one of the enemy planes. Wolf also got another fighter, the VF-10 pilots claiming seven in all. Ensign John I. Turner had already mixed it up with several Zekes, claiming a probable, when another pair of fighters made an overhead run on him. These two scored. Turner's oil line was cut and the fluid covered his windshield. He made it about 30 miles farther east before he had to ditch. Twenty-four hours later he was picked up by a *Wichita* floatplane.

"Usual story. Folly to dogfight Zekes," Kane later commented. "Jap pilots on this occasion better than those previously encountered, but our VF had no difficulty shooting them down if division and section tactics were followed."[46]

The *Enterprise* planes flew east. The bomber pilots were happy. They thought their bombs had mangled and possibly sunk the *Ryuho*. But they were wrong. Though damaged, the *Ryuho* was still steaming and fighting.

The third unit in Ozawa's Mobile Fleet, farthest to the south in the formation this day, was C Force. The three light carriers in this force were by far the best protected of any of the flattops in the Mobile Fleet, having four battleships and several cruisers as escorts. But, as related previously, earlier maneuverings had placed this potent unit out of position to do much damage to most of the attackers. The Americans were not going to let C Force off scot-free, however.

Actually, C Force was the first group in the Mobile Fleet to be attacked. Commander Ralph L. Shifley, Air Group 8's skipper, led forty-two planes from the *Bunker Hill, Monterey*, and *Cabot* against Kurita's vessels. At 1812 the oiler group had been sighted, but passed up in favor of better targets. Fifteen minutes later C Force was seen. At the same time a lookout on the *Chiyoda* saw the U.S. planes. His report was soon followed by a single antiaircraft shell, deep red in color, bursting over the center of the Japanese formation at 14,000 feet. This burst was in turn immediately followed by a barrage of shells. Though it appeared that the ships were not firing at specific targets but utilizing an area coverage, the display was every bit as fantastic—and deadly—as those by the other two forces. As only twenty-two planes were available, thirteen of which were Zekes, this antiaircraft fire was C Force's primary defense, and the ships "fiercely attacked [the Americans] by concentrating entire fire power."[47]

"The northern force contained two CVs, one was seen in the central force, and one in the southern force," Shifley thought. "Although accurate observation was difficult, a second CV may have been in the central force. Each force was screened with BBs, CAs, and DDs. A BB of the *Kongo* class was in the outer screen of the southern force. There was an additional BB on the north flank of the southern force, but it was too distant to be identified."[48] Shifley also noted that only a few destroyers were available to screen the big ships.

Since it appeared that the southern group had the largest carrier, Shifley ordered his fliers to attack those ships. Thus, the *Chiyoda*, with the *Kongo* and *Haruna* in attendance, drew the attention of virtually all the Americans. Lieutenant Commander James D. Arbes split his twelve-aircraft group into two units—Arbes taking a division of six planes against the *Chiyoda* from the southeast, while Lieutenant Arthur D. Jones led the remaining SB2Cs in from the north.

Shortly after 1830 Arbes pushed over from 13,000 feet and set his bombsight on the flattop. As his plane dropped like a rock in its 70-degree dive, the carrier began turning to the left. Going through 7,000 feet, Arbes felt his plane shudder and saw several holes appear on top of his wing. This did not deter him from his dive, and he kept going to 2,000 feet, where he released his bombs. He believed that one of them hit the carrier.

Following close behind were the other five planes of the division. As the *Chiyoda* was making the tight turn, each of the pilots had a slightly different setup on the ship. Releases were made around 2,000 feet, and several more hits were claimed.

Clouds and antiaircraft bursts darken the sky as smoke wreathes either the Kongo *or* Haruna. *The carrier in the right background is the* Chiyoda. *(National Archives)*

By the time the second division of Helldivers was starting down, the ships in the *Chiyoda*'s group were involved in wild independent maneuvers. An intelligence officer later commented that, "Apparently shortly after the first attack on the carrier the southern unit executed an 'Emergency 9 Turn', as all ships except one can be seen in the photographs to have executed approximately simultaneously a 90-degree turn to the left. While the straight course of the destroyer on the northern flank may have been part of the maneuver, it is probable that we can take comfort in the thought that in the Japanese Navy, too, there are some who do not get the word."[49]

The first section of Jones's division came in from the north. All three planes were hit by flak during the dive and on the pullout, but this did not stop them from dropping their bombs. Two or three more hits were claimed. Finally the last three dive bombers screamed down. Smoke wreathing the carrier impaired their aiming points so much that the pilots broke off their attacks to jump a battleship and a cruiser. All bombs missed, though one hit close enough to the *Maya* to set her port torpedo tubes on fire. Despite the claims of the pilots, the *Chiyoda* had emerged unscathed from these first attacks.

The *Chiyoda*'s evasive maneuvers had resulted in her heading slowly in the opposite direction to her original course. During these few moments the carrier was a sitting duck for any attack, but luck was with her and she was able to pick up speed again before the torpedo planes darted in.

Sixteen Avengers (four each from the *Monterey* and *Cabot* with 500-pound bombs and eight torpedo-carrying planes from the *Bunker Hill*) had been slightly behind the dive bombers. The oiler force had presented a tempting target, but the *Monterey*'s Lieutenant Ronald P. Gift had radioed his comrades, "To hell with the merchant fleet, let's go get the fighting Navy!"[50] The Avengers pressed on.

The attack by the VT-28 and VT-31 pilots got better results than that by their dive-bomber friends. Gift's four TBMs scooted down from 6,000 feet in 50-degree dives toward the *Chiyoda*. As they bored in, the flattop began to pick up speed and started a turn to starboard. To the *Chiyoda*'s crew the four-plane attack was made with "increasing fury" and "some tons" of bombs were dropped on them. Perhaps it seemed to the Japanese sailors that the attack was made with "increasing fury" because this time the Americans scored.[51]

The Torpedo 28 pilots caught the *Chiyoda* in her turn from two sides and walked their bombs across her stern. At least two of the 500-pounders ripped through the flight deck. Two planes were destroyed, a Jill and a Zeke in the hangar deck were damaged, twenty sailors killed and thirty more wounded. The *Monterey* fliers pulled out low over the water and retired to the southeast. As Gift pulled out, a lone Zeke was seen some distance away, but it soon disappeared.[52]

Meanwhile, Lieutenant E. E. Wood's four VT-31 torpedo planes were also making their presence felt. Wood and his wingman, Lieutenant (jg) J. B. "Beast" Russell, went after the *Chiyoda* and thought they both had planted bombs deep in the vessel's bowels. The last two pilots, seeing the flattop burning, selected the nearby *Haruna* as their target. This oft-"sunk" battleship took several hits. The number-four turret took a direct hit, and two near-misses caused the forward hull to bend. Two more bombs hit the quarterdeck, penetrating the upper, main, and middle decks before exploding. Heavy damage was caused and fifteen sailors killed and nineteen wounded. Nevertheless, the big ship continued steaming at 27 knots.[53]

Antiaircraft fire followed the planes as they zigzagged for home, but caused no damage. The *Monterey* and *Cabot* aircraft rejoined when out of gun range and took up a course of 100 degrees for home.

The next attack wave was the *Bunker Hill* torpedo planes led by Lieutenant Commander Kenneth F. Musick. These planes were armed with "pickle barrel" Mark 13 torpedoes. A false head allowed these torpedoes to be dropped at high speeds. But they would have little effect today. When VT-8 was still eight miles from the target, a Zeke made a half-hearted pass on the formation but was easily driven off by the combined fire of the turret gunners. Musick led his planes in a wave attack on the carrier's port side. The *Chiyoda* was now spinning around to starboard, and the torpedo pilots' favorite tactic of "anviling" the target would not work. Their high speed (over 250 knots) and constant jinking further complicated matters.

Musick and four of his fliers came in between 400 and 1,000 feet, heading almost due north. Black puffs of flak speckled the sky and geysers of water suddenly gushed up about the planes. But the Japanese gunners could not quite get the wildly careening gnats in their sights long enough to swat them. One after another the pilots toggled their deadly "fish" out. Then the Avengers broke away to begin their retirement. Behind them five torpedoes sliced through the water. Two explosions followed by towering columns of water appeared at the *Chiyoda*'s waterline. But there were no hits! Though the Avenger crews were sure they had seen the torpedoes hit, the waterspouts must have been caused by "prematures", bomb near-misses, or just plain wishful thinking. No hits were recorded by the Japanese in this attack.

The last three *Bunker Hill* pilots, believing the *Chiyoda* was doomed, shifted their attacks to other vessels. Two fliers picked out a *Nachi*-class cruiser maneuvering to the southwest of the carrier, but their torpedoes narrowly missed the fast-stepping ship. The last pilot zeroed in on a battleship on the opposite side of the force. The big ship turned into the attack, however, and the torpedo streaked past harmlessly.

In less than fifteen minutes the attack on C Force was over. The *Chiyoda* was burning, but the fire was soon put out. C Force regrouped and headed west at 24 knots.

Though they had been banged around by the heavy flak, none of the TG 58.2 planes had yet fallen. This was to change when they flew out of range of the antiaircraft fire. Waiting just outside the barrage was a covey of Zekes. Shifley and his wingman, Lieutenant (jg) Gerry Rian, had already encountered one Zeke that flew right in front of them. They both missed with their shots, and the enemy plane looped away and disappeared. Then, at the rendezvous 20 miles east of C Force they found six or seven Zekes darting around trying to pick off some *Cabot* and *Monterey* Avengers.

The two pilots immediately entered the fight. Shifley staggered one Zeke with several accurate bursts. As he passed over the fighter, it snapped over and smashed vertically into the sea. The action had now turned into a free-for-all, with Shifley and Rian squeezing off bursts at various Zekes as they flashed in front of them. Rian bagged another fighter which went down leaving a long trail of black smoke. Shifley blew some pieces off a third Zeke, but the plane dove away before any permanent damage could be done. Finally, three Zekes got on the Americans' tails and tracers began appearing "uncomfortably close." This prompted them to "pour the coal" to their Pratt and Whitneys. In 30 seconds they pulled away from the enemy.[54]

The *Bunker Hill* torpedo planes had little difficulty in retiring, with only one plane encountering and driving off a Zeke. The ship's Hell-divers were not so lucky. Five of them had just escaped from antiaircraft gunfire range when five or six fighters jumped them. The attack was well coordinated, with one fighter to each dive bomber. The Zekes attacked from behind and slightly below, where the gunners' .30-calibers were blanked out. Lieutenant (jg) Harwood S. Sharp's section was hard hit. Lieutenant (jg) James O. McIntire's SB2C slammed into the water and broke up; Lieutenant (jg) Charles D. Smith's plane went down in flames. The remaining dive bombers were all damaged.

The attack on the Mobile Fleet was over. The Americans now had over a two-hour flight in darkness to look forward to. For many it would be touch-and-go if they even made it back to their carriers. Behind them the *Hiyo* was sinking, as were two of the oilers. Four more carriers were damaged, along with the *Haruna*, *Maya*, *Shigure*, and another oiler.

Watching the *Hiyo*'s last moments were several interested spectators—Brown's crewmen, Babcock and Platz, and McLellan and his two crewmen, Hutchinson and Greenhalgh—in the water only a short distance from the doomed vessel. The *Nagato, Mogami*, and several destroyers rushed frantically about the stricken ship. Several times the men in the water were almost run down by the Japanese vessels.

The *Hiyo* was dead in the water and the raging fires spread quickly from deck to deck. As the ship began to list to port, the order to abandon ship was given. One group of sailors at the carrier's stern was beginning to go over the side when they were stopped by a sword-wielding young ensign. Using his sword for emphasis, the officer ordered the men to sing several traditional Japanese songs. The men sang until the water reached their knees, then they swept by the officer and abandoned ship. The ensign was last seen on the Hiyo's stern, still singing and brandishing his sword.[55]

The carrier was soon burning from stem to stern. Heavy explosions could be felt by those in the water, and she began to go down by the bow. Her screws came out of the water and the flames consuming her lit up the surrounding area. About two hours after she had been hit, the *Hiyo* plunged beneath the waves with a hiss and darkness returned. A lone destroyer combed the area with searchlights looking for any last survivors.

The attacks on the Mobile Fleet had not been as effective as they could have been. Unfortunately, the attacks had been uncoordinated, primarily because of the lateness in the day and the amount of fuel remaining. Also contributing to the relative ineffectiveness was the fact that only twenty-one of the the fifty-four Avengers engaged in the action carried torpedoes. (This was a lamentable state of affairs resulting directly from the SBD's success at Midway, but one that would soon be remedied.) Finally, the pilots had not had much practice in attacking high-speed vessels—and it showed.

But the dusk attack cannot be considered a failure. Though the number of ships sunk was not great, those sunk were valuable. And Japanese airpower suffered another crushing defeat. Eighteen U.S. planes had been lost over and around the Mobile Fleet, but the attackers had more than made up for these losses by destroying sixty-five enemy planes. When the day ended, Ozawa had only thirty-five planes left out of the 430 he had started with two days before. Though it was not recognized at the time, by the end of 20 June 1944 Japanese carrier aviation was finished for the rest of the war.

chapter 7

Chaos over the Task Force

As THE ATTACKERS LEFT THE AREA, Japanese seamen were busy fighting fires on several ships—to no avail on the *Hiyo* and the pair of oilers, but with commendable speed and success on the other vessels. Ozawa, no quitter, was still planning the destruction of the U.S. fleet. At 1900 he ordered the heavy cruisers *Haguro* and *Myoko* and most of DesRon 10 to join Kurita's C Force. After these ships joined, C Force was to head east, find the Americans and fight a night engagement with them. Ozawa took his remaining ships toward Okinawa. Though several of the vessels had been hit, their engineering spaces had suffered almost no damage and they were able to make a comfortable 20 knots.

In Tokyo, Admiral Toyoda and his staff had been following the last two days of fighting with increasing dismay. After discussing the situation with his staff, Toyoda ordered Ozawa to retire from the area. Ozawa received this dispatch at 2046. Since the carriers and screens of A and B Forces were already retiring, they continued northwest. However, Ozawa allowed Kurita to proceed east for over an hour before ordering him to turn back. Kurita had reached the vicinity of 16°05′N, 134°40′E when he received the recall at 2205 and turned about to rejoin the Mobile Fleet.

Darkness was complete when the last U.S. attacker began his plodding journey home. Not many would be racing this night. High-speed flight drank up too much gas. 20 June was the night of a new moon and it was as black as the inside of a coal barge. There was no horizon visible and patches of clouds hung wetly in the path of the planes. Far to the east, in the vicinity of TF 58, thunderstorms were building; the lightning shooting out of them would confuse some of the fliers when they arrived in the area.

The carriers were between 240 and 300 miles away (up to two and one-half hours of flying). Many of the planes had been damaged and some would not make it back. A number of pilots were novices at night flying, let along night carrier landings. They would certainly be getting on-the-job training this night. In small gaggles or sometimes just alone, the planes droned homeward. Some stayed low so as not to use fuel climbing; others climbed to get a little more breathing room. Generally, the fighters were in the best shape because, having carried belly tanks, they were reasonably fat on fuel.

The reaction set in as the planes plodded eastward. The pilots and their crews were suddenly very tired. They had just flown probably the longest mission they would ever fly, fought a wild battle at sundown, and still had a long way to go to reach a friendly flattop. The hypnotic hum of the engines enhanced their tiredness. Eyelids began to droop, finally closing. The flier would wake with a jerk, then begin making a minute inspection of every item in the cockpit, particularly the fuel gauge, in an effort to stay awake. Then the process would start again.

With no horizon to relate to, vertigo was a definite hazard. The aircraft that could had their wingtip and tail lights on so that pilots could stay in position with each other. But even this did not help sometimes. One pilot was trying to stay in level flight using a star as an "Up" reference only to discover the "star" was the tail light of another plane whose pilot was having just as much difficulty in staying level. Other pilots would feel they were banking and level the plane—only to find they were in a real bank, with the ocean just feet away.

Lieutenant Fanning had an especially hard time getting his damaged Hellcat back to the *Bataan*. Wounded in the left shoulder and over his left eye, Fanning found he had to hold the stick full forward and to the left to maintain level flight. With the fighter's engine pumping out 30 inches of manifold pressure and 2,050 RPM, he could indicate a little over 140 knots. However, if his speed dropped below 110 knots, his controls became sloppy, and at 98 knots the F6F would start to stall. Not helping his situation was the fact his compass had been shot out. Fortunately, he was able to tag along with a group of planes and made it back to the task force.[1]

But even in the damaged planes it was the fuel gauges, always the fuel gauges to which the pilot's eyes kept returning.

Over the radio some of the pilots were talking about their situation. A few were openly frightened, afraid they were lost and pleading for help. Others were quite matter-of-fact about their increasingly un- favorable fuel condition. Several joined forces and prepared to make water landings together.[2]

And the planes began to go in.

Faint patches of phosphorescence marked the ditchings. Those that could quickly scrambled out of their sinking planes and got into their rafts or bobbed about in their Mae Wests. Others were not so lucky. Wounded or perhaps knocked unconscious when their planes smashed into the swells, they were trapped in their cockpits and dragged down with the other planes.

The rest of the planes continued homeward.

Meanwhile, Admiral Mitscher had been preparing TF 58 for his returning airmen. He ordered his three task groups to open their interval to 15 miles so they would have sufficient room to maneuver during the recovery. He was still intent on pursuing the enemy, so at 1912 he proposed to Spruance that TG 58.7 be released to go after the Japanese. Spruance refused.

"Consider Task Force 58 should be kept tactically concentrated tonight," Spruance replied, "and make best practical speed toward the enemy so as to keep them in air striking distance."[3]

Spruance figured Admiral Lee's battlewagons had little chance of catching Ozawa's ships, over 250 miles away, and fuel was now becom- ing a big consideration for his ships. The destroyers were particularly low on fuel, with some as low as 24 percent of capacity.

By 2015 Mitscher's planes were beginning to near TF 58. On the ships' radars the blips could be seen; some of these blips obviously homing in on the task force's beacons. (A number of the planes first picked up the beacons 70 miles out.) It was just as obvious that others were lost. Some pilots were fooled by the lightning playing to the south and flew in that direction before discovering their mistake. A VF(N)- 101 Corsair was launched from the *Enterprise* to locate and bring back two groups of planes orbiting 80 miles from TG 58.3. The intercept was a success and the planes guided safely to the task force.

At 2030 the planes were arriving overhead. Task Force 58 turned eastward and upped speed to 22 knots. It quickly became apparent that the pilots were having a hard time picking out their home carriers. Each flattop had individually colored, foot-square glow lights to iden- tify themselves, but these were only visible from directly above, and the deck outline lights could only be seen from astern. About this time Admiral Clark ordered all his ships to turn on their lights. A few minutes later, a tense and tired, but willing to try anything to get his boys home, Mitscher ordered TF 58: "Turn on the lights!"[4] ("Smoke" Strean, who was trying to land on the *Yorktown* about this time, later claimed that it was his "bitching" loudly over the radio about his inability to find his carrier in the darkness that led to the lights being turned on.)[5]

It really doesn't matter whose idea it was; when the lights came on the effect was dazzling. All ships showed red truck lights and red and green running lights. The carriers' flight-deck lights were turned up to bright. On each group flagship a searchlight was pointed straight up in the air. Cruisers and destroyers fired star shells to light up the task force.

"It was a weird kaleidoscope of fast-moving lights forming intricate trails in the darkness," said an *Enterprise* pilot, "penetrated now and then by tracers shooting through the night as someone landed with his gun switches on, and again by suddenly brilliant exhaust flames as each plane took a cut, or someone's turtleback light getting lower and lower until blacked out by the waves closing over it. A Mardi Gras setting fantastically out of place here, midway between the Marianas and the Philippines."[6]

Another pilot said, "Our formation of ships (could) be described as similar to Atlantic City during convention week."[7]

Actually, if anything, TF 58 overdid the display. With so many lights on and star shells going off in bunches, pilots had a hard time picking out carriers and wasted much effort making passes on cruisers and destroyers. Still, in the middle of a supposedly unfriendly ocean— where Japanese submarines might be lurking—Mitscher had taken the gamble in order to get his airmen home. In those few moments he had endeared himself to his fliers forever.

The first planes to land did not have too much trouble. But then, as the bulk of the planes arrived with fliers tired, scared, wounded, or all three, the scene turned to utter chaos. (It would be confusing to try to cover this part of the action chronologically, so in an attempt to keep the narrative clear, each task group will be dealt with separately.)

Clark's TG 58.1 had been the first to turn on its lights, anticipating Mitscher's order by several minutes. Being farthest west, Clark's carriers began landing planes earlier than the other task groups, around 2015. Recovery was no easy task. "First the wind hauled and then backed, varying between 060 degrees true and 200 degrees true, making night landings even more difficult."[8]

Ensign H. G. Lewis brought his Helldiver aboard the *Hornet* on his first approach, although he had made only twenty-three previous carrier landings and *none* at night. However, deck crashes at 2035, 2124, and 2146 hampered operations considerably. The last plane to land on the *Hornet* was the F6F of the air group commander, Jackson D. Arnold. Having carried extra drop tanks instead of bombs in order to remain high, take pictures, and direct the attack of his fliers, Arnold had arrived over the *Hornet* with plenty of fuel. Seeing the situation, he had waited until everyone else had landed before making his approach. Unfortunately, he came in too fast and slashed through the arresting gear and barriers. Arnold escaped from his burning plane with just bumps and bruises. The fire was soon extinguished, but before Arnold had a chance to say anything, his plane and the valuable photographs were pushed over the side.

The *Yorktown* began landing planes at 2043 with an F6F and ended at 2205 with an SBD. The "Fighting Lady" was pretty lucky; she had only two "closed decks." The first accident, however, was tragic. Lieutenant M. M. Tomme had just landed and was preparing to get out of his plane, when a visiting aircraft ignored a waveoff and dove at the deck with its hook up. The plane hit hard, bounced over the barrier and smashed into Tomme's Hellcat, killing him instantly. Three other planes were also destroyed in the pileup. The next "closed deck" was a belly landing that tied up the deck for twenty valuable minutes.

When the *Bataan*'s Lieutenant (jg) Irwin finally landed on the *Yorktown*, he had been flying over the task group for forty-five minutes waiting for an open deck. As he taxied past the ship's island, his engine sputtered to a stop—out of gas! Eventually the *Yorktown* landed eight fighters and two bombers from her own air group, plus six fighters from the *Bataan*, four *Hornet* fighters and torpedo planes, two SBDs from the *Enterprise*, and one fighter each from the *Bunker Hill*, *Belleau Wood*, and *Lexington*.

The first two planes to land on the *Bataan* were from the *Yorktown* and both crashed. "I've just landed two and both cracked up," the light carrier radioed the *Yorktown*. "Can you get your planes over your ship?"

"We will do what we can," the *Yorktown* replied.

"They're mixed up which carrier is which," the *Bataan* shot back. "We can't take them into the landing circle. Our planes are in someone's landing circle, I don't know whose."[9]

In the meantime, the *Belleau Wood* took aboard three of her own fighters, a *Lexington* Avenger, and one Hellcat apiece from the *Hornet* and *Yorktown*. Lieutenant (jg) Christensen, from the ship's own VF-24, had a very difficult time getting his damaged fighter aboard the flattop. During the fight over the enemy fleet, his plane had been riddled badly. Both rudder cables had been shot away and his hydraulic system knocked out. His right aileron was shredded and several instruments, including his compass, were destroyed. Christensen was shepherded back to the carrier by another pilot. Over the ship, he found the landing circle in shambles. Four times he made approaches using full right rudder tab for directional control; four times he was waved off. On the fifth try he made it. His plane was junked.[10] Two more of the *Belleau Wood* fighters went to other carriers, while the lone TBF that returned (Lieutenant Omark's) landed on the *Lexington* with one gallon in its tanks!

With planes running out of fuel every minute, or so it seemed, TG 58.1's screen was soon reduced to only the cruiser *Oakland*, all the destroyers being on rescue work. DesDiv 92 was detached at 2351 to search for survivors, returning to the task group late the next day. All the destroyers did yeoman work the next few days pulling fliers out of the water.

One such flier was VF-2's Ensign W. H. Vaughan, Jr. Flying an F6F without an artificial horizon, he had his hands full trying to keep straight and level on this moonless night. Unable to get aboard a carrier, he decided to ditch. Almost immediately following this decision, the Hellcat's engine began to detonate and then burst into flames. This reinforced his plans. Just before he touched down, the engine cut out. Vaughan had no trouble getting out of his plane; it remained afloat for over a minute. It was after he got out that he had problems.

In the water he took off his chute, inflated his Mae West, and separated his raft from the chute harness. But then, raft, chute, and sea anchor line became entangled. Though he tried for twenty minutes to free his raft, he finally had to let it go. In his fight with the raft, Vaughan had also lost his waterproof flashlight. Now he had only a whistle, revolver, and dye marker with him. Luck did not desert him, however, for a nearby destroyer heard his whistle and picked him up a short time later.[11]

Montgomery's TG 58.2 had its share of troubles, and the ship hardest hit by them was the *Bunker Hill*. She began landing planes at 2033, with a number of planes from her own air group first aboard. Landings went smoothly for awhile, then at 2056 a *Hornet* pilot brought in his SB2C too fast. Ignoring a waveoff and red flares, he slammed down and missed the arresting wires. The plane hit the barrier and toppled over on its nose, leaving its prop implanted firmly in the deck. As the deck crew struggled to dislodge the dive bomber, an anxious young ensign from the *Cabot* tried to land his Avenger on the *Bunker Hill*. Like the previous pilot, he ignored warnings and forced his aircraft on the deck.

The Avenger hit hard and veered to starboard. The right wing was torn off when it hit a gun mount. The TBM continued down the deck, smashing into the still immobile Helldiver. The *Cabot* plane flipped over on its back and crashed into the island and flight-deck crash crane. A fire broke out but was quickly put out by the crash crew. Though badly burned, the Avenger pilot survived. Not so fortunate were Commander Wayne O. Smith, the ship's air officer, and three of the deck crew. Three were killed outright and one more succumbed the next day. One of the bodies was so entangled in the wreckage that it could not be removed before the planes were pushed over the side.

Valuable minutes flashed by before the *Bunker Hill* could begin landing planes again at 2144. At 2236 a *Wasp* Hellcat took the barrier, once again fouling the deck. The deck crew worked swiftly and efficiently and jettisoned the plane. The carrier landed her last plane at 2305. In the one and a half hours of landings the *Bunker Hill* had taken aboard ten of her own fighters, four *Wasp* fighters, a *Cabot* Avenger, two *Hornet* Helldivers, and an *Enterprise* SBD, plus two of her own night fighters that had been on CAP.

The *Bunker Hill*'s air group had been mangled badly. Her fighter squadron had come through in fine shape (only Lieutenant (jg) P. J. Wilson was lost, his plane being seen to crash and explode near the task force), but her bomber and torpedo squadrons were hurting. Only three of the eight Avengers launched made it back to some carrier. Only one of the twelve Helldivers sent out made it back safely. Two had been shot down over the Mobile Fleet and nine others had to land in the water after running out of gas.

The *Wasp* began landing planes at 2046 and continued for two hours. Two "closed decks" hampered operations. One of the crashes involved the *Bataan*'s Lieutenant Fanning, who made it back after getting shot up over the Japanese ships. Fanning made no less than seven passes on the *Wasp* before being able to land. He was high as he landed and his plane glided into the barrier. The Hellcat flipped over on its back and the engine tore away from the fuselage. When the deck crew lifted his plane, Fanning released his seat belt and dropped out on his head. Besides the wound in his shoulder, he now had a bump on his head.[12]

When the last plane landed at 2245, the ship had received five of her own fighters, one fighter each from the *Lexington*, *Bunker Hill*, and *Bataan*, one *Yorktown* dive bomber, and five Dauntlesses from the

Enterprise. As with the *Bunker Hill*, the *Wasp* had her Helldiver squadron roughly handled. Five of the big planes had to ditch and five more were missing. Except for the pilot of one of these last planes, none of the latter five crews were recovered.

The *Cabot* had an interesting night, landing nine planes, only two of which were her own. Two of the planes were big SB2C's, a type that was not supposed to be able to operate from the narrow-deck light carriers. But the *Cabot* got them on, though a *Yorktown* dive bomber that took the barrier had to be pushed over the side to make room for the rest of the carrier's "guests."

One of the funnier moments of the night involved a *Cabot* pilot. When he arrived over TF 58, "Beast" Russell decided he was going to pick out the biggest carrier he could find to land on. The *Cabot* was just a bit short and narrow for his peace of mind. After searching for a few

Lieutenant (jg) Logan J. Phillips, a Bunker Hill *pilot, describes the attack on the Mobile Fleet in the* Monterey *ready room. He landed on the light carrier during the chaos of the night landings. (National Archives)*

Lieutenant R. P. Gift relaxes in his ready room after returning from the attack. Note the inscription on the blackboard.

minutes, he found a carrier that suited him. As he clambered out of his Avenger following the landing, he was greeted with, "That was a beautiful landing, Mr. Russell—just like daytime!"

Surprised, Russell shot back, "What ship is this?"

"Why the *Cabot*, of course! What did you think it was?"

"That's all I want to know!" Falling to his knees, "Beast" Russell bent over and planted a kiss on his ship's deck.[13]

The fourth carrier in TG 58.2. the *Monterey*, landed only a few aircraft during the madhouse and had a fairly easy time. One plane that was not allowed to land on her belonged to her own torpedo squadron. Ensign R. W. Burnett had tried to land on the *Monterey* but had been waved off. A second try at a pair of lights turned out to be a pass at a destroyer. With fuel almost exhausted, Burnett set his Avenger down alongside the destroyer. He and his crew scrambled out of their sinking plane, and hardly got their feet wet before a boat from the destroyer *Miller* picked them up.

The action was no less frantic in TG 58.3. The first plane to land on the *Enterprise* came aboard at 2055. The Helldiver's 20-mm guns went off just as it touched down, sending everyone to the deck. Fortunately no one was hurt. Four Avengers were next to land, none being from the *Enterprise*. Following closely behind was a *Lexington* SBD. The plane was high at first, then dipped below the carrier's ramp. Suddenly appearing again at the ramp, the Dauntless got a quick "fast" and a "cut" from the Landing Signal Officer. The plane bounced over the wires, then slid off the barrier into the island. It took the feverishly working crew ten minutes to clear the wreckage and push it over the side. During that time several planes just flying on fumes had to set down in the sea.

With the deck open again, the stampede (for that was what the landings throughout the task force had turned into) resumed. Planes charged up to the end of the deck only to be waved off when another plane cut in too close. Lieutenant Walter R. Harman landed his Hellcat and caught the fifth (the next to last) wire. The hook man could not get Harman's tailhook released. The plane was stuck as "Tip" Mester's Dauntless thundered in to land. Lieutenant Walt Chewning, the catapult and arresting gear officer, sized up the situation and jumped up from the catwalk to help release the fighter's hook.

As Chewning and the hook man worked furiously, Mester was given the "cut" by the LSO. Mester planted his SBD and his hook caught the third wire. As the Dauntless pulled the wire taut, Chewning heard the roar of its engine and glanced back to see the plane surging forward. He rolled off to one side to get out of the way of the impending crash. Mester's SBD stopped a few feet short of Harman's fighter. No one was hurt, but plenty of grey hairs were added to the heads of those concerned.[14]

Cook Cleland landed his VB-16 Dauntless on the *Enterprise* shortly after the ship's narrow escape with the "double cut." As he and his gunner prepared to climb out of their cockpits, the deck crew (nervous and tense over the last few minutes' encounters) rushed up screaming that they had to push the battered plane overboard. Cleland tried to talk them out of it, but to no avail. His plane was going over the side.

Tired and strung out with nervous tension, he reached for his pistol and waved it at the deck crew. His beloved Dauntless remained on the *Enterprise*.[15]

Landings went relatively smoothly (if there was such a word for this night) for the next few minutes, then Lieutenant (jg) Joseph A. Doyle brought his VT-10 plane in. Doyle's landing was very smooth, then the Avenger's gear collapsed. It was another ten minutes before the deck crew had the heavy plane over the side.

At 2210 the *Enterprise*'s LSO, Lieutenant Horace I. Proulx, brought the last plane aboard. Only six of the planes aboard belonged to her air group. One of Air Group 10's planes that never found a deck to land on was the Avenger of Lieutenant (jg) Cummings. This is what the evening looked like to him:

Our gasoline supply was as much concern to us as anything else we had to consider after we returned to our floating city of lights. Confusion became more apparent as we reduced those last 50 miles, and by the time we arrived there was bedlam. It was too pitiful to be disgusting. Planes made passes at everything floating. I circled too long myself and was forced to go down to find a carrier. I squared away on the starboard side of the *Enterprise* and seemed to be part of a four-plane landing circle. My center face gauge registered about five gallons less than empty but I felt I could make one pass. I didn't get the chance to do so. The *Enterprise* informed us that her deck was foul; that we must hunt some other base. Well I could see the curtains then and struck out for the screening vessels. At about the same time I remember a carrier calling up and announcing she was shooting star shells, and I saw some fresh ones go up. These seemed to be ahead so I decided to stretch out into the wind. The engine still ran beautifully and I went beyond the screening vessels forward of the *Enterprise*. Just as I reached the most promising lights, I saw it was a large ship—possibly a BB searching for survivors with her searchlight.

Just then the engine on gallant old 52 gave us forewarning that she had started 'burning the hydraulic fluid' by coughing violently. The shipboard people below heard that and also heard us fly on. We didn't go over 2,000 yards up wind however until our old dependable had to stop running on her reputation and quit entirely. We tried to engineer a dead stick landing. Although we were very slow it was still not a perfect landing for we slid off on our right wing and the nose dropped. We hit somewhat nose down. My instinct was to lean forward and curve to the left and when we hit that was my position. I felt an impact equal to a rugged carrier landing.

Our exit from the plane was speedy enough and the water pleasant. My greatest difficulty was getting all the way out of my harness when I found I couldn't break the chute riser loose from my back pack. Old 52 gave her final salute by sweeping her tail around and nearly taking Lindsay and me with her. It *was* a sad parting. Terry paddled around like a duck and even after Lindsay and I were squared away in the raft he played around outside.

I signaled to the *Baltimore* (we learned her name later) with my water-filled flashlight and the hands aboard saw the dull red glow. It hurried our rescue. In about fifteen minutes from the time we hit the water the big dark form of the heavy cruiser was sliding alongside to pick us and the raft up. Rescued! Treated like kings and returned to the Big E two days later by the DD *Bradford*."[16]

Proulx had brought in twenty-three planes that hectic night. Besides the six *Enterprise* planes, Proulx had handled six *Lexington* SBDs and one F6F, three Avengers and two Helldivers from the *Hornet*, one fighter and one torpedo plane from the *Yorktown*, a *Wasp* Hellcat and dive bomber, and one *Bunker Hill* TBF. Proulx almost landed a twenty-fourth visitor.

Toward the end of the evening he picked up another plane in the landing circle. However there was something odd about the behavior of this plane. Instead of following normal landing procedures, this pilot did everything in reverse; with a "high" signal he would fly higher, etc. Disgusted after a third waveoff, Proulx shone a light on the plane and was amazed to see red "meatballs." Others aboard the flattop were equally surprised to see this apparition. The visitor finally flew off and was not seen again.[17]

(An apparition it may have been. Though both the *Wasp* and the *San Jacinto* also claimed seeing an enemy plane in their landing patterns, there has been no definite proof there actually was one. And yet— stranger things have happened in wartime.)

Things were and had been pretty hectic in TG 58.3 by the time the Japanese plane appeared. The destroyers were particularly busy, as a look at the task group's radio log shows.

Mitscher got a close look at the chaos around TF 58 when the planes started landing on the *Lexington*. The first plane to land was a *Hornet* Avenger. Realizing the difficulty his pilots were having finding their own carriers, at 2052 Mitscher told them to land on any available flattop.

The next plane to land on the *Lexington* was also a visitor, an F6F. Up to this point things had been relatively quiet for the ship. Then the rat race began. Incoherent gaggles of planes rushed the ship, each pilot hoping to force his way onto the deck. They had to be waved off, their precious fuel becoming more precious by the second.

Another Hellcat was brought aboard, this one from the *Enterprise*, followed shortly by another fighter. Next, an Avenger came lumbering out of the darkness astern. Flying the big plane was Torpedo 10's Lieutenant Eason. Eason had already made one pass at the carrier and was almost hit by a unlighted plane, then he was cut out of the pattern by a second plane. On this try he was in the groove and the LSO was about to give him a "cut" when the Avenger's engine sputtered and died. Now just a flying brick, the plane staggered and fell off on its left wing. The LSO dived into his safety net as the tons of steel, aluminum, and rubber hurtled over him to splash into the water. As the *Lexington* raced on, Eason and his crew could be seen tumbling out of the sinking plane. After about fifteen minutes in the water, they were picked up by the destroyer *Cogswell*.

Time	To	From	Message
2103	CTG 58.3	*Knapp*	"Am dropping out to pick up plane."
2105	CTG 58.3	*Knapp*	"We are going after one on our port side. How about the flare."
2106	*Healy*	ComDesRon 50	"Drop astern and find that man in area astern then trail 2,000 yards astern."
2108	*Braine*	CTG 58.3	"Did you see plane just outside screen to port about abreast of *Lexington?*"
2117	TG 58.3	CTG 58.3	"One in water on port bow of *Enterprise.*"
	CTG 58.3	*Birmingham*	"Plane astern of *Lexington* about 6,000 yards."
2130	CTG 58.3	?	"*Birmingham* has plane in water about 3,000 yards port quarter."
		Lexington	"Small boy on port, stay clear."
2141	CTG 58.3	*Cotten*	"We are backing down—picking pilot that crashed on starboard beam."
2144	CTG 58.3	*Cotten*	"Plane on starboard side—pilot out in life raft. Flare in water 100 yards bearing about 260."
2145			"Plane in water port side of *Lexington*. *Cogswell* acknowledge."
	Gatling	CTG 58.3	"There's one passing now."
	Birmingham	*Cogswell*	"We are slowing to pick up man now."
	Gatling	CTG 58.3	"There is one on starboard side of *Enterprise*—There is flashing light right close to him."
2222	CTG 58.3	*San Jacinto*	"I believe there is a Jap plane over *San Jacinto.*"
		San Jacinto	"The plane with bright red light over formation appears to be a Zeke dead ahead of me now."
2226	CTG 58.3	*San Jacinto*	"That plane passed low over us and his red circles were quite discernible on his lower wing."
	CTG 58.3	*Caperton*	"That plane flying overhead has red balls. He is a Val. He went close enough to our searchlights to see those balls."[18]

The madness continued. More planes queued up to try and land on the big carrier. Time after time the LSO had to wave them off. Air discipline had almost completely broken down now. Pilots jockeyed for position right up to the ramp, hoping to force other pilots out of the pattern. Waveoffs were sometimes ignored, generally with tragic results. If the pilots did accept a waveoff, they did so in ways they would never have usually done—pulling out straight up the deck or cutting to the right, just missing the carrier's island.

A fourth Hellcat landed on the *Lexington*, then a *Hornet* SB2C was brought aboard. The dive bomber trundled forward to its parking spot. Roaring out of the blackness astern came another Bombing 2 Helldiver, its pilot intent on landing. The plane was coming in too fast. The LSO frantically tried to wave off the onrushing plane, but his signals were ignored and the dive bomber kept coming.

Forward on the *Lexington*'s flight deck the six planes already landed were parked. Two Hellcats had been spotted to starboard, but the last planes were still parked nose to tail. With the help of Plane Handling Crew No. 6, the SB2C was just moving into its parking slot. Its crew was probably thankful this mission was over.

Then the second Helldiver swept past the LSO. The screech of the ship's crash siren split the air.

It was 2110.

"Clear the deck!" came a cry.

There was a grinding, ripping crunch as the "rogue plane" slammed into the parked dive bomber. The *Lexington* blacked out—a warning of a foul deck. Another cry was heard, "Loose bomb!"

The gunner in the parked Helldiver was dead, chopped to pieces by the landing plane's propeller. The impact drove the parked plane forward into the other three aircraft, destroying them all. The pilot of the struck plane was trapped in his cockpit with a smashed foot. One of the plane handlers had been crushed to death and five others injured. The pilot and gunner of the other dive bomber were unhurt.

With the hiss of fire extinguishers as an accompaniment, the deck crew threw themselves into the task of clearing the wreckage. Only a few flashlights and a sickly green spotlight illuminated the scene. The mobile crane was brought forward and began dipping into the wreckage. Planes still congregated to the rear of the ship, hoping they would be first to land when the lights were turned on again. The minutes ticked by. Finally the crane dropped the last piece of junk over the side.

The lights flashed back on. It was 2120.[19]

An Avenger was first to land, then the gaggle of aircraft started racing for the ship again. At this time none of the *Lexington*'s planes had yet landed, but not for lack of trying. When Air Group 16's planes had returned they had found mass confusion. Many of the pilots made three or four passes at a carrier before landing or ditching. Ensign Edward G. Wendorf came close to disaster as he tried to land.

Wendorf was starting his turn to downwind when he saw the exhaust flames of a plane rushing toward him. He nosed over and the other plane roared by only feet away. A mid-air collision had been avoided, but Wendorf was in serious trouble. He had been low to begin with; now he was too low! The Hellcat's left wheel and wingtip dug into the water. The plane began "several cartwheels and some unrecognizable gyrations."[20]

The F6F came to a sudden stop on its back with its nose six to ten feet under the water. The canopy had slammed shut, but water poured through broken parts of it. Wendorf frantically pushed and pulled at the canopy. Finally it budged and he began to drop out of the plane. He was halfway out when the canopy slid forward again, catching on his chute and raft. Once more Wendorf kicked and pried and the canopy opened. He fell clear, but was held against the fighter by the rapidly building water pressure. His lungs were bursting and red-hot pokers seemed to be searing every part of his body. It was almost half a minute before he was able to kick free. Wendorf floated to the surface where he lay weakly.

After a few minutes he inflated his lifejacket, then spent an agonizing hour before he could get his raft inflated. In his weakened condition it took him four tries to finally climb in his raft. Paroxysms of nausea brought on by the oil and water he had swallowed rolled over him as he lay in the raft. After a time he used his one remaining shoe to bail out the raft. As he finished, he noticed several shapes in the water nearby. Thinking these were more downed pilots, Wendorf called out and reached for them. Suddenly he realized they were sharks! Wendorf "began to beat the water madly with (his) shoe, and having no particular use for one shoe, finally threw it at them."[21] Remembering his pistol, Wendorf drew it and fired several shots at his escorts. The sharks eventually moved off.

During this time several destroyers had passed close by, but Wendorf was unable to get their attention by shouting or firing his pistol. He kept wishing he had kept his back pack with its flares and flashlight, but it had apparently gone down with his chute and harness when he had discarded them. Wendorf settled into a fitful sleep.

He was awake when a light carrier neared his raft. At first he was unable to speak, but he finally croaked out an "Ahoy!" Someone on the carrier heard him and a smoke pot was thrown over to mark his position. Soon the destroyer *Clarence K. Bronson* sidled up, and at 0415 Wendorf was pulled aboard. As he unbuckled his Mae West aboard the destroyer, he discovered he had been wearing his back pack all night![22]

Lieutenant (jg) Arthur P. Whiteway had initially missed TF 58 when he had arrived over the force and had flown off toward the lightning flickering to the southeast. Realizing his mistake, he turned back, flying in and out of clouds. Star shells bursting inside the clouds blinded him and he went into a spin, finally recovering only 200 feet above the water. Eventually, he planted his Hellcat on a light carrier at 2150. The plane that landed ahead of Whiteway had to be jettisoned to make room for his F6F.

Some of Air Group 16's planes finally made it aboard the *Lexington*. Like so many others sent out on the strike, the *Lexington* pilots and crewmen were completely drained by their experiences. Many sat dazed in their cockpits after landing. Even after they had reached the ready rooms, nervous tension kept such a hold on them that some could not sit still for more than a few minutes. A gunner coming into his ready room threw his camera onto a chair. With an anguished cry he vowed he would never fly again. When handed a shot of brandy to calm him down, a pilot refused it, claiming his belly was already too full of war.[23]

Of the twenty-one planes that landed on the *Lexington*, only nine were hers. The *San Jacinto* also had her share of visitors during the night (including the wandering Japanese plane) and wound up landing ten aircraft. One Avenger deadsticked into the barrier and had to be jettisoned. She also had one of the few amusing moments during the recovery. Ensign John F. Caffey, from the *Lexington*, was among the many being waved off repeatedly. With his SBD almost out of gas, Caffey told his gunner, AOM2c Leo D. Estrada, to prepare for a water landing. Estrada doffed his chute and got his gear ready for a quick exit.

Shortly the Dauntless touched down and stopped. Estrada leaped from his cockpit to find himself face to face with an astonished *San Jacinto* sailor. Mastering the situation, Estrada told the seaman, "This water landing business isn't as bad as I thought it'd be."[24]

Caffey found that the light carrier's deck crew was not too knowledgeable about the SBD, which did not have folding wings. He was told to fold his plane's wings and he tried to explain that SBDs just were not built that way. "God damn it," the reply shot back. "Fold 'em anyway!"[25]

About 2020 the *San Jacinto* reported a Japanese plane, identified as a Val or Judy, in its landing circle. The plane was waved off three times because its tailhook was not down. "It is worthy of note," the flattop later reported, "that only the studied refusal of the pilot to lower his hook prevented his ship from capturing a wandering Jap 'Val' who thrice attempted to land on board."[26]

The *Princeton* had not launched any planes that afternoon, but offered to take aboard as many as she could. The offer was gratefully accepted and she wound up landing three Avengers. The last plane to land was VT-10's Lieutenant (jg) Lawton. He shut down his engine with twelve gallons of gas remaining. "It was a fairly exciting night," Lawton said.[27] Because more strikes against the enemy were anticipated the next day, Admiral Reeves approved the use of the three planes with *Princeton* crews if needed for these strikes.

By 2250 it was evident that no more planes would be landed. The destroyers, already busy, now took over with a will. There were lots of fliers in the water and, as Samuel E. Morison colorfully put it, the sea looked like "a meadow full of fireflies"[28] from the blinking of their waterproof flashlights. To add to the scene, a chirping sound floated across the water, caused by the whistles blown by the fliers. Destroyers darted here and there picking up soggy aviators. One of those rescued was Torpedo 8's skipper, Lieutenant Commander Musick. Musick had already ditched several days earlier and had been picked up by the destroyer *Hickox*. Running out of gas this time and again having to ditch, Musick was picked up by—the *Hickox*. As he was brought aboard, Musick saw painted on the ship's stack a caricature of himself. A sailor was already adding a hash mark under it for the second rescue.[29]

The attack on the Mobile Fleet had not cost the TF 58 many planes, but the long flight back and the night recovery had been disastrous. Six Hellcats, five dive bombers, and six Avengers had probably been lost in combat; seventeen more fighters, forty-two dive bombers, and twenty-three torpedo planes had been lost in deck crashes and ditchings. Of the 226 planes that had reached the Mobile Fleet, 99 had been lost— close to half of the attackers. Personnel losses were fortunately much less. On the 21st fifty-one pilots and fifty crewmen were rescued, while thirty-three more pilots and twenty-six crewmen were pulled from the water the next few days. Thus, only sixteen pilots and thirty-three crewmen had been lost, along with two deck officers and four ship's enlisted men. These were sad losses, but nothing compared to what could have been, if every effort had not been exerted to rescue the downed airmen.

chapter 8

Frustrating Victory

THE RECOVERY OF TF 58's PLANES had taken almost four hours, and during this time the force had to steam east at 22 knots. When TF 58 finally came back west it was making only 16 knots in order to rescue as many fliers as possible, and was heading almost due west. Since the Mobile Fleet was heading northwest at 20 knots, TF 58 was losing ground.

The search for Ozawa's ships went on, however. The Americans had no way of yet knowing that the *Shokaku*, *Taiho*, and *Hiyo* had gone down, but figured there had to be cripples to go after. A report received at 0130 on the morning of 21 June from a VP-16 PBM tended to confirm this point. The plane told of shadowing many ships, some of them trailing oil, at 16°15′N, 133°05′E at 2305. A few minutes after receiving this message Admiral Mitscher ordered deck-load strikes readied for launch as soon as possible after dawn.

On the afternoon of the 20th Bill Martin had proposed to Mitscher a night minimum-altitude attack on the Mobile Fleet using eight VT-10 snoopers, plus the Avengers recovered from the afternoon strike. It was planned to launch two snoopers at midnight, followed by the remaining planes at 0200. Mitscher had approved the plan; but because of the confusion during the recovery and the fact that the five planes in the attack were now unavailable, he cancelled the strike shortly before 0200.[1] However, two of the *Enterprise*'s torpedo planes, carrying full bomb-bay tanks, were launched at 0230 to pick up the Mobile Fleet where the PBM had left off. Once again Lieutenant Nelson, with Lieutenant (jg) Moore flying wing, found the enemy. Following is Nelson's report of the mission:

Two snoopers were originally scheduled to go out . . . with belly tanks to find and shadow their retreating fleet, and aid an approved night bombing attack by VT-10.

Because of confusion of planes of the previous evening strike returning at night, take-off time was postponed. We busied ourselves perfecting plans, trying to think of every detail to mutually aid each other in the event of plane equipment failure, how to report satisfactorily what would be seen or picked up by radar, the use of extra flares and floatlights we would carry to illuminate for identification, leading in attacking planes, or turning the Jap fleet and slowing their withdrawal.

Word finally came to man planes about 0030. . . . Our best and only enemy position was: 1900, Lat. 15-30N, 133-05E. As no course and speed was known, I decided to advance that 100 miles on 270 was an average possible retirement course. . . . Just as the catapult officer was about to wave us off, we were told to cut engines. In a few moments we were told to return to ready room. The night strike for VT-10 was cancelled and the pilots who had been up all night were bitterly disappointed. At 0145, word was passed that snoopers would go out immediately, and a strike launch about 0500. Just before take-off a note was brought to our planes reading "Saipan snooper now reports enemy fleet at 16-15N, 133-05E, course 180, speed 15, at 2330K, 20th." This corroborated a report given us in ready room half an hour earlier about snooper picking up a "suspicious ship trailing oil" in that direction. I did not have time to plot or rework our course prior to take-off at 0230. At 0235 we departed formation. In a few minutes, Moore called on VHF with a (coded) new position of enemy which my radioman (decoded) as 16-30N, 132-48E, course 330, which the ship had sent. . . . We held our original track while I replotted a course to this latest position 40 miles advanced; a course 295°, 252 miles from our 0305 position when we turned. We were flying blacked out, no moon, no horizon, hazy, sky .6 covered by scuddy clouds getting worse toward the target forcing us to stay below 1500 feet, whereas I wanted to get higher for longer range radar pickup. Before leaving the ship, the call of the PBM snooper 8V211 was given us, his frequency 3755, and that he intended to stay on station until 0230. At about 0330 I tried desperately to raise him by both voice and CW hoping to get some further report. We received no answer, but I want to say he did a fine job and his reports helped us considerably in picking up the Jap fleet.

I expected to intercept about 0440; I began climbing slowly about 0435. Moore and I had been in good VHF communication up to this time. Suddenly he did not answer back and my gunner lost sight of him as we entered a cloud. I was very worried thinking he might have gotten vertigo so I descended to the water within five minutes, dropped a smoke light, turned on all my plane lights and started searching for any evidence of him on the water. I called him on VHF and 6420 continually telling him to return to our 0440 position, what steps I was taking to find him, and that I would keep looking for him for about 45 minutes. I even tried to tell him how to continue our search to cover more area as we were separated anyhow. I dropped several more smoke lights and in my searching for Moore ran across an oil slick wake running 300° which I mentally noted knowing there would be good hunting on the end of it. Finally as I was about to give up hope, at 0512 Moore joined up. He reported that during his search for me his radarman had picked up blips. Another hectic period ensued wherein we lost and found the blips several times. We then proceeded up the oil wake about 10 minutes and again got echoes 90° starboard about 16 miles. Knowing attack planes might be enroute we dropped smoke light, plotted and sent this report about 0530, "First enemy force time 0522K, Long. 131-35E, Lat. 17-15N, 6 medium, heavy oil wake course 300. We will search further for other forces." As the sky was beginning to lighten we proceeded toward our radar contact and saw DDs (6). Then this report was sent, "Correction Long. 138-03E, Lat. 17-30N, course 320, speed 20, 6 DD's, 1 lagging, oil wake from another group will report further HF." Neither of these CW reports seem to have been received by the ship.

We then turned left to angle toward the oil slick when I saw the CA group ahead of the DD group. Again I started toward our slick when ahead about 10 miles appeared the CV force on about 030(T). After a few minutes contemplating this awesome sight I looked to the left (south) about 10 miles and beheld the BB group on course 300° at about the point where the carrier oil wake turned. It was about 0605 by this time. We found ourselves in the center of the diamond described in "A." We orbited around clouds, alert for air opposition, replotting our position, and sent in amplifying reports. Although I only saw the BB shoot at us, the crew report DDs in the CV formation also fired. At one time a DD between us and CVs started laying smoke screen of brownish smoke in expectation of our coordinated attack, no doubt, but ceased after about 500 yards. We took departure at 0655, as I thought there were a few planes on the stern of the rear (leaking) CVL and they seemed to be turning into the wind, and further delay seemed to be stretching our luck.

Further attempts at identification beyond that given in "A" would lead to seeing pink elephants, except to say that all the CVLs looked alike, low, long, no appreciable difference in length, and no apparent distinguishing features between them, and no apparent open spaces between hull and deck either fore or aft. The cruisers we are agreed were heavy from massed superstructure characteristics. The BB identification is positive, the *Yamoto*s looking a great deal like recognition sketches and our own *Iowa* class. When last seen the CVLs were heading into a heavy rain squall.
. . . Along about 0730 I began sending in amplifying reports on voice

(6740) and also began hearing VHF from Rebel 1, (*Bunker Hill* VF). We then repeated our reports on VHF through Rebel 1 and Rebel 32 who acknowledged and retransmitted to our forces. 81 Sniper's call to us was heard and he picked up our transmissions. Even a greater disappointment than that we did not have a couple of bombs in place of half of our belly tank gas, was the realization that our striking planes would not be able to reach those sitting duck targets. We heard a Rebel plane call base "enemy position out of range we will carry out alternate plan."

About 0820 started climbing to 5000 feet for YE signal and began sweating when 0830 and 0840 passed without results. Finally about 0850 the YE was picked up. Arrived over base at 0915; landed at 1010 exhausted, with about 150 gallons left, having started with 605."[2]

As Nelson and Moore looked for the Japanese, Mitscher radioed Spruance, "With wind to easterly, it will not be possible to close enemy at option speed greater than 15 knots. Enemy appears to be escaping northwest with idea of fueling. Some damage done. Yesterday, antiaircraft fire extremely heavy and accurate. Many planes damaged. We hope to find a few crippled ships today."[3]

Between 0545 and 0615 the task groups launched deckload strikes, with the Hellcats carrying 500-pound bombs. The pilots were told to fly about 300 miles and if finding nothing, return rather than risk water landings again. And nothing is what they found, for Ozawa's ships were at least 70 miles farther to the northwest by this time. Though Nelson sent the attackers a heartfelt "It's a beautiful day. I hope you sink them all,"[4] there was nothing the TF 58 planes could do.

At 0800, with his planes still looking for the enemy, but now with information gleaned from Nelson's reports, Mitscher gloomily told Spruance, "Report of special scouts equipped with special fuel tanks and without bomb load, the enemy heading northwest, speed 20 knots, distance 360 miles. Maximum range of plane with bomb load is 250 miles. Strike now in air ordered to hit cripples within range. If they go farther many of them will again make water landings. Air strikes cannot reach target at present range."[5]

Although sure there was now no chance to catch the enemy, Spruance decided to send TG 58.7 ahead to look for cripples while the rest of TF 58 followed searching for survivors of the action the night before. Task Group 58.2 joined forces with TG 58.7, minus the *Cabot* which went to TG 58.3 and the *Monterey* which went to TG 58.1. (Both carriers rejoined TG 58.2 the next day.) The combined task groups did not proceed with great haste westward, however. Fuel for TG 58.7's destroyers was urgently needed, so these ships were topped off, starting after noon. Not until 1516 was a course of 280 degrees resumed.

While little Japanese air activity was evident throughout the day, a few snoopers did make appearances. *Cowpens* planes downed one Betty, while seven *Belleau Wood* fighters, returning from the abortive search/strike, ganged up on another of the twin-engined bombers and sent it cartwheeling into the water. The cruiser *Vincennes* picked up another kind of snooper when she reported capturing three Japanese carrier pigeons. Unfortunately for the intelligence officers, the birds were not carrying any messages. The cruiser did not report the fate of the pigeons.

More searches flown in the afternoon again failed to turn up anything, and it was now obvious that the enemy had gotten away. As the day wore on, TF 58 approached the area of the battle the day before. To a casual observer flying high over the Philippine Sea, it might not have appeared that a naval battle had been fought here during the last couple of days. But, though the sea had scoured much of itself clean, there were signs. If this observer looked closer he might have seen clots of oil clinging tenaciously to the surface of the water, some areas of debris, and, here and there, yellow specks in the water—fliers in life jackets and rafts. Rescue efforts began immediately and continued for several days, with a number of aviators (including McLellan and his crew and Brown's crew) being picked up.

Task Force 58 suffered a number of operational losses during the rescue phase, but most crews were picked up. One who was lost was the *Lexington*'s Ensign William J. Seyfferle. Seyfferle had flown all the way to the Mobile Fleet and back on the 20th, landing on another carrier during the madhouse around TF 58. Now the next day, he was returning to his ship. As he settled into the groove for the approach, his plane suddenly went into a spin and slammed into the water. Only a patch of foam marked the spot. There was another tragedy that evening when a PBM not showing any IFF began to approach TG 58.1. Destroyers of DesDiv 92 opened fire and brought the plane down. There were no survivors.

At 1920 on 21 June Admiral Spruance issued orders that if the last search of the day did not spot anything, TF 58 would retire. Nothing was seen and at 2050 the task force turned east and speeded up to 18 knots. At the time the task force began its retirement, TG 58.7 had reached 133 55'E to become the westernmost American unit.

Meanwhile, in hurrying northwestward the Japanese had also launched a pair of small searches to their rear, with equally negative results. As Ozawa led the Mobile Fleet toward Okinawa, he called in his chief of staff, Captain Toshikazu Ohmae, to record his letter of resignation to Admiral Toyoda. Ozawa wrote his superior that he regretted he had not led his forces to victory, but his own "inadequacies" and the lack of training for his aircrews had been a big factor in the defeat. Toyoda refused to consider Ozawa's request and Ozawa remained to serve, along with his carriers, as a sacrificial lamb at the battle of Leyte Gulf.[6]

The Mobile Fleet anchored in Nakagasuku Wan, Okinawa, on the afternoon of the 22nd. Survivors from the *Hiyo* and *Taiho* were transferred to the *Zuikaku*, while those from the *Shokaku* were taken to the *Maya*. At 0515 on 23 June A-GO was terminated. The carriers, plus the *Haruna* and *Maya*, went to Japan for repairs, while most of the other vessels returned to Singapore.

After it turned back, TF 58 headed for a fueling rendezvous with TG 50.17 some 220 miles to the east. Fueling was begun as soon as possible on the afternoon of the 23rd and was completed the next day. Following the fueling Spruance took the *Indianapolis* and the ships borrowed from TF 52 back to Saipan. Task Force 58 would go back to Eniwetok in bits and pieces, for a fully deserved rest. Task Group 58.2 was the first to head back, while TGs 58.3 and 58.4 remained off the Marianas until the first days of July, supporting the operations on Saipan and Tinian. Task Group 58.1 was ordered to hit Pagan on the way back to the Marshalls. Clark, though willing to do this, had bigger things in mind. Not satisfied with the pounding that his and Harrill's groups had given Iwo Jima, Clark asked Mitscher on the 23rd for permission to strike Iwo Jima again. Mitscher quickly gave his permission and "Operation Jocko" was on.

Clark's carriers struck Pagan on the afternoon of the 23rd. Little of value was found there but the deadly antiaircraft fire knocked one Hellcat out of the sky. *Bataan* pilots had a profitable afternoon, however, bagging four Zekes and a Betty on the last CAP of the day.

After striking Pagan, TG 58.1 turned north for the run to Iwo Jima. In the path of the group bobbed a tiny raft carrying an American pilot shot down on 13 June. Lieutenant Commander Bob Price, the *Cowpens* air group commander, had survived in his cramped raft, living on a few fish and sparse water. Now, on the 23rd, the *Boyd* spotted his raft and crept in so quietly that Price did not see her until she was only 300 yards away. He was soon aboard the destroyer and just as quickly aboard the *Hornet*. Rapidly regaining lost weight, Price returned to command of Air Group 25 on 6 July. (Tragically, Bob Price had only five more months to live. On 18 December he was washed overboard from the *Cowpens* and lost when Halsey's Third Fleet stumbled into the path of a typhoon.)

Clark's foray against Iwo Jima was well timed. Sitting on the Iwo and Chichi Jima airfields were 122 aircraft waiting for the word from Kakuta to move to the Marianas. At 0600 on the 24th, TG 58.1 was about 235 miles southeast of Iwo Jima. The day was cloudy with scattered showers. From the *Hornet*'s, *Yorktown*'s, and *Bataan*'s decks rose fifty-one Hellcats, each laden with 500-pound bombs. The *Belleau Wood* supplied the CAP and ASP chores for the group.

The Japanese were not fooled this time, having snooped Clark's group earlier; they were waiting for the Hellcats. But the warning did them little good. Admiral Sadaichi Matsunaga sent almost sixty fighters and even a few bombers of his 27th Air Flotilla to intercept the Americans. The two forces collided about halfway between Iwo Jima and TG 58.1. All but four of the Americans jettisoned their bombs and joined the fight. The four pilots who kept their bombs proceeded to Iwo Jima, where they dropped them on the airfield.

The Japanese defenders were generally inexperienced but their ranks were leavened with a scattering of veterans, including a one-eyed fighter pilot named Saburo Sakai. (Sakai had lost his right eye in combat over Guadalcanal; now his experience was needed so badly that he was in combat again. He survived the war to become Japan's greatest living ace with sixty-four confirmed victories.) Sakai was amazed at the speed and maneuverability of the Hellcats, but that did not stop him from throwing himself into the fight. Sakai, who claimed several aircraft himself, believed his friends had also done well.[7] But when the fracas was over, the 27th Air Flotilla had lost twenty-four Zekes and five Judys. The TG 58.1 group had lost only six planes. Seventeen *Bataan* fighters had a good workout, claiming seventeen kills and three probables, but losing two pilots. Now without bombs, the remaining fighters returned to their ships.

The Hellcats arrived over TG 58.1 in enough time to get into another fight. Along with the abortive interception, Matsunaga had sent two strikes against Clark's ships. The first wave of twenty torpedo planes was annihilated by the CAP and ships' fire. At one point two *Belleau Wood* pilots chased a Kate down through the black puffs of antiaircraft fire to finally splash it in the middle of the formation.

Nine Jill and nine Judys, escorted by twenty-three Zekes, made up the second attack. They fared somewhat better than the first group. Only ten Zekes and seven Jills were lost, nine of these to the *Bataan* fliers. VF-50's skipper, Lieutenant Commander R. S. Lemon, got one of the Jills in this afternoon attack but was himself missing after the fight. When the Japanese fliers returned to Iwo Jima they reported, "The results were vague and the target was not sighted."[8] Obviously, the Americans didn't think the results were vague. Following these attacks Clark released the *Baltimore*, *McCall*, and *Helm* to proceed to Eniwetok. At 1900 the rest of TG 58.1 turned for Eniwetok. Matsunaga, however, had kept a few planes in the area all day, and when five small attacks occurred between 2142 and 2305, Clark recalled the cruiser and her escorts. Then, when things finally calmed down, Clark was able to take all his ships to the Marshalls, anchoring there on the 27th.

As the sounds of gunfire faded from the waters of the Philippine Sea, another battle—this one with words—flared up.

The outcome of the battle left both sides with a bitter taste in their mouths—the Japanese, not surprisingly, because they had lost the battle; the Americans because the bulk of the Japanese fleet had escaped. Admiral Ozawa had fought a good battle, but he had been operating with too many handicaps. His air units were especially green, and this was all too obvious when they were chewed up on 19 June. Ozawa had also been hurting for destroyers to flesh out the antiaircraft fire of his ships and to provide a better antisubmarine screen. This latter point was brought home forcibly to the Japanese when the *Taiho* was torpedoed out from under Ozawa by the *Albacore* and the *Shokaku* sunk by the *Cavalla.*

"It is admitted that the antisubmarine defense (especially during a battle) should be re-examined," the Japanese commented afterwards. "Since a battle of a fleet is now mainly carried out by the aerial battle by its planes, the fleet is frequently staying in the same combat area to launch or receive the planes. Therefore, the antisubmarine defense must be carried out more strictly than ever before. In spite of this situation the fleet observes practically no other precaution than posting lookouts for submarines in a circular fleet formation, and cruises unconcerned at a high speed with the blind trust that the submarine danger is not much to worry about. This is indeed a serious misconception which makes us really worried."[9]

This report went on to mention that the three carriers lost had been sunk by submarines (erroneous in the *Hiyo*'s case for she had been torpedoed by the *Belleau Wood* aircraft, and had sunk following internal explosions) and that antisubmarine measures needed to be tightened up, possibly incorporating a small carrier specifically for these operations.

Nevertheless, it appears that the Japanese failed to heed the recommendations in "Impressions and Battle Lessons (Air) in the 'A' Operation." Effective antisubmarine warfare continued to elude them the rest of the war. Even worse than their antisubmarine tactics during the battle were the operations of their own submarines. In this area the Japanese suffered a complete debacle.

"During the operation No. A," the Japanese said, "enemy sub-marines were sighted, yet our submarines engaged in the battle very little, out of proportion to damages done to them. This was admittedly due to lack of improvement in the radio instruments of submarine detection at the base, while the enemy submarines were equipped with improved radars. Furthermore, in order to avoid confusion among our submarines, their field of operation was restricted to the water east of the line joining the archipelago. This was very regrettable. It would admittedly have been better, if the submarines had not been subjected to restriction to the operational field and ordered about where to go according to the development of the battle."[10] Unfortunately for them, Japanese submariners throughout the war were hampered by the lack of true strategic goals. Thus, their operations were ineffective and, except for early successes, their attacks on U.S. fleet units were general-ly lackluster.

But the Japanese had excelled in long-range search. Throughout the battle their search efforts continually outshone those of their American counterparts. Ozawa, knowing Spruance's innate caution and figuring that Spruance would tie his force to Saipan, held his ships out of the U.S. search planes' range while his long-legged searchers pinpointed the enemy's position. Except for two errors in plotting on 19 June which led to some abortive missions, Ozawa's fliers were reasonably accurate in their position reports.

But the A-GO plan fell apart completely when Ozawa had to use his ill-trained air groups. They were incapable of fighting a major engage-ment that early in their air-group life. Then, the idea of shuttling planes between the Mobile Fleet and Guam was an idea built of sand, which crumbled in reality. The A-GO planners labored under the false assumption that the Americans would be tied up elsewhere and would allow the Japanese to complete the circuit with impunity. Also a very important part of the plan was the use of land-based planes to attack the enemy fleet. This overly-ambitious portion of A-GO was thrown into almost complete disarray in the first few days of action. Later attacks by the remaining planes accomplished little while losing more of the valuable aircraft.

Admiral Kakuta's glowing, but totally false, reports of aircraft avail-able and safe bases on Guam, plus reports of great damage to TF 58, played a not inconsiderable part in the Japanese defeat. If Kakuta had been honest, Ozawa might have changed his tactics, perhaps sending his strikes out in larger numbers in hopes of breaking through the U.S. defenses in greater mass. Whether new tactics would have worked is debatable, but Ozawa might not have lost so many of his valuable pilots.

In the end, Kakuta must be assigned much of the blame for the disaster that enveloped the Japanese.

Did the Japanese have a choice in fighting or not fighting this battle? Not really. Although a delay would have been beneficial to the air groups, the odds were mounting daily against the Japanese. Any war of attrition could only go against them and, therefore, a "decisive" battle where they could destroy the offensive power of the U.S. Navy—the carriers of TF 58—seemed to be the only way to slow the American juggernaut. Finally, the Marianas were an important part of the inner defense line, an area that required the strongest defense measures.

While the Japanese were upset over the outcome of the battle, they might have been very surprised if they had known the feelings of the victors, who were no less upset about the results. A feeling of frustration swept through TF 58 immediately after the battle. It was obvious that Japanese airpower had been rudely handled. Not so obvious, however, was how much damage had been done to the enemy's ships. The *Hiyo* had been counted sunk, but the fate of the other carriers was still unknown. The *Shokaku* and *Taiho* had not been seen to go down by their attackers. Also, pilot reports could not be considered as the final word on damage to the ships. So there were still at least six, and maybe as many as eight, carriers available to the Japanese.

In his action report Mitscher regretfully concluded, "The enemy escaped. He had been badly hurt by one aggressive carrier strike, at the one time he was within range. His fleet was not sunk."[11]

Admiral Montgomery was blunter. "Results of the action were extremely disappointing to all hands," he wrote, "in that important units of the enemy fleet which came out in the open for the first time in over a year and made several air attacks on our superior force, were able to escape without our coming to grips with them. It is true that our troops on Saipan were well screened and protected against the enemy surface force, but it is considered unfortunate that our entire strength was deployed for this purpose until too late to prevent the enemy's retirement."[12]

Back at Pearl Harbor many on the CinCPac staff harbored feelings of dissatisfaction, too. Admiral Nimitz never criticized Spruance's actions in the Philippine Sea, but he also must have felt a twinge of disappointment. Some of Nimitz's subordinates, however, were harsh in their statements about Spruance, particularly if they leaned toward aviation. Many of these people felt that if an aviator (which Spruance was not) had been in charge, the Japanese would have suffered tremendous losses. Much of the criticism was just unjustified, but some was stingingly relevant.

Did Spruance blunder in the Philippine Sea? Did he take too cautious an approach—an approach that wasted the overwhelming superiority of his forces? It is this observer's belief that he did; and because the majority of the enemy's ships (including the all-important carriers) were permitted to escape, a confrontation with nearly tragic consequences for the Americans was allowed to take place, in the Battle for Leyte Gulf.

To understand fully Spruance's handling of TF 58 off the Marianas (for it was he, not Mitscher, calling the tactical shots),[13] we need to go back to 1942 and Midway. When Halsey became ill just before that battle, he recommended the brilliant Spruance to command the *Enterprise/Hornet* group. Admiral Frank Jack Fletcher was to be in tactical command of the entire operation. Spruance, a "big gun" man fresh out of a cruiser command and "knowing only vaguely the fine points of carrier-group command,"[14] inherited Halsey's staff, led by the exceptionally knowledgeable, but also exceptionally temperamental, Captain Miles Browning. Midway was Spruance's battle, not Fletcher's, and the decisions he made there led to that great victory. In his biography of Admiral Spruance, Thomas B. Buell shows that Spruance made the decision to attack the Japanese carriers on his own.[15] However, it should be noted that this decision most likely was based upon strong advice from his aviation-oriented staff.[16]

Spruance's stay with the carriers was short. His command at Midway, though brilliant, was a fluke and he never again was *intimately* involved in the "nuts and bolts" aspects of carrier operations. Following Midway Spruance went to CinCPac as Nimitz's chief of staff. There his gifted and analytical mind was put to good use planning future operations. Unfortunately, at a time when the carrier was becoming the major weapon of the Navy, and the battleship had begun a slow slide to oblivion, Spruance apparently never took the time or never really understood the need to become conversant with carrier operations. Perhaps his success at Midway unduly shaped his conception of the way carrier operations and tactics should be handled.

From his job at CinCPac Spruance moved to Commander Central Pacific Force. In this capacity during the Gilberts operations in November 1943, his inherent caution led him to restrict carrier activities to a limited area around the islands. Not being as mobile, the carriers were needlessly exposed to enemy air and submarine attacks and suffered unwarranted damage in the operation. In particular, the *Independence* was torpedoed and put out of action for several months. The fast carriers could have been more useful with greater freedom of action, beating down Japanese airpower in the Marshalls.

By the time June 1944 rolled around, Spruance (as Commander Fifth Fleet) should have had ample opportunity to observe and take notice of carrier tactics in the Gilberts, Marshalls, Truk, and other operations. The somewhat "free-wheeling" nature of these actions, however, did not lend themselves to Spruance's own character. Thus, when the Japanese sortied to fight in the Philippine Sea, Spruance, a tidy and cautious man, was not about to fight a battle that possibly involved taking risks; his battle would be like the man—tidy and cautious.

Spruance's staff might have had some effect on him, but they were too homogenous. Most of them were surface sailors like Spruance, and their thought processes ran right alongside their commander's. Burke believes this may have been an elemental error in Spruance's command.[17] A little healthy disagreement from those with different outlooks might have been beneficial.

Samuel Eliot Morison states in his semi-official history of the U.S. Navy during the war that Mitscher's only responsibility was to TF 58, while Spruance's responsibilities were greater—that of the entire operation, including TF 58, the troops, and transports. Therefore, Spruance had to play it close to the vest in order to protect his mission, the securing of the Marianas. Apparently Mitscher's only worry was the enemy carrier force that "menaced" his own vessels.[18]

Morison's interpretation is fine up to a point; obviously Spruance had the greater responsibility. But does greater responsibility necessarily go hand in hand with greater caution? Morison also seems to place more importance on the danger to the American carriers than did Mitscher or even the Japanese. The very tactics the Japanese used shows their wariness of the American flattops. They knew the shortcomings of their fliers. On the other hand, Mitscher realized his fliers and planes were better than most of their opponents, and his TF 58 gunners had gotten good practice in previous months shooting Japanese planes out of the sky. Task Force 58 clearly was *the* force with which to contend.

"I think that going after the Japanese and knocking their carriers out would have been much better and more satisfactory than waiting for them to attack us," Admiral Spruance told Morison some years after the battle, "but we were at the start of a very important and large amphibious operation and we could not afford to gamble and place it in jeopardy. The way Togo waited at Tsushima for the Russian fleet has always been in my mind. We had somewhat the same basic situation, only it was modified by the long-range striking power of the carriers."[19]

But the Philippine Sea was not Tsushima. Those carriers that Spruance mentioned had changed the nature of naval warfare; that "long-range striking power" meant that one could not sit and wait. Carriers were meant to be mobile and aggressive, not static and passive as they were too often in the Philippine Sea.

Spruance was also unduly concerned with a flank attack (a favorite gambit of the Japanese, but one that could be countered) and the safety of the transports that were supposedly lying to off Saipan. He had apparently read the captured Japanese Z Plan and from it "assumed the Japanese were after Turner's transports."[20] Spruance was very confident that he could read the character of his opponent and divine his intentions. His confidence was misplaced. Ozawa, on the other hand, was much more skillful in guessing what Spruance would do and planning accordingly.[21] Spruance apparently missed in the Z Plan the far-from-new Japanese adherence to the theory of destroying the American carriers first.[22] Basically, the Japanese were still seeking a "decisive" battle with the American fleet, and the destruction of the transports, though important, was secondary to the battle with TF 58.

In Admiral King's memoirs it is said that, "King's first act on stepping ashore (at Saipan) was to tell Spruance that he had done exactly the correct thing with the Fifth Fleet in the Battle of the Philippine Sea, no matter what anyone else might say, especially since he had to remember that the Japanese had another fleet ready in the Inland Sea to pounce upon the many American transports that had not entirely discharged their cargoes at Saipan. Consequently King repeated to Spruance that his decision had been, in King's view, entirely correct, for which Spruance thanked him."[23]

But where, actually, were most of the transports that Spruance felt compelled to protect? Two hundred miles east of Saipan and completely out of the danger area![24] And, unfortunately unknown to Admiral Spruance because he had not been conveyed General Holland Smith's optimism, the transports probably would not have been needed en masse for the two days it took to fight the battle.[25]

And what of a flank attack? King must have known from intelligence reports that little of the remaining Japanese naval power was based in Japan. King's statement, therefore, must be taken with a grain of salt, and was probably only intended to show Spruance that King still stood behind him in spite of any criticism. An attack around the southern end of the American forces was a better possibility, but it would have been more susceptible to detection by Admiralties-based PB4Ys, not to mention searchers from the carriers. If an attack did get through to

Saipan, the enemy would not find a defenseless force. A flanking move would most likely mean a divided force on the enemy's part; thus, neither unit would be at full strength. Even if the heavy forces (the *Yamato*, etc.) got through, they would be met by seven old battleships which, though outranged, could still inflict damage and would not be sitting ducks. Six escort carriers were also available. They carried about eighty Wildcat fighters and over fifty Avengers. If needed, the five escort carriers of the Southern Attack Force were nearby. Three of these carried Hellcats. The "jeep" pilots were not so well trained as their TF 58 counterparts, but as they proved later in the war, they could certainly hold their own.

Mitscher was not greatly concerned with a flanking attack, saying in his action report, "The decision was then reached that even if the Japanese chose to make such a suicidal attempt (a flanking attack) our forces could still attack the main Japanese fleet if it approached directly from the west or southwest. *It was believed that this decision was in accord with the desires of the Commander in Chief to fight a decisive battle.* [Italics added.] It appeared that there was nothing the Japanese could do with their fleet to affect seriously the occupation of the Marianas, so long as the Fast Carrier Task Forces were intact. Even the slight possibility of damage to our landing forces could be avoided if the Fast Carrier Task Forces did not go more than 300 miles from the Marianas without some definite indication as to the location of the main Japanese force, for we could attack a diversionary force as easily from a position 300 miles west (down wind) of the Marianas as we could from the near vicinity of Saipan."[26]

The portion of Mitscher's report regarding a decisive battle is crucial, for it is obvious that Mitscher believed that such a battle *should* be fought, and it is a fair assumption that in his message to Spruance and Mitscher, Nimitz believed that a decisive battle *would* be fought.[27] In a message to King prior to Forager, Nimitz said, "Your [message] concerns questions to which both Spruance and I have continuously given extensive consideration. Destruction of the enemy fleet is always the primary objective of our Naval Forces."[28] Spruance's obsession with the protection of the invasion fleet apparently obscured his understanding of this basic point.

If Spruance was still concerned with his defenses around Saipan in case of a flanking movement, why didn't he return all or part of TF 58's battleships to the island? Except as antiaircraft ships, the big vessels played little part in the battle. The battlewagons might have been better used split between the task groups (especially since Lee thought it unwise to fight a night surface action with his ships, and it would have been virtually impossible to fight a daylight battle with enemy planes present), or with some left behind at Saipan.

What if TF 58 had headed west on the 18th? Would Mitscher have been sticking his neck out for the Japanese cleaver? Doubtful, because of the tactics the Japanese actually used. At all times Ozawa wanted to keep TF 58 at arms' length (his own arms—his planes' range—having more reach than his enemy) and most likely would have retreated for a while to stay out of range. If Ozawa had retreated, then headed back east in two groups to try a flanking maneuver, he would have been crisscrossing an area of heavy American submarine activity, and might have lost more ships to these opportunistic hunters.

By heading west on the 18th, Mitscher might have just pushed Ozawa away from the Marianas and kept the Mobile Fleet from doing any damage at Saipan. In other words, a little aggressiveness on the part of the Americans would very likely have protected the Saipan beachhead just as easily, and more emphatically, than merely waiting for the first blow.

Finally, if TF 58 had headed west and closed the distance with the Mobile Fleet enough to launch a strike on the morning of the 19th, would the results have been less in TF 58's favor? Morison seems to think so, believing that massed Japanese planes and antiaircraft fire would have exacted a much greater toll of U.S. planes. Also, some U.S. carriers could have been sunk by the enemy. Then, with TF 58 occupied with the enemy ships, the Guam-based planes would have had a field day.[29]

American aircraft losses probably would have been greater than the combat losses they actually suffered, but would they have exceeded the eighty-two planes lost "operationally" following the 20 June attack? This is extremely doubtful. Japanese antiaircraft gunnery was not so effective as it could have been at this stage of the war (radar-controlled gunnery was still in its infancy in the Japanese Navy); the amount of flak thrown up by a unit like C Force often looked more awesome than it was. And as has been mentioned repeatedly throughout this book, the caliber of most of the Japanese fliers made heavy losses of U.S. planes unlikely. Conversely, the quality of American radar-controlled gunnery and aircraft intercepts would have made enemy attacks on TF 58 quite dangerous, and almost suicidal. (This was actually the case in the 19 June raids.) The enemy might have been able to hit a few carriers, but it is highly unlikely they would have sunk any. The *Essex*-class carriers were very tough, as were the light carriers, and American damage control techniques had improved considerably since the early days of the war.

An attack on the Mobile Fleet on the 19th would have been much better organized than the attack that was actually made. Being better organized, it would have had a greater chance of inflicting heavier damage on the enemy. Sunk or damaged carriers would have been of little use to the pilots in the air, and a flight to Guam past TF 58 would not have been easy. And this brings us to another point by Morison— the Guam-based planes. How many of these were there? Only about fifty. Almost all of the Marianas-based planes had been destroyed during the preinvasion operations. Yap, Palau, and Truk shuttled in replacements that created some problems on the morning of the 19th, but these were soon beaten down. If they had been left alone on the 19th, these fifty planes might have irritated TF 58, but being of such a small number (just a little over half of what just *one* fast carrier had), they can not be considered a major threat. Much of the activity over Guam on 19 June was caused by planes from Ozawa's force trying to reach the dubious safety of Orote field. Even these planes probably would not have reached Guam if Mitscher had attacked their ships that day.

"The greatest loss (to TF 58) was one of position," Land and Van Wyen concluded, "which even during the battle had not been too desirable. The Task Force was caught between two forces, being to the lee of the enemy's land bases and holding the enemy carrier force downwind. The necessity of heading into the wind for the rotation of fighters during the battle resulted in the relative position of the two carrier forces remaining about the same, both moving closer to the Japanese land bases as the battle progressed. At the end of the day the Japanese Fleet was still beyond the range of our carrier planes."[30]

On the 17th Spruance had issued his battle plan, saying, "Our air will first knock out enemy carriers. . . . Action against the retreating enemy must be pushed vigorously by all hands to insure complete destruction of his fleet." Aggressive sounding, but the next day he had already settled into a defensive posture. Instead of pressuring the Japanese, he was allowing himself to be pressured. It is hard to reconcile Spruance's aggressive ardor of one day, and his defensive pallor of the next. It is interesting to note that in his battle plan he gave no thought to an enemy flanking maneuver, considering his concern for that possible tactic. It also appears that Spruance, still the surface sailor, did not comprehend the possibility that the Japanese would use to advantage the range of their planes, and attempt to destroy or damage the U.S. ships before closing for a purely surface action.[31]

To Spruance a "fleet action" still meant battleship against battleship. This conception was not that unusual; there were still many in the U.S. Navy who thought that way. But naval warfare was changing, and a fleet action could now mean either a surface or an aerial action.[32] If Spruance had been more conversant with the aviation capability of his fleet perhaps he would have headed west for the "decisive" action.

Besides Spruance's fateful decision not to head west, there was another factor that hindered the Americans during the battle. This was the relatively poor performance of American searchers. Not just the carrier planes, but the land- and sea-based patrol planes fell far short of what was required. Carrier search endeavors had fallen by the wayside as the war continued, and the other patrol planes had been unable to take up the slack. Still, in the Philippine Sea the PBMs may have had some excuse. "The PBMs were buffeted about considerably at their open sea moorings," ComAirPac said later, "were attacked on the water by enemy planes, and on account of the rugged operating conditions, suffered radio and IFF failures which may have hindered their contact reporting as well as subjected them to attack by F6Fs and our own forces (which shot down two).[33]

The Battle of the Philippine Sea brought home hard the deficiencies of U.S. search techniques. Because of communications problems the PMB and PB4Y searches too often provided information to Spruance and Mitscher too late to be of use. Commenting on the initial contact report from Lieutenant Arle which was not received until eight hours later, ComAirPac said, "During this delay the Japs hit TF 58 first from a fleet of then unknown exact location. Their force, then out of round-trip range of ours, could possibly have been closed sufficiently to permit an early morning attack if the message had been received."[34]

Also in the matter of searches, Mitscher and his carrier admirals seemed to be operating under the idea that the battle was just another tactical exercise. Except in the last stages of the fight, little effort was expended in extending the range beyond the normal distances the search planes always flew. Eventually, using Avengers with bomb-bay tanks or utilizing the Hellcat's remarkable range, the distances were extended; but by that time it was too late. "Our carrier planes can reach the limits of their versatility, and inflict maximum damage on the enemy," ComAirPac stated after the battle, "only if their capabilities are realized and exploited by flexible minds. In 1942 'more range' was the cry of the entire carrier force; now that we possess the range, it should be used."[35] Task Force 58's commanders also did not seem to attach great importance to the fact that enemy carrier planes had been seen (and shot down) at fairly great distances from TF 58. There appears to have been no attempt to follow up on these sightings by sending more long-range searches to these areas.

Following the battle, numerous recommendations based on various aspects of the fighting began their slow way up the chain of command. Among the many recommendations were several complaints about the relatively poor performance of the torpedo planes in the shipping attack role. These complaints soon led to the Avengers' carrying of smaller bombs and a reversion back to their original weapon, the torpedo.[36] The various problems that surfaced during Forager were eventually overcome as U.S. forces slugged their way to Japan.

Though there had been problems in various areas, there were also some bright spots. One such "star" was the activity of the U.S. submarines. Constantly harassing the Japanese at Tawi Tawi, then reporting their movements; providing lifeguard service for downed pilots in the Marianas; and finally, topping it off by sinking two enemy carriers—in all these, the submariners proved invaluable. Working the other side of the street from the submarines, but equally important, were the U.S. antisubmarine units. With the *England* leading the way, they decimated the Japanese undersea forces and prevented them from being of any use during the battle.

However, in the final analysis, it was the pilots of TF 58 that broke the back of the Japanese in the Philippine Sea. In the Turkey Shoot they completely controlled the sky, and only small remnants of the enemy escaped to fight again. Then on the 20th they attacked the Mobile Fleet and, though not doing as much damage as was hoped, reduced enemy airpower to an insignificant factor, and battered some Japanese ships.

The Battle of the Philippine Sea was a great, though frustrating victory for the Americans. However, had Spruance been more aggressive, it could have been decisive and the Battle of Leyte Gulf might never have taken place. That it could have ended the war in a few days, as Jocko Clark thought,[37] is very unlikely considering the vast amount of territory Japan still controlled, the time period during which the battle was fought (mid-1944), and the state of Japanese civilian and military politics at that time.

Yet Operation Forager, in which the Battle of the Philippine Sea played such an important part, probably did help shorten the war. Repercussions in Japan over the Battle of the Philippine Sea and the occupation of Saipan were immediate. "Hell is on us," remarked one anguished Japanese official following the fall of Saipan.[38] Many knowledgeable Japanese agreed with this assessment of the situation. To these people, the war had become increasingly unfavorable to Japan, and Premier Hideki Tojo's government had drawn more and more

blame for the country's predicament. The loss of Saipan further in-
flamed the situation. Tojo made an effort to compromise by offering
some of his positions in the government to others, but was unable to get
anyone to accept. On 18 July 1944 (the day the fall of Saipan was finally
announced to the Japanese public) Tojo and his cabinet resigned. A
new cabinet was formed under General Kuniaki Koiso. Koiso vowed to
fight the Allies with all his power, but the fall of Saipan had allowed a
peace party to slowly gain strength in the inner circles of the Japanese
government.

In a militaristic government such as that in Japan during World War
II, the peace movement had to be circumspect, for many of the military
firebrands used assassination as a tool to eliminate opposition or dis-
sent. But as the war continued to go against Japan, the peace movement grew and would eventually prevail. Thus Forager and the Battle
of the Philippine Sea had played an enormously fateful role in the
internal development of the Japanese government.[39]

What had the Battle of the Philippine Sea cost the combatants during
the two days of action, the 19th and 20th? American losses were
remarkably light for the ferocity of the fighting. On the 19th TF 58 lost
three planes on search missions, one plane to an enemy fighter and
seven to flak over Guam, fourteen to enemy planes on interception
missions, and six operationally. With these thirty-one planes were lost
twenty-seven pilots and crewmen. While the next day's loss of aircraft
tripled, the number of fliers lost did not quite double. Only six planes
were shot down by flak, while eleven fell to the Zekes. Listed as operational losses were an incredible eighty-two planes; many of these
planes had run out of gas or made water landings. But with superlative
search and rescue work by TF 58 and the Saipan-based PBMs, only
sixteen pilots and thirty-three crewmen were lost.[40]

One high-ranking officer in TF 58 might be considered an indirect
loss. On 29 June Rear Admiral "Keen" Harrill was felled with acute
appendicitis and had to undergo surgery. He never returned to a
command in the fast carriers. Although his operation provided a
convenient excuse to ease him out of the carriers, the real reason was
Harrill's less-than-acceptable handling of his task group throughout
the battle and—unforgivable to some fire eaters—his apparent non-
aggressiveness.

While American losses were relatively light, Japanese losses were
overwhelming. When dawn broke on 19 June Ozawa had 430 carrier
planes and 43 floatplanes available. During the day he launched 355
carrier planes and 19 floatplanes. Only 130 of these returned to the
Mobile Fleet! Twenty-two planes had also been lost when the Taiho and

Shokaku went down. Some of the planes that did not return to the Mobile Fleet made it to Guam and Rota, where most were wrecked upon landing or were too damaged for further use. The next morning Ozawa could report only 100 carrier planes and 27 floatplanes operational. Many of the planes that had made it back to their ships were too shot up to use on the 20th. On 19 June the Japanese had lost about 300 fighters and bombers and 16 float planes!

Following the action on the 20th, Ozawa could report only 25 Zekes and 10 other carrier planes, plus 12 floatplanes, in operational condition. According to the Japanese, Ozawa lost only 19 carrier planes in combat on the 20th, but an amazing 46 carrier planes and 15 floatplanes operationally. It seems incredible that 61 Japanese planes could have been lost "operationally" during combat over their own fleet; Morison estimates that about 40 planes were shot down by the Americans.

No matter what the cause of the losses, Japanese naval airpower had suffered a blow from which it would never recover. On 19 and 20 June the Mobile Fleet lost 426 aircraft, plus about 50 more from Kakuta's land-based units. With these 476 planes went approximately 450 aviators. It was a terrible loss. When the Japanese sortied again in October to fight at Leyte Gulf, the carriers would be used only as decoys, for there were few planes or aviators to man them.[41]

When the sun went down in the Philippine Sea on 20 June it did not mark just the passing of another day. It also prefigured the end of Japanese aspirations in the Pacific. The two-day Battle of the Philippine Sea had shorn the Japanese Navy of its most potent weapon—its airpower. Now there would be no more great victories; only the slow, inexorable slide into the darkness of defeat. Japan's red sun was setting.

Appendix I

United States Units Engaged in the Battle of the Philippine Sea

(NOTE: This listing includes only those units actively participating in the battle, either through combat or in the search role. Although TF 58's composition changed several times following the sortie on 6 June 1944, this listing shows TF 58's organization for 19 and 20 June 1944. Asterisk (*) indicates killed in battle.)

Fifth Fleet
Admiral Raymond A. Spruance in *Indianapolis*

Task Force 58
(Fast Carrier Task Force)
Vice Admiral Marc A. Mitscher in *Lexington*

TASK GROUP 58.1
(Carrier Task Group One)
Rear Admiral Joseph J. Clark (ComCarDiv 13) in *Hornet*

(Carriers)

Hornet			Capt. W.D. Sample
Air Group 2		1 F6F-3	Comdr. J.D. Arnold
VF-2	36 F6F-3 (Hellcat)		Comdr. W.A. Dean
VB-2	33 SB2C-1C (Helldiver)		Lt. Comdr. G.B. Campbell
VT-2	14 TBM-1C (Avenger)		
	4 TBF-1C		Lt. Comdr. L.M.D. Ford
VF(N)-76			
(Det. B)	4 F6F-3N		Lt. R.L. Reiserer

	Yorktown	Capt. R.E. Jennings
	(Rear Admiral Ralph E. Davison, ComCarDiv 2, on board)	
	Air Group 1 1 F6F-3	Comdr. J.M. Peters
VF-1	41 F6F-3	Comdr. B.M. Strean
VB-1	40 SB2C-1C	Lt. Comdr. J.W. Runyan
	4 SBD-5 (Dauntless)	USNR
VT-1	16 TBM-1C	
	1 TBF-1C	Lt. Comdr. W.F. Henry
VF(N)-77		
(Det. B)	4 F6F-3N	Lt. A.C. Benjes
	Belleau Wood	Capt. J. Perry
	Air Group 24	Lt. Comdr. E.M. Link
VF-24	26 F6F-3	Lt. Comdr. Link
VT-24	6 TBM-1C	
	3 TBF-1C	Lt. R.M. Swensson
	Bataan	Capt. V.H. Schaeffer
	Air Group 50	Lt. Comdr. J.C. Strange
		USNR
VF-50	24 F6F-3	Lt. Comdr. Strange
VT-50	9 TBM-1C	Lt. Comdr. L.K. Swanson
	267 planes in TG 58.1	

(Support Unit)

Cruiser Division 10	Rear Admiral L.H. Thebaud
Boston	Capt. E.E. Herrmann
Baltimore	Capt. W.C. Calhoun
Canberra	Capt. A.R. Early

(Group Screen)
Capt. W. K. Phillips

Oakland	Capt. Phillips

Destroyer Squadron (DesRon) 46

Destroyer Division (DesDiv) 91	DesDiv 92
Izard	*Boyd*
Charrette	*Bradford*
Conner	*Brown*
Bell	*Cowell*
Burns	

DesRon 6 (less DesDiv 12)

DesDiv 11	
Maury	*Helm*
Craven	*McCall*
Gridley	

TASK GROUP 58.2
(Carrier Task Group Two)
Rear Admiral Alfred E. Montgomery (ComCarDiv 3) in *Bunker Hill*

(Carriers)

	Bunker Hill		Capt. T.P. Jeter
	Air Group 8	1 F6F-3	Comdr. R.L. Shifley
VF-8	37 F6F-3		Comdr. W.M. Collins
VB-8	33 SB2C-1C		Lt. Comdr. J.D. Arbes
VT-8	13 TBF-1C		
	5 TBM-1C		Comdr. K.F. Musick
VF(N)-76			
(Det. A)	4 F6F-3N		Lt. Comdr. E.P. Aurand
	Wasp		Capt. C.A.F. Sprague
	Air Group 14	1 F6F-3	Comdr. W.C. Wingard
VF-14	34 F6F-3		Lt. Comdr. E.W. Biros USNR
VB-14	32 SB2C-1C		Lt Comdr. J.D. Blitch
VT-14	15 TBF-1C		Lt. Comdr. H.S. Roberts
	3 TBF-1D		USNR
VF(N)-77			
(Det. C)	4 F6F-3N		Lt. J.H. Boyum
	Monterey		Capt. S.H. Ingersoll
	Air Group 28		Lt. Comdr. R.W. Mehle USNR
VF-28	21 F6F-3		Lt. Comdr. Mehle
VT-28	8 TBM-1C		Lt. R.P. Gift USNR
	Cabot		Capt. S.J. Michael
	Air Group 31		Lt. Comdr. R.A. Winston
VF-31	24 F6F-3		Lt. Comdr. Winston
VT-31	8 TBM-1C		
	1 TBF-1C		Lt. E.E. Wood
	244 planes in TG 58.2		

(Support Unit)

Cruiser Division 13	Rear Admiral L.T. Dubose
Sante Fe	Capt. J. Wright
Mobile	Capt. C.J. Wheeler
Biloxi	Capt. D.M. McGurl

(Group Screen)
Capt. G.W. Clark

San Juan	Capt. Clark
DesRon 52	

DesDiv 103	DesDiv 104
Owen	*Hickox*
Miller	*Hunt*
Tingey	*Lewis Hancock*
The Sullivans	*Marshall*
Stephen Potter	

DesRon 1
   DesDiv 1
      MacDonough   *Hull*
      Dewey

TASK GROUP 58.3
(Carrier Task Group Three)
Rear Admiral John W. Reeves, Jr., (ComCarDiv 4) in *Enterprise*
(Carriers)

	Enterprise		Capt. M.B. Gardner
	Air Group 10		Comdr. W.R. Kane
VF-10	31 F6F-3		Lt. Comdr. R.W. Schumann, Jr.
VB-10	21 SBD-5		Lt. Comdr. J.D. Ramage
VT-10	9 TBF-1C		
	5 TBM-1C		Lt. Comdr. W.I. Martin
VF(N)-101			
(Det. C)	3 F4U-2 (Corsair)		Lt Comdr. R.E. Harmer
	Lexington		Capt. E.W. Litch
	Air Group 16	1 F6F-3	Comdr. E.M. Snowden
VF-16	37 F6F-3		Comdr. P.D. Buie
VB-16	34 SBD-5		Lt. Comdr. R. Weymouth
VT-16	17 TBF-1C		
	1 TBM-1C		Lt. N.A. Sterrie USNR
VF(N)-76			
(Det. C)	4 F6F-3N		Lt. W.H. Abercrombie USNR
	San Jacinto		Capt. H.M. Martin
	Air Group 51		Lt. Comdr. C.L. Moore
VF-51	24 F6F-3		Lt. Comdr. Moore
VT-51	6 TBM-1C		
	2 TBM-1D		Lt. Comdr. D.J. Melvin
	Princeton		Capt. W.H. Buracker
	Air Group 27		Lt. Comdr. E.W.Wood*
VF-27	24 F6F-3		Lt. Comdr. Wood
VT-27	9 TBM-1C		Lt. Comdr. S.M. Haley USNR

228 planes in TG 58.3

(Support Unit)

Cruiser Division 12	Rear Admiral R.W. Hayler
Montpelier	Capt. H.D. Hoffman
Cleveland	Capt. A.G. Shephard
(Also Assigned to Support Unit)	
Birmingham	Capt. T.B. Inglis
Indianapolis	Capt. E.R. Johnson

(Group Screen)
Capt. R.C. Alexander

Reno   Capt. Alexander
DesRon 50
   DesDiv 99   DesDiv 100
     Clarence K. Bronson   Cogswell
     Cotten   Caperton
     Dortch   Ingersoll
     Gatling   Knapp
     Healey
   DesDiv 90
     Anthony   Terry
     Wadsworth   Braine

TASK GROUP 58.4
(Carrier Task Group Four)
Rear Admiral William K. Harrill (ComCarDiv 1) in Essex

(Carriers)

	Essex		Capt. R.A. Ofstie
	Air Group 15	1 F6F-3	Comdr. D. McCampbell
VF-15	38 F6F-3		Lt. Comdr. C.W. Brewer*
VB-15	36 SB2C-1C		Lt. Comdr. J.H. Mini
VT-15	15 TBF-1C		
	5 TBM-1C		Lt. Comdr. V.G. Lambert
VF(N)-77			
(Det. A)	4 F6F-3N		Lt. R.M. Freeman
	Langley		Capt. W.M. Dillon
	Air Group 32		Lt. Comdr. E.C. Outlaw
VF-32	23 F6F-3		Lt. Comdr. Outlaw
VT-32	7 TBF-1C		
	2 TBM-1C		Lt. D.A. Marks
	Cowpens		Capt. H.W. Taylor
	Air Group 25		Lt Comdr. R.H. Price
VF-25	23 F6F-3		Lt. Comdr. Price
VT-25	6 TBM-1C		
	3 TBF-1C		Lt. R.B. Cunningham USNR

163 planes in TG 58.4

902 carrier planes in TF 58

(Support Unit)

Cruiser Division 14   Rear Admiral W.D. Baker
Vincennes   Capt. A.D. Brown
Houston   Capt. W.W. Behrens
Miami   Capt. J.G. Crawford

(Group Screen)
Rear Admiral L.J. Wiltse

San Diego   Capt. L.J. Hudson

DesRon 12
    DesDiv 4†   DesDiv 23
      Lang   *Lansdowne*
      Wilson   *Case*
      Sterett   *Lardner*
      Ellet   *McCalla*
DesRon 23
    DesDiv 45   DesDiv 46
      Charles F. Ausburne   *Converse*
      Stanly   *Spence*
      Dyson   *Thatcher*

TASK GROUP 58.7
(Battle Line)
Vice Admiral Willis A. Lee Jr., (ComBatPac) in *Washington*

(Battleships)

Battleship Division (BatDiv) 6   Vice Admiral Lee
    Washington   Capt. T.R. Cooley
    North Carolina   Capt. F.P. Thomas
BatDiv 7   Rear Admiral O. M. Hustvedt
    Iowa   Capt. J.L. McCrea
    New Jersey   Capt. C.F. Holden
BatDiv 8   Rear Admiral G.B. Davis
    Indiana   Capt. T.J. Keliher
BatDiv 9   Rear Admiral E.W. Hanson
    South Dakota   Capt. R.S. Riggs
    Alabama   Capt. F.D. Kirtland

(Support Unit)

Cruiser Division 6   Rear Admiral C.T. Joy
Wichita   Capt. J.J. Mahoney
Minneapolis   Capt. H.B. Slocum
New Orleans   Capt. J.E. Hurff
San Francisco   Capt. H.E. Overesch

(Group Screen)

DesRon 45
    DesDiv 12   DesDiv 89
      Mugford   *Halford*
      Conyngham   *Guest*

†There has been some confusion over the identities of DesDivs 4 and 24. Actually, the two units traded designations on 20 June 1944. DesDiv 24 stayed in the Southwest Pacific and was not in the battle.

Patterson	*Bennett*
Bagley plus	*Fullam*
Selfridge	*Hudson*
DesRon 53	
DesDiv 106	
Yarnall	*Stockham* plus
Twining	*Monssen*

Long Range Search Planes Used In The Battle

(At Saipan)

	Ballard	Lt. Comdr. G.C. Nichandross USNR
VP-16	5 PBM-5 (Mariner)	Lt. Comdr. W.J. Scarpino
	(At Mokerang Field, Los Negros)	
VB-101	12 PB4Y (Liberator)	Comdr. J.A. Miller

Submarines Operating in Support of Forager

Task Force 17 Submarines

Vice Admiral Charles A. Lockwood

"Dunkers Derby" (Bonin Islands)

Gar	*Plaice*
Archerfish	*Swordfish*
Plunger	

"Convoy College" (Southeast and east of Formosa)

Pintado	*Tunny*
Pilotfish	

"Pentathlon" (West and southwest of the Marianas)

Albacore	*Finback*
Seawolf	*Stingray*
Bang	

"Speedway" (Ulithi and Philippines)

Flying Fish	*Seahorse*
Muskallunge	*Pipefish*
Cavalla	*Growler*

Seventh Fleet Submarines

Rear Admiral Ralph W. Christie

Southeast of Mindanao

Hake	*Paddle*
Bashaw	

Tawi Tawi

Harder	*Redfin*
Haddo	*Bluefish*

Luzon

Jack	*Flier*

Appendix II

Japanese Units Engaged in Operation A-GO, 1-20 June 1944

(Asterisk indicates man killed or ship sunk in battle.)

Mobile Fleet
Vice Admiral Jisaburo Ozawa in *Taiho*

"A" FORCE
Vice Admiral Ozawa

Carrier Division One   Vice Admiral Ozawa
  601st Naval Air Group   Lt. Comdr. Akira Tarui

*Taiho**

27 A6M5a	(Zeke)
27 D4Y1	(Judy)
18 B6N1	(Jill)
3 D4Y1c	(Judy)

*Shokaku**

27 A6M5a
27 D4Y1
18 B6N1
 3 D4Y1c

Zuikaku

27 A6M5a
27 D4Y1
18 B6N1
 3 D4Y1c
___

225 planes in "A" Force

(Force Screen)

Cruiser Division Five   Vice Admiral Shintaro Hashimoto
    Myoko   Haguro
              Destroyer Squadron 10 (less DesDiv 4)
           Rear Admiral Susumu Kimura in *Yahagi* (CL)

DesDiv 10   DesDiv 17
    Asagumo   Urakaze
    Tanikaze*   Isokaze
DesDiv 61
    Hatsuyuki   Shimotsuki
    Wakatsuki   Minazuki*
    Akizuki

"B" FORCE
Rear Admiral Takaji Joshima in *Junyo*

Carrier Division Two   Rear Admiral Joshima
    652nd Naval Air Group   Lt. Comdr. Jyotaro Iwami
                        Junyo
                   18 A6M5a
                    9 A6M5a (fighter-bombers)
                    9 D4Y1
                    9 D3A2 (Val)
                    6 B6N1
                        *Hiyo**
                   18 A6M5a
                    9 A6M5a
                   18 D3A2
                    6 B6N1
                        Ryuho
                   18 A6M5a
                    9 A6M5a
                    6 B6N1
                   ___
                   135 planes in "B" Force

(Force Screen)
        Nagato (BB)   *Mogami* (CA)
DesDiv 4
    Michishio
    Yamagumo   Nowaki
DesDiv 27
    Shigure   Hamakaze

Samidare   *Akishimo*
*Shiratsuyu**   *Harusame**
Hayashio

"C" or Van Force
Vice Admiral Takeo Kurita in *Atago*

Carrier Division Three   Rear Admiral Sueo Obayashi in *Chitose*
  653rd Naval Air Group   Lt. Comdr. Masayuki Yamagami

Chitose

6 A6M5b
15 A6M5b
3 B6N1
6 B5N2 (Kate)

Chiyoda

6 A6M5b
15 A6M5b
3 B6N1
6 B5N2

Zuiho

6 A6M5b
15 A6M5b
3 B6N1
6 B5N2

—

90 planes in "C" Force

—

450 planes available at start of A-GO

(Force Screen)

Battleship Division One   Vice Admiral Matome Ugaki
  Yamato   *Musashi*
Battleship Division Three   Vice Admiral Yoshio Suzuki
  Kongo   *Haruna*
Cruiser Division Four   Vice Admiral Kurita
  Atago   *Chokai*
  Takao   *Maya*
Cruiser Division Seven   Vice Admiral Kazutaka Shiraishi
  Kumano   *Chikuma*
  Suzuya   *Tone*

Destroyer Squadron 2 (less DesDiv 27)
Rear Admiral Mikio Hayakawa in *Noshiro* (CL)

DesDiv 31
  Asashimo   *Kishinami*
  Okinami

DesDiv 32
  Tamanami   *Hamakaze*
  Fujinami   *Hayanami**
  Shimakaze

Supply Forces
1st Supply Force
Oilers
  Hayusui   *Kokuyo Maru*
  Nichiei Maru   *Seiyo Maru**
Destroyers
  Hibiki   *Yunagi*
  Hatsushimo   *Tsuga*

2nd Supply Force
Oilers
  *Genyo Maru**   *Azusa Maru*
Destroyers
  Yukikaze   *Uzuki*

Submarine Force
Vice Admiral Takeo Takagi* on Saipan

I-5*	I-10*	I-38	I-41	I-53	I-184*	I-185*	RO-36*
RO-41	RO-42*	RO-43	RO-44*	RO-47	RO-68	RO-104*	RO-105*
RO-106*	RO-108*	RO-112	RO-113	RO-114*	RO-115	RO-116*	RO-117*

Base Air Forces
Vice Admiral Kakuji Kakuta* on Tinian

61st Air Flotilla
   121st Naval Air Group
      Tinian   10 D4Y1 (Judy)
      Peleliu   10 D4Y1
   261st Naval Air Group
      Saipan   80 A6M5 (Zeke)
   263rd Naval Air Group
      Guam   80 A6M5
      Yap   40 A6M5
   265th Naval Air Group
      Peleliu   40 A6M5
      Guam   15 A6M5
   321st Naval Air Group
      Tinian   15 J1N (Irving)

343rd Naval Air Group
   Tateyama   40 N1K (George)
521st Naval Air Group
   Guam   80 P1Y (Frances)
   Tinian   40 P1Y
523rd Naval Air Group
   Tinian   40 D4Y1
   Yap   40 D4Y1
761st Naval Air Group
   Peleliu   40 G4M (Betty)
1021st Naval Air Group
   Tinian   20 L2D (Tabby)
22nd Air Flotilla
   151st Naval Air Group
     Harushima   20 D4Y1
   202nd Naval Air Group
     Harushima   40 A6M5
     Mereyon   40 A6M5
   251st Naval Air Group
     Takeshima   20 J1N
   253rd Naval Air Group
     Takeshima   80 A6M5
   301st Naval Air Group
     Yokosuka   40 J2M (Jack)
   503rd Naval Air Group
     Kaedeshima   40 D4Y1
   551st Naval Air Group
     Harushima   80 B6N1 (Jill)
   755th Naval Air Group
     Guam   40 G4M
26th Air Flotilla
   201st Naval Air Group
     Davao   80 A6M5
   501st Naval Air Group
     Lasang   40 A6M5/D4Y1
   751st Naval Air Group
     Davao   40 G4M
23rd Air Flotilla
   153rd Naval Air Group
     Sorong   60 A6M5/D4Y1

732nd Naval Air Group
    Wasile   40 G4M
753rd Naval Air Group
    Menado   40 G4M
                                           ─────────
                                           1290 aircraft

(NOTE: Information on Japanese air strength is based on figures given in *Campaigns of the Pacific War* and represents assigned strength. Operational strength was actually much less. Morison estimates the actual strength in the Marianas-Palaus-Philippines-Bonins area in early June as only 540 aircraft.)

Appendix III

U.S. Air Operations on 19 June

I-Interceptions

TG	Carrier	Sqdn	Missions/ Sorties	Aborts	Number Engaging Enemy Aircraft
58.1	Hornet	VF-2	4/36		32
	Yorktown	VF-1	2/30	2	22
		VF(N)-77	1/1		1
	Bataan	VF-50	2/35		7
	Belleau Wood	VF-24	2/16		12
58.2	Bunker Hill	VF-8	3/26		24
	Wasp	VF-14	2/25		16
	Monterey	VF-28	3/21		19
	Cabot	VF-31	5/36		23
58.3	Enterprise	VF-10	2/24		14
	Lexington	VF-16	3/38	2	31
	San Jacinto	VF-51	5/25		10
	Princeton	VF-27	2/20	2	19
58.4	Essex	VF-15	4/42	2	37
	Cowpens	VF-25	2/22		13
	Langley	VF-32	1/16		4
Totals			43/413	8	284

(NOTE: Charts based on those in "Naval Air Operations in the Marianas" and squadron ACA reports.)

| Enemy Aircraft | | | | | | | U.S. Aircraft Lost | | |
Engaged	Dest.	Air Prob.	Dam.	Dest.	Ground Prob.	Dam.	AA	A/C	Ops
53	37	5	2					1	
36	32	5						2	
1	1								1
20	11	2							
35	10	3	6						
34	18	3	1			3		2	
14	11		4					1	
21	19								1
67	26	1	1						
19	19								
60	26	5			5				1
12	9	2						1	
44	29	6						2	
137	63	12						4	
11	9	3						1	1
2	2								
566	322	47	14		5	3		14	4

II-Bombing Missions

TG	Carrier	Sqdn	Missions/ Sorties	Aborts	Number A/C Attacking	Tons Bombs Dropped
58.1	Hornet	VF-2	2/20		8	
		VB-2	2/31	3	21	9
		VT-2	2/16	1	15	8.5
	Yorktown	VF-1	2/13			
		VB-1	2/24		24	20
		VT-1	3/12		12	3
	Bataan	VF-50	2/7		7	1
		VT-50	1/4		4	4
	Belleau Wood	VF-24	1/7		7	
58.2	Bunker Hill	VF-8	1/14		6	
		VF(N)-76	1/3		2	
		VB-8	1/16	1	15	11
	Wasp	VB-14	1/14		14	9.75
		VT-14	1/11	3	8	8
58.3	Enterprise	VB-10	1/11		11	5.5
		VT-10	1/10	1	9	9
	Lexington	VF-16	1/8		8	
		VB-16	1/17	1	16	8
	Princeton	VF-27	1/4			
58.4	Essex	VB-15	1/12	2	10	5
	Cowpens	VF-25	1/8		8	
Totals			29/262	12	205	101.75

Number Engaging Enemy A/C	Enemy Aircraft		Air		Ground			U.S. A/C Lost		
	Engaged	Dest.	Prob.	Dam.	Dest.	Prob.	Dam.	AA	A/C	Ops
5	30	15	1		1					
								2		
					4			3		
					2					
3	11	8							1	
								1		1
6	2	1		1						1
3	6	5	1		3					
					2			1		
4	1				1					
					1		5			
21	50	29	2	1	14	0	5	7	1	2

III-Search and Rescue Missions

TG	Carrier	Sqdn	Missions/ Sorties	Number Engaging Enemy Aircraft	Enemy A/C Engaged
58.1	Yorktown	VF-1	2/2	2	4
		VB-1	2/2		
58.2	Bunker Hill	VF-8	2/2	1	1
		VB-8	2/2	2	1
		VF(N)-76	2/2	2	1
	Wasp	VF-14	1/1	1	1
		VB-14	1/1	1	1
58.3	Enterprise	VF-10	1/1	1	1
		VF(N)-101	1/1	1	1
	Lexington	VF-16	7/7	7	15
		VT-16	7/11	4	5
58.4	Essex	VF-15	1/3	2	4
		VB-15	1/3	1	3
Totals			30/38	25	38

Enemy Aircraft			U.S. Aircraft Losses
Dest.	Air Prob.	Dam.	A/C
4			
1			
			1
1			1
		1	
1			
			1
		1	
14			
1	2	1	
4			
1	—	1	—
27	2	4	3

Appendix IV

U.S. Air Operations on 20 June: The Attack on the Mobile Fleet

TG	Carrier	Sqdn	Sorties	Aborts	Number Attacking Enemy Ships	Number Engaging Enemy Aircraft
58.1	Hornet	VF-2	15	1	14	1
		VB-2	14		14	1
		VT-2	8	2	6	
	Yorktown	VF-1	15	1	11	1
		VB-1	15	2	13	1
		VT-1	10	2	8	5
	Bataan	VF-50	10		6	4
	Belleau Wood	VF-24	8	2	2	3
		VT-24	4		4	2
58.2	Bunker Hill	VF-8	14		4	14
		VB-8	12		12	6
		VT-8	8		8	8
	Wasp	VF-14	16		16	11
		VB-14	12		12	5
		VT-14	7		7	1
	Monterey	VT-28	4		4	1
	Cabot	VT-31	4		4	2
58.3	Enterprise	VF-10	12		8	12
		VB-10	11		10	11
		VT-10	5		5	5
	Lexington	VF-16	11	2	9	2
		VB-16	16	1	15	15
		VT-16	7	1	5	6
	San Jacinto	VT-51	2		2	2
Totals			240	14	199	118

| Engaged | Enemy Aircraft | | | U.S. Aircraft Lost | | | Weapons Dropped | |
	Dest.	Prob.	Dam.	AA	A/C	Ops	Bombs (Tons)	Torp. (No.)
1		1				7	3	
2		1		1		11	9·75	
						2	2	4
1			1			3	2·75	
1						9	9·75	
5				2		4	3	5
17	4		3		2	1	1·5	
10	3	3			1	1	·25	
4			2	3				4
10	2	2	1			1		
5		2	1		2	9	9	
2			1			5		8
5	5				1	1		
5			2		1	10	9	
1						3	7	
2			1			1	4	
2			2			2	4	
20	7	1	1		1	1		
10						1	5	
12	1		1			4	4·5	
2	1		1		1	1		
21	2		8		1	2	12.5	
11	1		6		1	2	5	
4						1	2	
153	26	10	31	6	11	82	94	21

Notes

Chapter 1

1. Lt. Grace P. Hayes, "The History of the Joint Chiefs of Staff in World War II: The War Against Japan" (hereafter cited as Hayes) Vol. I, pp 142, 194; Maurice Matloff, *Strategic Planning for Coalition Warfare, 1943–1944* (hereafter cited as Matloff), p 186; Louis Morton, *Strategy and Command: The First Two Years* (hereafter cited as Morton), p 33.
2. Wesley Frank Craven and James Lea Cate, "The Army Air Forces in World War II" Vol. IV *The Pacific: Guadalcanal to Saipan, August 1942 to July 1944*, p XIV; John Miller, Jr., *Cartwheel: The Reduction of Rabaul*, p 1.
3. Hayes, Vol. I, p 142.
4. Major Carl W. Hoffman, *Saipan: The Beginning of the End* (hereafter cited as Hoffman), p 14.
5. Hayes, Vol. I, p 388.
6. Ibid; Samuel Eliot Morison, *History of United States Naval Operations in World War II*, Vol. VIII, *New Guinea and the Marianas* (hereafter cited as Morison), p 5.
7. Hayes, Vol. I, p 388.
8. E. B. Potter, *Nimitz* (hereafter cited as Potter), p 237; Morison, p 5.
9. Morton, p 589.
10. Hoffman, pp 14–15.
11. Potter, pp 237–238.
12. Morison, p 4; Morton, pp 457–460.
13. Potter, p 279.

14. Hoffman, p 15.
15. Commander in Chief U.S. Pacific Fleet and Pacific Ocean Areas, "Narrative and Appendix," p 110.
16. Ibid., pp 111–112; Matloff, p 186; Hayes, Vol. II, pp 7–8.
17. CinCPac/POA, "Narrative and Appendix," pp 111–112.
18. Ibid., p 112; Hayes, Vol. II, pp 13–14; Matloff, p 191; Morton; p 467, also see pp 447–452.
19. Miller, *Cartwheel*, pp 212–213; Morton, p 547.
20. Hoffman, p 15.
21. Matloff, pp 308–309; Hayes, Vol. II, p 103; Morton, p 596.
22. Hayes, Vol. II, p 24; Hoffman, p 15; Morison, p 6.
23. Potter, p 241.
24. Morison, p 6.
25. Hoffman, p 16.
26. Morison, p 7.
27. Potter, pp 242–243; Craven and Cate, *Guadalcanal to Saipan*, p 553.
28. Hoffman, p 17.
29. Matloff, pp 376–377; Morton, pp 602–603.
30. Hoffman, p 18.
31. Morton, pp 668–672; Hoffman, p 18.
32. Hoffman, p 18.
33. Ibid.; Granite, Serial 0004, p 7; CinCPac/POA "Narrative and Appendix," p 121.
34. Granite, Serial 0004, p 8.
35. Potter, pp 280–281; CinCPac/POA "Narrative and Appendix," p 126; Hayes, pp 170–171.
36. Potter, p 281.
37. Hoffman, p 19; Craven and Cate, *Guadalcanal to Saipan*, p 571.
38. Mafloff, p 455.
39. Potter, p 281.
40. Ibid.
41. Matloff, p 456.
42. Potter, p 283.
43. Ibid.
44. Hoffman, pp 19–20; Vice Adm. George C. Dyer, *The Amphibians Came to Conquer*, p 856.
45. CinCPac/POA "Narrative and Appendix," p 127.
46. Hoffman, p 19.
47. CinCPac Command Summary, p 2314.
48. Ibid., also see pp 2312-2314; Matloff, pp 458–459.
49. Hoffman, p 21.
50. Granite II Serial 00071, p 9.

Chapter 2

1. Paul S. Dull, *A Battle History of the Imperial Japanese Navy, 1941–1945* (hereafter cited as Dull), pp 95–98.
2. *Campaigns of the Pacific War*, pp 205, 221; Dull, p 302.
3. Clark G. Reynolds, *The Fast Carriers* (hereafter cited as Reynolds), p 160; W. D. Dickson, *The Battle of the Philippine Sea* (hereafter cited as Dickson), p 26.
4. *Campaigns*, pp 226–227.
5. Ibid., p 227.
6. Morison, p 219.
7. Ibid., p 217
8. Clay Blair, Jr., *Silent Victory*, p 625.
9. Escort Division 40 Action Report, Serial 08, 27 May 1944, p 11.
10. Ibid., p 18.
11. *Campaigns*, pp 209, 222–223.
12. Dickson, pp 45–46.
13. "Magic" Far East Summaries, 12 February 1944–18 September 1944, SRS 73, 75, 77.
14. Morison, pp 118–132; Dull, pp 302–303; Dickson, pp 48–53; "Magic" Summaries, SRS 79.
15. "Magic" Summaries, SRS 87.

Chapter 3

1. Fleet Adm. King and Walter Muir Whitehill, *Fleet Admiral King: A Naval Record*, p 491.
2. CTF 58 Action Report, Serial 00388, Enclosure B, p 4.
3. *Hornet* Action Report, Serial 0020, Enclosure D, p 1.
4. Lt. W. G. Land and Lt. A. O. Van Wyen, *Naval Air Operations in the Marianas* (hereafter cited as Land and Van Wyen), p b–11.
5. Philip A. Crowl, *Campaign in the Marianas*, p 72.
6. CTG 58.2 Action Report, Serial 00223, p 7.
7. VF-24 ACA Report No. 23–44.
8. *Yorktown* Action Report, Serial 0020, Enclosure C, p 2; *Essex* Action Report, Serial 0029, Part V, pp 3–4.
9. *Princeton* Action Report, Serial 0239, p 13.
10. VB-14 ACA Report No. 16.
11. *Lexington* Action Report, Serial 0217, Comments.
12. VT-16 ACA Report No. 37.
13. VT-1 ACA Report No. 2.
14. Morison, p 180; see Charles A. Lockwood and Hans C. Adamson, *Battles of the Philippine Sea*, pp 69–71, for a defense of this bombardment.
15. COMINCH Secret Information Bulletin No. 20, p 74–25.

16. Comdr. Edward P. Stafford, *The Big E*, p 328.
17. Ibid., p 324–330; Morison, pp 176–178.
18. VT-16 ACA Report No. 37.
19. VF-14 ACA Report No. 23.
20. *Stingray*, Report of Patrol No. 11, pp 10–12.
21. CTF 58 Action Report, Enclosure B, p 7.
22. Land and Van Wyen, p b-1.
23. Morison, p 253; Potter, p 296; W. J. Holmes, *Double-Edged Secrets*, pp 179–180, 182.
24. *Campaigns*, pp 221–224.
25. Reynolds, p 166, also see pp 161–169 for an excellent discussion of "Formalist" versus "Meleeist" tactics.
26. Ibid., pp 177–178.
27. Adm. J. J. Clark, with Clark G. Reynolds, *Carrier Admiral* (hereafter cited as Clark), p 163.
28. CinCPac Chrono Files, message 142355 Com5thFlt to CTG 58.4.
29. Lt. Kenneth Clayton, "Iwo Never Was a Pushover", p 48.
30. Reynolds, p 78.
31. Clark, p 167.
32. Ibid., pp 165–167; Reynolds, pp 181–182; Theodore Taylor, *The Magnificent Mitscher*, pp 212–213.

Chapter 4

1. "A-GO Operations Log, Supplement," No. 91, p 14.
2. CinCPac Chrono Files, message 131812 CTF 17 to all subs; E. B. Potter and Flt. Adm. Chester W. Nimitz, *The Great Sea War* (hereafter cited as Potter and Nimitz), p 350.
3. *Campaigns*, p 260; 1st Mobile Fleet Classified No. 1048, p 2.
4. Dickson, p 63.
5. John Toland, *The Rising Sun*, p 498.
6. CinCPac Chrono Files, message 151411 *Seahorse* to ComSubPac.
7. *Lexington* War Diary, Serial 0135, Enclosure A, p 2.
8. Morison, pp 202–203; Land and Van Wyen, p b-10; Crowl, *Campaign in the Marianas*, pp 98–99.
9. Reynolds, pp 168, 181.
10. Land and Van Wyen, p b-2.
11. CTF 58 Action Report, Annex E, pp 1–2.
12. Ibid., Enclosure B, pp 7–8; Burke Interview, pp 13–15.
13. CTF 58 Action Report, Enclosure B, p 8.
14. Ibid., Enclosure B, p 11.
15. Lt. Comdr. J. Bryan III and Philip Reed, *Mission Beyond Darkness* (hereafter cited as Bryan and Reed), p 14.

16. Dickson, p 221.
17. CinCPac Chrono Files, message 162204 ComSubPac to *Cavalla*.
18. *Cavalla* Patrol Report No. 1; CinCPac Chrono Files, message 171345 *Cavalla* to ComSubPac; Dickson, p 80; Burke, "Decision Not to Force an Action on the Night of 18–19 June," p 7.
19. CinCPac Chrono Files, message 171856 CTF 17 to all subs, message 180016 CTF 17 to specific subs.
20. CinCPac Chrono Files, message 171639 ComSubPac to *Cavalla*.
21. A-GO No. 90, pp 38–39.
22. CTF 58 Action Report, Enclosure B, pp 12–13.
23. Ibid., Enclosure B, p 14.
24. Com5thFlt Action Report, Serial 00026, p 5.
25. Thomas B. Buell, *The Quiet Warrior* (hereafter cited as Buell), p 265.
26. CTF 58 Action Report, Enclosure B, p 15.
27. Com5thFlt Action Report, Serial 00026, p 5.
28. Burke, "Decision Not to Force an Action . . .," p 7.
29. Burke Interview, p 19.
30. A-GO No. 91, p 20.
31. Burke, "Decision Not to Force an Action . . .," p 7.
32. Com5thFlt War Diary, Serial 00398, p 16.
33. Com5thFlt Action Report, Serial 00026, p 6; Potter and Nimitz, p 351.
34. CinCPac Chrono Files, message 190453 CTF 17 to all subs.
35. A-GO Operation "Detailed Summary of Reconnaissance and Air Attacks," p 2; Morison, p 246.
36. *Campaigns*, p 242.
37. A-GO Operation "Detailed Summary," p 3.
38. Morison, pp 246–247.
39. Ibid., p 247.
40. *Campaigns*, pp 265–266.
41. CinCPac Command Summary, p 1964.
42. Land and Van Wyen, p b–15.
43. CTF 58 Action Report, Enclosure B, p 17.
44. Ibid., also see Burke, "Decision Not to Force an Action . . .," pp 8–9.
45. Reynolds, p 183.
46. Com5thFlt Action Report, Serial 00026, p 6; Potter and Nimitz. pp 352–353.
47. Burke, "Decision Not to Force an Action . . .," p 9.
48. VF-25 ACA Report No. F8.
49. *Campaigns*, p 265.
50. CTF 58 Action Report, Enclosure B, p 20.
51. CinCPac Chrono Files, message 181106 CTF 17 to *Stingray*.
52. Com5thFlt Action Report, Serial 00026, p 7; Potter and Nimitz, pp 352–353.
53. Stafford, *The Big E*, p 337.

Chapter 5

1. A-GO Operation "Detailed Summary," p 3; Dickson, pp 100–102; Morison, Chart No. III.
2. Burke Interview, p 24.
3. *Stockham* Action Report, Serial 006, p 2.
4. Ibid.
5. CTF 58 Action Report, Enclosure B, p 22.
6. CTG 58.2 Action Report, p 10.
7. *Yorktown* Action Report, Enclosure C, p 2.
8. Dickson, p 108; Morison, p 269; Dull, p 307.
9. Dickson, p 108; Morison, p 269; *Campaigns*, p 245. Dull, p 307, has 35 Judys instead of 53.
10. Morison, pp 271–272; Dickson, pp 110–111.
11. CTG 58.3 Action Report, Serial 00116, Enclosure B, TBS Log, p 2.
12. Ibid., p 3.
13. VF-15 ACA Report No. 29.
14. Ibid.
15. Ibid.
16. Ibid.
17. VF-2 ACA Report No. 59–44.
18. Stockham Action Report, p 2.
19. CTG 58.3 Action Report, Enclosure B, TBS Log, p 3.
20. Ibid.
21. Ibid.
22. *Albacore*, Report of War Patrol No. 9, Serial 013, p 7.
23. Toland, *The Rising Sun*, p 500.
24. James H. and William M. Belote, *Titans of the Sea*, p 308; Morison, p 269; Dickson, p 110.
25. VF-15 ACA Report No. 30.
26. Ibid.
27. Ibid.
28. Ibid.
29. Taylor, *The Magnificent Mitscher*, p 229; Edward H. Sims, *Greatest Fighter Missions*, pp 140–145.
30. CTG 58.3 Action Report, Enclosure B, TBS Log, pp 4–5.
31. VF-8 ACA Report No. 57.
32. VF-50 ACA Report No. 26.
33. Ibid.
34. VF-1 ACA Report No. 36.
35. *Stockham* Action Report, p 3.
36. *Indiana* Action Report, Serial 075, p II-3.
37. *San Francisco* Action Report, Serial 0042, Enclosure G, p 60.
38. CinCPac Command Summary, p 1965.
39. *Cavalla*, Report of War Patrol No. 1, p 11.
40. Robert Sherrod, *On to Westward*, p 118.

41. CinCPac Chrono Files, message 191005 *Cavalla* to ComSubPac.
42. CinCPac Chrono Files, message 191123 ComSubPac to *Cavalla*.
43. Morison, p 280.
44. Dull, p 308.
45. Stafford, *The Big E*, p 345.
46. Morison, p 273.
47. VF-15 ACA Report No. 31.
48. Ibid.
49. Maj. O. R. Lodge, *The Recapture of Guam*, pp 108–109.
50. CinCPac/POA, "Operations in the Pacific Ocean Areas During June 1944," Serial 003623.
51. Morison, p 274; Burke, "Decision Not to Force an Action," p 15. Strean believes this anecdote to be, at the least, embellished.

Chapter 6

1. Com5thFlt Action Report, Serial 00026, p 10.
2. Reynolds, p 195.
3. Clark, p 171.
4. *Essex* Action Report, Part V, p 4.
5. A-GO. No. 90, p 46.
6. Ibid., pp 46–47.
7. VT-10 ACA Report No. 61–44.
8. Com5thFlt Action Report, Serial 00026, p 11.
9. VT-10 ACA Report No. 62–44, Nelson Narrative.
10. Ibid., Jones Narrative.
11. CTG 58.3 Action Report, Enclosure B, TBS Log, p 14.
12. Ibid.
13. Bryan and Reed, p 15.
14. CTF 58 Action Report, Enclosure B, p 27.
15. CTG 58.3 Action Report, Enclosure B, TBS Log, p 14.
16. CTG 58.1 Action Report, Serial 0052, p 10.
17. CTG 58.3 Action Report, Enclosure B, TBS Log, p 15.
18. Bryan and Reed, pp 26–27.
19. CAG 2 Report, Serial 082, p 2.
20. AG-14/VB-14 ACA Report No. 24.
21. VF-24 ACA Report No. 33–44.
22. *Belleau Wood* Action Report, Serial 0019, 2nd Endorsement.
23. VB-2 ACA Report No. 50–44.
24. Ibid.
25. *Yorktown* War Diary, Serial 0199, p 25.
26. Ibid.
27. VF-50 ACA Report No. 29.
28. *Campaigns*, p 245.

29. Ibid., pp 246, 263.
30. CAG 1 Report, Serial 001, p 6.
31. *Yorktown* War Diary, pp 24–25.
32. CAG 1 Report, pp 5–6.
33. *Campaigns*, p 245.
34. VT-24 ACA Report No. 1.
35. VF-24 ACA Report No. 33–44
36. Ibid.
37. Bryan and Reed, p 29.
38. AG-16/VT-16 ACA Report No. 42, McLellan Narrative.
39. *Campaigns*, p 245.
40. AG-16/VB-16 ACA Report No. 46.
41. VT-51 ACA Report No. 2.
42. Bryan and Reed, p 49; AG-16/VB-16 ACA Report No. 46.
43. VB-10 ACA Report No. M-13.
44. VT-10 ACA Report No. 63–44.
45. Ibid.
46. VF-10 ACA Report No. 46-44.
47. Tabular Record of Movements—*Myoko*.
48. CAG 8 ACA Report No. 10.
49. CTG 58.2 Action Report, Appendix 1, pp 3–4.
50. Morison, p 298.
51. *Campaigns*, p 252.
52. Ibid., Dickson, p 157.
53. Tabular Record of Movements—*Haruna*.
54. CAG 8 ACA Report No. 10.
55. Toland, *The Rising Sun*, p 503.

Chapter 7

1. VF-50 ACA Report No. 29.
2. Bryan and Reed, pp 63–64.
3. CTF 58 Action Report, Enclosure B, p 28.
4. Taylor, *The Magnificent Mitscher*, p 234; Clark, p 173.
5. Strean Narrative, p 122.
6. VT-10 ACA Report No. 63–44, Lawton Narrative.
7. VB-10 ACA Report No. M-13.
8. *Belleau Wood* War Diary, Serial 0116, p 10.
9. CTG 58.3 Action Report, Enclosure B, TBS Log, p 17.
10. VF-24 ACA Report No. 33–44.
11. VF-2 ACA Report No. 66–44.
12. VF-50 ACA Report No. 29.
13. Comdr. Robert A. Winston, *Fighting Squadron*, p 162.
14. Stafford, *The Big E*, pp 355–356.

15. Bryan and Reed, p 96.

16. VT-10 ACA Report No. 63–44.

17. Stafford, *The Big E*, p 356.

18. CTG 58.3 Action Report, Enclosure B, TBS Log, pp 18–23.

19. Bryan and Reed, pp 73–78.

20. AG-16/VF-16 ACA Report No. 53, Wendorf Narrative.

21. Ibid.

22. Ibid.

23. Bryan and Reed, p 105.

24. Ibid., p 97.

25. Ibid.

26. *San Jacinto* Action Report, Serial 004, Executive Officer's Report.

27. VT-10 ACA Report No. 63-44.

28. Morison, p 304.

29. Ibid.

Chapter 8

1. VT-10 ACA Reports 65-44 and 64-44.

2. VT-10 ACA Report No. 64-44.

3. CTF 58 Action Report, Enclosure B, p 30.

4. VT-10 ACA Report No. 64–44, Radio Log.

5. CTF 58 Action Report, Enclosure B, p 32.

6. Morison, p 309.

7. Saburo Sakai, with Martin Caidin and Fred Saito, *Samurai*, pp 282–295.

8. A-GO No. 91, p 29.

9. *Campaigns*, pp 266–267.

10. Ibid., p 267.

11. CTF 58 Action Report, Enclosure B, p 32.

12. CTG 58.2 Action Report, pp 9–10.

13. Burke, "Decision Not to Force an Action . . .," pp 7, 24–25; Reynolds, pp 169, 386; Buell, pp 265–266.

14. Potter, p 266.

15. Buell, p 131.

16. Reynolds, pp 28–29.

17. Burke, "Decision Not to Force an Action . . .," pp 11–12.

18. Morison, p 314.

19. Ibid., p 315.

20. Buell, p 263.

21. Ibid., p 279.

22. *Campaigns*, p 221.

23. King and Whitehill, *Fleet Admiral King: A Naval Record*, p 563; Potter and Nimitz, p 360.

24. Reynolds, p 186; Crowl, *Campaign in the Marianas*, pp 123–126.

25. Buell, pp 278–279.
26. CTF 58 Action Report, Enclosure B, pp 8–9.
27. Ibid.; Buell, p 271.
28. CinCPac Command Summary, p 2323.
29. Morison, pp 315–316.
30. Land and Van Wyen, p b-32.
31. Buell, p 265.
32. CinCPac/CinCPOA, Operations in the Pacific Ocean Areas During June 1944, Serial 003623, Annex B, p 3.
33. ComAirForPacFlt, Analysis of Pacific Air Operations, June 1944, Serial 00888, pp 10–11.
34. Ibid., p 11.
35. ComAirForPacFlt, Analysis of Pacific Air Operations (Marianas Operations, 11–30 June 1944), Serial 001224, p 27.
36. AG-24 ACA Report No. 23-44. Most of the Action Reports, ship or aircraft, had recommendations of varying quality for the improvement of equipment, tactics, or operating procedures.
37. Clark, p 176.
38. *Interrogations of Japanese Officials*, Vol. II, p 356.
39. Toland, *The Rising Sun*, pp 523–530; Morison, p 340; Potter and Nimitz, pp 362–363; Crowl, *Campaign in the Marianas*, p 1.
40. Land and Van Wyen, charts; Squadron ACA reports; Morison, p 321.
41. Morison, pp 319–321; Dickson, pp 247–249; *Campaigns*, pp 246–248.

Bibliography

Documentary Sources: American

Action Reports, Commander Fifth Fleet
  Serial 00026, 13 July 1944; Serial 0051, 3 August 1944.
Action Report, Commander Task Force 58
  Serial 00388, 11 September 1944.
Action Report, Commander Task Group 58.1
  Serial 0052, 14 July 1944.
Action Report, Commander Task Group 58.2
  Serial 00223, 10 July 1944.
Action Report, Commander Task Group 58.3
  Serial 00116, 16 July 1944.
Action Report, Commander Task Group 58.4
  Serial 0054, 13 July 1944.
War Diary, Commander Fifth Fleet
  Serial 00398, 14 July 1944.
War Diary, Carrier Division One
  Serial 0046, 8 July 1944.
War Diary, Carrier Division Three
  Serial 00251, 21 July 1944.
War Diary, Carrier Division Four
  Serial 0229, 8 July 1944.
Action Reports and War Diaries of the carriers *Bataan, Belleau Wood, Bunker
  Hill, Cabot, Cowpens, Enterprise, Essex, Hornet, Langley, Lexington, Monterey,*

Princeton, San Jacinto, Wasp, Yorktown
Various serials.
Action Reports and War Diaries of the battleships *Alabama, Indiana, Iowa, New Jersey, North Carolina, South Dakota, Washington*
Various serials.
Action Reports and War Diaries of the cruisers *Indianapolis, Minneapolis, Mobile, San Francisco*
Various serials.
Action Reports of the destroyers *Stockham* and *Yarnall*
Various serials.
ACA Reports of Air Groups 1, 2, 8, 14, 15, 16, 25, 27, 28, 50
Various serials.
ACA Reports of VF's and VT's 10, 24, 31, 32, 51
Various serials.
Action Reports, Commander Escort Division 39
Various serials.
Action Reports, Commander Escort Division 40
Various serials.
Action Reports of the destroyer escort *England*
Various serials.
Albacore, Report of War Patrol No. 9
Serial 013, 16 July 1944.
Cavalla, Report of War Patrol No. 1
No serial, 3 August 1944.
Stingray, Report of War Patrol No. 11
Serial 09, 10 July 1944.
Command Summary, Book 5, Vols. 1 and 2, 1 January 1944—31 December 1944 Headquarters, Commander in Chief, Pacific.
Campaign plan GRANITE
Serial 0004, 15 January 1944; Serial 00071, 3 June 1944.
Joint Staff Study—Marianas Islands Operation
Preliminary draft, no serial, 29 February 1944; Final draft, Serial 00031, 20 March 1944.
CinCPac Operations Plan 3-44 for FORAGER
Serial 00275, 23 April 1944.
CinCPac Secret and Confidential Chrono Files
13–16 June 1944, 17–20 June 1944.
Battle Experience: Supporting Operations for the Capture of the Marianas Islands (Saipan, Guam and Tinian) June-August 1944.
COMINCH Secret Information Bulletin No. 20.
Operations in the Pacific Ocean Areas During June 1944.
CinCPac/CinCPOA, Serial 003623, 7 November 1944.
Air Operations Memorandum No. 36.
ComAirForPacFlt, Serial 02438, 25 June 1944.
Analysis of Pacific Air Operations June 1944.
ComAirForPacFlt, Serial 00888, 27 July 1944.

Analysis of Pacific Air Operations (Marianas Operations, 11-30 June 1944)
ComAirForPacFlt, Serial 001224, 20 September 1944.
Land, Lt. W. G., USNR, and Lt. A. O. Van Wyen, USNR. *Naval Air Operations in the Marianas*.
Deputy Chief of Naval Operations (Air), 1945.
Hayes, Lt. Grace P., USN. "The History of the Joint Chiefs of Staff in World War II: The War Against Japan."
Vol. I *Pearl Harbor through TRIDENT*.
Vol. II *The Advance to Victory*.
Historical Section, Joint Chiefs of Staff, 1953 and 1954.
U.S. Naval Administration in World War II
"Narrative and Appendix," two volumes.
CinCPac/POA, 23 January 1946.
U.S. Naval Administration in World War II, DCNO (Air)
Aviation in the Office of the Chief of Naval Operations
"Carrier Warfare"
Part I: "Remarks on the Development of the Fast Carrier Task Force." Lt. Andrew R. Hilen, Jr., USNR.
Operational Experiences of Fast Carrier Task Forces in World War II.
Weapons System Evaluation Group Study No. 4, 15 August 1951.
Narratives on Marianas operations:
Commodore Arleigh A. Burke, Interview, 20 August 1945: "Decision Not to Force an Action on the Night of 18-19 June," 1945.
Comdr. David McCampbell and Lt. Wayne Morris, 29 November 1944.
Comdr. Robert A. Winston, 7 August 1944.
Oral Histories:
Vice Adm. J. B. Colwell
Vice Adm. Olaf M. Hustvedt
Vice Adm. Fitzhugh Lee
Vice Adm. Bernard M. Strean
Rear Adm. Charles Wheeler

Documentary Sources: Japanese

"Operation A-GO."
Japanese Monograph No. 90.
"The A-GO Operations Log, Supplement."
Japanese Monograph No. 91.
"Outline of Third Phase Operations, February 1943-August 1945."
Japanese Monograph No. 117.
Tabular Records of Movement (TROM) and Action Reports of Japanese battleships and cruisers.
Microfilm JT 1. (in English)
"Detailed Battle Report of A-GO Operations: Battles in Seas West of Saipan

from 13 June to 22 June 1944, including Detailed Summary of Reconnaissance and Air Attacks, 15–22 June 1944."
1st Mobile Fleet Classified No. 1048, 5 September 1944. (WDC 161517)
U.S. Strategic Bombing Survey (Pacific).
The Campaigns of the Pacific War.
Interrogations of Japanese Officials, two volumes.
Washington: Government Printing Office, 1946 and 1947.
"Magic" Far East Summaries, 12 February 1944–18 September 1944.
SRS 1 thru 260.
Translation Reports of Japanese Intercepts, World War II, March 1942–September 1944.
SR-01 thru SR-1182.

Books

Belote, James H. and William M. *Titans of the Sea.*
New York: Harper and Row, 1975.
Blair, Clay, Jr. *Silent Victory.*
Philadelphia: Lippincott, 1975.
Bryan, Lt. Comdr. J., III, USNR, and Philip Reed. *Mission Beyond Darkness.*
New York: Duell, Sloan and Pearce, 1945.
Buell, Thomas B. *The Quiet Warrior.*
Boston: Little, Brown, 1974.
Clark, Adm. J. J., USN (Ret.), with Clark Reynolds. *Carrier Admiral.*
New York: McKay, 1967.
Craven, Wesley Frank, and James Lea Cate, editors. *The Army Air Forces in World War II,* Vol. 4, *The Pacific: Guadalcanal to Saipan, August 1942 to July 1944.*
Chicago: University of Chicago Press, 1950.
Crowl, Philip A. *Campaign in the Marianas.*
Washington: Ofice of the Chief of Military History, Department of the Army, 1960.
Dickson, W. D. *The Battle of the Philippine Sea, June 1944.*
London: Ian Allan, 1975.
Dull, Paul S. *A Battle History of the Imperial Japanese Navy, 1941–1945.*
Annapolis: Naval Institute Press, 1978.
Dyer, Vice Adm. George C., USN (Ret.). *The Amphibians Came to Conquer: The Story of Admiral Richmond Kelly Turner,* Vol. II.
Washington: Government Printing Office.
Forrestel, Vice Adm. E.P., USN (ret.). *Admiral Raymond F. Spruance: A Study in Command.*
Washington: Government Printing Office, 1966.
Francillon, R. J. *Japanese Aircraft of the Pacific War.*
New York: Funk & Wagnalls, 1970.

Hoffman, Maj. Carl W., USMC. *Saipan: The Beginning of the End.*
  Washington: Historical Division, Headquarters, U.S. Marine Corps, 1950.
Hopkins, Capt. Harold, RN. *Nice to Have You Aboard.*
  London: George Allen & Unwin, 1964.
Hoyt, Edwin P. *How They Won the War in the Pacific: Nimitz and His Admirals.*
  New York: Weybright and Talley, 1970.
Ito, Masanori, with Roger Pineau. *The End of the Imperial Japanese Navy.*
  New York: Macfadden, 1965.
Jensen, Lt. Oliver, USNR. *Carrier War.*
  New York: Simon and Schuster, 1945.
Karig, Capt. Walter, USNR, et al. *Battle Report* Vol. IV, *The End of an Empire.*
  New York: Rinehart, 1948.
King, Fleet Adm. Ernest J., and Walter Muir Whitehill. *Fleet Admiral King: A Naval Record.*
  New York: Norton, 1952.
Lockwood, Charles A. and Hans C. Adamson. *Battles of the Philippine Sea.*
  New York: Crowell, 1967.
Lodge, Maj. O. R., USMC. *The Recapture of Guam.*
  Washington: Historical Branch, Headquarters, U.S. Marine Corps, 1954.
Matloff, Maurice. *Strategic Planning for Coalition Warfare, 1943–1944.*
  Washington: Office of the Chief of Military History, Department of the Army, 1959.
Miller, John Jr. *Cartwheel: The Reduction of Rabaul.*
  Washington: Office of the Chief of Military History, Department of the Army, 1959.
Morison, Samual Eliot. *History of United States Naval Operations in World War II,* Vol. VIII, *New Guinea and the Marianas.*
  Boston: Little, Brown, 1964.
———— *The Two-Ocean War.*
  Boston: Little, Brown, 1963.
Morrissey, Lt. Thomas L., USNR. *Odyssey of Fighting Two.*
  Privately printed, 1945.
Morton, Louis. *Strategy and Command: The First Two Years.*
  Washington: Office of the Chief of Military History, Department of the Army, 1962.
Naval History Division. *United States Naval Chronology, World War II.*
  Washington: Government Printing Office, 1955.
Parish, Thomas, editor. *The Simon and Schuster Encyclopedia of World War II.*
  New York: Simon and Schuster, 1978.
Polmar, Norman. *Aircraft Carriers.*
  Garden City: Doubleday, 1969.
Potter, E. B. *Nimitz.*
  Annapolis: Naval Institute Press, 1976.
Potter, E. B. and Fleet Admiral Chester W. Nimitz, USN, editors.
  The Great Sea War. New York: Bramhall House, 1960.

Reynolds, Clark G. *The Fast Carriers*.
  New York: McGraw-Hill, 1968.
Roscoe, Theodore. *United States Submarine Operations in World War II*.
  Annapolis: United States Naval Institute, 1949.
————— *United States Destroyer Operations in World War II*.
  Annapolis: United States Naval Institute, 1953.
Sakai, Saburo, with Martin Caidin and Fred Saito. *Samurai*.
  New York: Dutton, 1957.
Sherrod, Robert. *On to Westward*.
  New York: Duell, Sloan and Pearce, 1945.
Silverstone, Paul H. *U.S. Warships of World War II*.
  London: Ian Allan, 1965.
Sims, Edward H. *Greatest Fighter Missions*.
  New York: Harper, 1962.
Stafford, Comdr. Edward P., USN. *The Big E*.
  New York: Random House, 1962.
Taylor, Theodore. *The Magnificent Mitscher*.
  New York: Norton, 1954.
Tillman, Barrett. *The Dauntless Dive Bomber of World War Two*.
  Annapolis: Naval Institute Press, 1976.
————— *Hellcat: The F6F in World War II*.
  Annapolis: Naval Institute Press, 1979.
Toland, John. *The Rising Sun*.
  New York: Random House, 1970.
Watts, Anthony J. *Japanese Warships of World War II*.
  London: Ian Allan, 1968.
Winston, Comdr. Robert A., USN. *Fighter Squadron*.
  New York: Holiday House, 1946.

Articles

Busch, Noel F. "Task Force 58."
  Life, 17 July 1944.
Clayton, Lt. Kenneth, USNR. "Iwo Never Was a Pushover."
  Flying, June 1945.
Macintyre, Capt. Donald, RN. "The Last Great Carrier Battle."
  Part 67 of *History of the Second World War*, BPC Publishing, 1974.
Miller, Thomas G., Jr. "Anatomy of an Air Battle."
  American Aviation Historical Society *Journal*, Summer 1970.
Pratt, Fletcher. "Two Little Ships."
  United States Naval Institute *Proceedings*, July 1947.
Williamson, Capt. John A., USNR (Ret.), and William D. Lanier. "The Twelve
  Days of the *England*."
  United States Naval Institute *Proceedings*, March 1980.
Zimmerman, Ens. Sherwood R., USN. "Operation Forager."
  United States Naval Institute *Proceedings*, August 1964.

Index

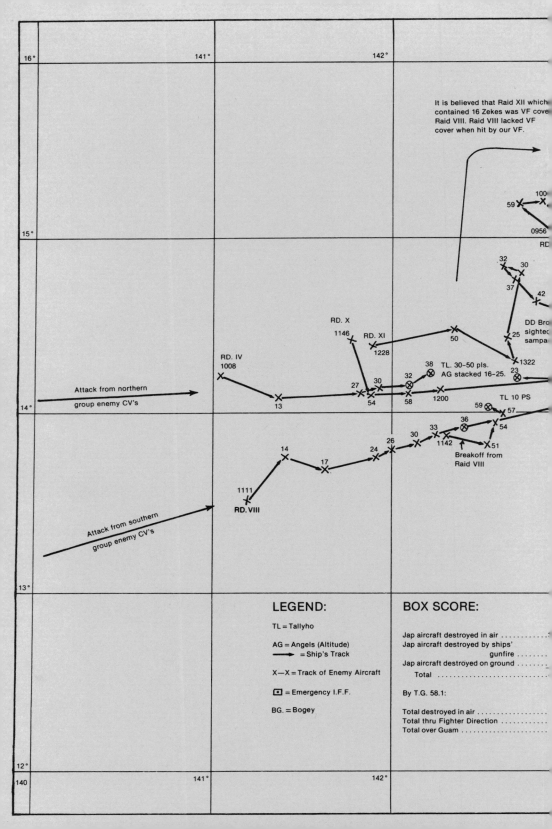

It is believed that Raid XII which
contained 16 Zekes was VF cove⟨
Raid VIII. Raid VIII lacked VF
cover when hit by our VF.

16°   141°   142°

59 ✕━━✕ 100
0956
RD⟨

15°

32
30
37
42
25
✕1322
23

RD. X
1146
RD. XI
1228
50

DD Bro⟨
sighted
sampa⟨

RD. IV
1008

38 TL. 30–50 pls.
AG stacked 16–25.

Attack from northern
group enemy CV's

27 30   32
54   58   1200

13

59   TL 10 PS
57
36   54
33   51
30   1142
Breakoff from
Raid VIII

14°

14
17
24   26
1111
RD. VIII

Attack from southern
group enemy CV's

13°

LEGEND:

TL = Tallyho

AG = Angels (Altitude)
━━━▶ = Ship's Track

✕—✕ = Track of Enemy Aircraft

⊡ = Emergency I.F.F.

BG. = Bogey

BOX SCORE:

Jap aircraft destroyed in air . . . .⟨
Jap aircraft destroyed by ships'
                    gunfire . . . .⟨
Jap aircraft destroyed on ground . . . .⟨
    Total . . . .⟨

By T.G. 58.1:

Total destroyed in air . . . .⟨
Total thru Fighter Direction . . . .⟨
Total over Guam . . . .⟨

12°

140   141°   142°